# The Times Of My Life

# THE
# TIMES
## OF MY LIFE

REVEREND JAMES R. SQUIRE

Mill City Press

Mill City Press, Inc.
2301 Lucien Way #415
Maitland, FL 32751
407.339.4217
www.millcitypress.net

Printed in the United States of America

ISBN-13: 978-1-5456-5518-4

Symbols on the Cover: The wheel gears indicate how past, present, and future come together. They represent the inner workings of a clock and demonstrate how past, present, and future operate as one to get the correct ingredients for meaning, faith, and purpose in the times of our life. The gears could also be the cogs of a machine that power a person forward in life.

The orange background stands for those volumes of the history of famous people that were the first books I took out of a public library. They filled a shelf. The covers of those books were orange. I was not old enough to have a library card so I had to borrow my older brother's card. I read every volume in that history collection.

# *Table of Contents*

# *DEDICATION*

"You Light Up My Life
You Give Me Hope To Carry On
You Light Up My Days and Fill My Nights With Song"
- Joseph Brooks

This is Dedicated To My Family

Vicki, Thaddeus, Meredith, Joanna, Adam, Courtney,
and Spencer

And to my School Family of the Episcopal Academy

# ACKNOWLEDGEMENTS

One of the special gifts presented to me at my retirement ceremony was a table built by Stephen Muir, a member of our Plant Operations staff. Thank you, Steve. I am also grateful to my colleague, The Reverend Albert E. R. Zug, '78 who salvaged the wood from the pulpit in Christ Chapel on the Merion Campus to be used in the building of the table. The following inscription is on a gold plaque on top of the table.

> The table was made from the Christ Chapel pulpit
> From The Episcopal Academy Merion Campus
> Consecrated May 15, 1960;
> Deconsecrated June 6, 2008
> Presented to
> The Reverend James R. Squire in 2016
> In appreciation for his thirty eight years of service as
> Head Chaplain of the Episcopal Academy.
> The pulpit was "Rev's" pulpit for twenty-nine years
> And he preached in it more than any other person.

> And a glad sound comes with the setting sun, "Servant
> Well done."

> Jane Laurie Borthwick

There are areas in the Class of 1944 Chapel given to honor people. I am grateful to the Jannetta Family for giving a waiting area in the rear of the chapel given in my honor. This room is a place where people gather before a service. It is used a great deal by others as well who need a special place to meet. It became an area that helped me a in a very direct way.

I have injured many of the parts of my body while running, from the top of my head to my feet. These injuries include a serious head injury, various ankle injuries, and everything in between. During one run I tore my Achilles tendon. This limited my mobility to walk. I had to carefully consider how I would navigate from one part of the campus to another. Hence I asked my Ethics classes to meet with me in that waiting area and corridor to cut down on some of the distances I had to cover. My office was down the corridor from this area so I didn't need to travel far for class. This use of the space made me even more grateful for this recognition by a very special family that I have known for many years. The Jannettas have supported me in many ways. I think the family may have a record for the number of members who have attended Penn (The University of Pennsylvania) with thirteen Penn degrees among eight of them. They also have four EA (The Episcopal Academy) diplomas.

I am also indebted to Betsy Williams, '93 and Jenny Williams Weymouth, '96 for giving the Chapel in the Sky, an outside garden, dedicated to honor me and former Assistant Chaplain, The Reverend Anita Schell-Lambert.

There is a group of people who understand the importance of financial back up for students in need. They have played a major supportive role in Vicki's and my life for many years. These friends gave money to establish a scholarship fund named for Vicki and me to support EA students in need of financial aid. This large group of people included April C. Crockett, Walter W. and Marjorie Buckley, the family of The Honorable Constance H. and Dr. Sankey V. Williams, Dr. J. Brien and Maggie Murphy, Tobias, '90 and Kristin Welo, Frederick C. Haab, '57 and the Stewart Huston Charitable Trust. These gifts continue to come in and I am grateful to EA's Office of Institutional Advancement for informing us when a gift to the fund occurs. Recall that aphorism that "we never stand taller than when we stoop to help a child."

Last spring Vicki and I attended the Scholar's Luncheon. This is an opportunity for the givers of a scholarship and the recipients to meet. It was obviously very moving for Vicki and me to hear from across our table, "Thank you for making it possible for me to attend EA. It is a terrific place. I wouldn't be here without the support of your Scholarship Fund." Yes, life does come full circle.

The glue in any institution is the people who operate behind the scenes. This glue at EA included secretarial staff, Plant Operations staff, the dining room team, members of the Parents Association, the Alumni Society, members of the Board of Trustees and the Altar Guild. I am grateful for all they do.

The Altar Guild functions to work with the chaplaincy staff behind the scenes. This dedicated group works with flower arrangements, silver polishing and any endeavor to make the Class of '44 Chapel the special place it is. Since the chapel is one of the most frequently used churches in the Philadelphia area, there is always much to be done. In addition to the daily use by the school community, the chapel is also a place where special events occur. People have traveled from far and wide to see this remarkable sacred space due to the fame of the architects who designed it, Robert Venturi, a member of the class of 1944, and Denise Scott Brown. We, as a school community, are grateful for the support of the Class of 1944 for providing the funds to build it.

I am grateful for the set of Advent purple hangings and stoles that were given to the chapel in honor of my ministry by the Altar Guild.

Richardson Merriman is the Founder and Chairman of the First Pennsylvania Trust, father of Peter, '01, a great friend, and a lay theologian. Matters of the spirit and the hard questions of the religious life concern him. Rich made a generous gift to support and expand the religious programs at EA, making possible a National Conference on Understanding Islam, the development of a vigorous program in bioethics, and other important endeavors.

## SETTING THE STAGE

This is a memoir. This means I have tried to be as honest as my psyche and soul would permit me to be in describing important events in my life. This book is also about you. It would be self-serving if it were just about me. If it helps just one person who reads it, then it will be worthwhile. We all tell a story with our lives. And I want my memoir to be for you, as the reader, a mirror for reflection on your own life.

I have included what I have learned about important aspects of being human, recognizing the central role that relationships play in our lives. I do not try to separate my life as a teacher from who I am as a person. As a result, this book has three core elements. It is a memoir. It is a chronicle of lessons I learned that may benefit others, and it is an instrument for self-reflection.

This memoir shows my life in a linear fashion beginning with my youngest memories right to the present day. Along the way, it draws themes and lessons learned with sections following chapters to inspire self-reflection in the reader.

So consider the narrative of the book as a friend that may help you to see something new about yourself to help you to be more effective, creative, happy, and filled with meaning to create a more meaningful relationship with yourself, others and your God.

Close friends will share their inner self with one another. You have my innermost thoughts and feelings in this book, so it is safe for you to share your thoughts as you address the opportunity for reflection in the questions that appear throughout.

We all have things in our life that have been challenging for us. Some have more challenges than others. We can feel that we are the only one who has struggles making us feel isolated because we have certain issues that are painful to us. We can also have personal victories that are known only to us that we have kept from others. It is all in the perspective. What one person may see as challenging may not be a challenge for another.

The following paragraph from my previous book, <u>Watch Your Time</u>, focuses on how we view our own personal challenges.

> We will realize the grass is not greener on the other side of the fence. We can only grow in a relationship when we come to accept our own sorrows. There is a story about the Tree of Sorrows. Once people die and reach heaven, they are free to walk around the Tree of Sorrows and place their

sorrows on the tree. After they place their sorrows on the branches, they must walk around the tree and remove someone else's sorrows from it. Once they circle the tree and see the sorrows of others, they wind up picking their own back off the tree. (Squire 2017)

I spent 38 years as Head Chaplain at The Episcopal Academy (EA, Episcopal) where I was the chief pastor and Head of the Religion Department. For the most part I taught Ethics and Biblical Studies. I feel that I have seen it all and have found myself in the middle of circumstances that required operating in the gray of decision making. For many reasons it was like being the doctor in the ER. No day ever went as I thought it would when I left home for the office. I know that I am very comfortable being in the middle of difficult situations. I also have a need and desire to be helpful to others.

In my roles as a priest and pastoral psychologist, I am a secret bearer. People have trusted me with their deepest secrets and concerns. I could only be helpful if they knew that trusting in me was a core value for me. Trust is at the heart of all relationships. For me it is paramount!

I once had a woman student at our school come for dinner. She was a friend of one of my sons. She was an athlete who came to the dinner table hungry after an exhausting practice. She dove directly into her meal with head down. She was known for saying exactly what was on her mind at the time. She had no filters. She looked up from her plate, looked me directly in the eye as I was seated across from her, and apropos of nothing said, "You know, if you ever shared all the secrets that you know, there would be a ton of people who would become part of a rumor mill."

She then went back to eating her meal with her head and vision transfixed on the next bite. She looked up at me again and said, "But everybody knows you would never do that."

That sentence, "But everybody knows you would never do that", was a statement at the heart of everything I did. So most of you will never find your name in this book, but at times you will know who you are in the narrative.

## The Three Freedoms

I was traveling to a meeting at a college in mid Pennsylvania when I became unsure if I was going in the right direction. I called a colleague of mine who was studying in a community nearby to this college and asked him if he could give me directions. He was from the Midwest, had a mid-western accent, and was filled with sayings from living in the heartland. He responded to my request for directions by saying, "Jim, it isn't the end of the world, but you can see it from there."

I reflect on his words in a different way as I reach an age where it is certainly not the end of my life, but I can see it clearer from where I am at this time in my life.

I read an article written by Jack Riemer that appeared in the *Houston Chronicle* in 2001, describing the following experience. On November 18, 1995 Itzhak Perlman, the famous violinist, was giving a concert at the Lincoln Center in New York City. Shortly after the concert began one of his strings broke. The sound of it could be heard throughout the hall. Everyone thought that he would stop, but he signaled the conductor to keep on going as he played the rest of the concert with just three strings instead of four. He did this with great passion. The audience gave him a thunderous applause. He smiled and using a humble voice said to the audience, "You know sometimes it is the artist's task to find out how much more music you can still make with what you have left." (Riemer 2001) That is what I am doing at this stage of my life. I am figuring out how much music I have left.

I wonder about how I sought direction in my own life from the beginning to now and how that has shaped who I have become. Have future considerations had anything to do with where I find myself today? I think of the Machiavellian notion that the "ends justify the means". According to him it is what is in the future that makes right anything that we are doing in our past or present decision making.

So the question becomes, Are we pushed through life by being informed by the past and "watching our time" in the present or are we pulled into the future by future considerations? I believe we are both pushed and pulled in each moment of our lives as we attempt to hold onto the present moment. I have looked back on my life to examine this push/pull phenomenon and have done so through the lens of theology (a study of God), Christology (a study of Christ) and psychology (a study of why we do what we do). I am both a priest and a pastoral counselor.

There is an important story by James Thurber titled <u>The Sea and the Shore</u> (Thurber 1970) that speaks to finding purpose as we think about "freedom from" and "freedom to" as well as "freedom in", the freedom to dwell and reflect in the moment. The story is about lemmings. The rodents live in Norway and periodically they have migrations from the land to the sea and certain death. One lemming leads the way proclaiming, "Fire, the world is coming to an end." The other lemmings panic and follow rushing headlong to their death. As they die some say, "We are lost!" Others shout, "We are saved!" We should all be on a quest to strive to learn before we die what we are running from and what we are running to, and when we should take time and repose to be in the moment.

We all seek freedom and the freedom, in particular, to choose and make decisions that fall under three categories. One is the "freedom to" which has future considerations at its heart and "freedom from" which focuses on our past and present as well as "freedom in". All three are happening at the same time so we are always caught between the push and pull of life and the importance of balancing past and present moments with what we hope the future will bring. I don't think we are as aware of these motivations as we should be.

Like all of us fellow travelers along this life's troubled way I have been struggling all my life to balance past, present, and future. Looking back I now see "freedom from" and "freedom to" as a pattern for my life. As you look at the years you have lived and will continue to live, what will be a pattern that is true for you?

The three freedoms introduced above are in constant play throughout our lives, but may dominate in one phase or another.

There are anecdotes included in this book that will help you to walk in my shoes a bit.

Remember that as we look back on our life as a memoir, we tend to remember things in the way we wish they were. We also shape memories in a way that will enable our past to conform to how we want to be perceived by others. Once we admit this to ourselves, it will open the door to more honesty regarding the path that has brought us to where we are and we will see how the future pulls us into our tomorrows.

The time in my life that was least accessible to my memory was the period between first grade and graduation from a public high school. To address this issue I sent a draft of this book to a classmate of mine who was with me in grade one through graduation from high school. I also asked him to write a review of the book. I said, "David, keep me honest!" David Spence, who later in life became a chemical engineer, wrote the following to me in his email that included his review. "From the historical perspective, I can't dispute any of your recollections of our shared wonder years."

# FREEDOM FROM

# CHAPTER 1: THE EARLY YEARS

## *Pre-school*

Some people say that our earliest memory forms a template for how we will live. If it is a happy memory then our path will be woven with happiness. If it is a sad memory then our path will be woven with a sense of struggle and despair. For me, my first memory is crawling on a cold linoleum floor in the kitchen of the home where I was born and raised. The doctor came to the house to bring me into the world. It was a gray day.

I can't remember once being held by either of my parents. I can't remember any time that I was told that they loved me. In my home there was a sense of doom and gloom that held in a balance against unbridled joy. Today I am a hugger and a lover. Because it was missing in my life, I am the classic example of psychological over reach, hugging many and saying "I love you" to those I love. I am effusive in this regard. What we missed in the early years, we tend to want later in life. I always looked forward to relatives visiting for then my father and mother seemed happier.

I remember that birthdays in our family were glossed over fairly quickly. The only ritual for the day was a homemade birthday cake. There were never gifts beyond the gift of cake and candles. There were never any parties to include anyone in the celebration beyond my immediate family. To this day I could not tell you the birthday of either parent. I do, however, remember the birthday of my brother, Walter (nicknamed Buddy), because his birthday is January 1.

Today I realize how important birthdays are to people. There is much focus on plans for the day. I try to act like birthdays are important to me but it is just that, an act! This demonstrates that there are times when we try to become the opposite of what we experienced in childhood. Facebook keeps a running commentary of who has a birthday in your friend group. I can't relate to that aspect of Facebook. If someone forgets my birthday, I never feel deprived because the celebration of birthdays was not part of my early life. We assume that what happened to us in our younger years is the norm.

The neighborhood was our playground. There was so much to do. The television was rarely on. Hide and Go Seek was a popular game. We all had a low key attitude toward neighborhood games. No one paid that much attention to the winners or losers. It was just fun.

## Elementary School

I remember the smell of my elementary school days. I have experienced that smell a few times since. When I do experience it, I am immediately brought back to a wonderful time of learning and of being cared for by teachers. The smell was a combination of many things such as paper tablets, crayons, construction paper, ink, pencils, chalk, paint, and play dough.

Today when I experience that smell, I feel a warm sensation and excitement about learning new things. My teachers opened up a whole new world for me. I can picture each one and haven't forgotten even the sound of their voices.

## Learning

I love to learn. I was too young for a public library card but borrowed my brother's card. I was a fixture at the library and focused on a series of history books. All the book covers in the series were orange. This particular set of books were biographies of famous historical figures. They filled an entire shelf. I read every one of them. They transported me to another world of people who were brave and who lived life as an adventure.

Once I finished that series I moved on to the Hardy Boys who were teenage detectives. The theme again was adventure and mystery. I could literally picture their brave actions and was awed by their ability to solve mystery after mystery. My friends and I exchanged the books once we finished reading one and discussed how the Hardy Boys were so good at solving crimes. I read a good many of Robert Louis Stevenson's works. My favorite was Treasure Island. I can still picture the layout of the library. I can see the librarian at her desk, stamping book after book as people checked out their new reading adventures.

## On Competition

I received constant praise from teachers and was popular with my peers. Relationships became important to me and I had close friends. It was then that I learned how competitive I am. I wanted to be the best. I wanted to always be on top.

My friends were all different. They were not as competitive as I was in the classroom, but they certainly were in other areas such as in athletics. I didn't realize until later in life that the competitive spirit I have was ingrained. It is in my DNA. Competition of any kind did not interfere with our friendships. Whether it was sports, or the academic life, our common bond was that we liked being together. A book title describes us perfectly, Where Are You Going? Out! What Are You Going to Do? Nothing.

One of my close friends was a girl who was better than I was at school. She was tops in everything. No matter what I did or how hard I worked I could not beat her. She was always the best! She was the most popular as well.

We had recess twice a day on a macadam playground. I was regarded as one of the fastest runners in my class. One day she and I decided to race to see who was the fastest. All eyes were on us in the playground. Go! We raced from one end of the playground to the other. She was very athletic and beat me handily in the race for all to see. I can still remember her purple and blue checked dress waving in the wind always yards ahead of me. All cheered for her.

I cheered as well for I had a secret crush on her. After winning she doubled back walking and just smiled at me as she passed by.

I loved to run and was pretty fast. As I got older my friends became faster and I was relegated to being average. They were good on short distances. I recall, though, that I could run longer distances than they could. Running would become a theme in my life. I gave it up for many years and then found it again in my thirties.

Later in life running became a time when I could be alone with my thoughts, process the day, pray for people who were undergoing great challenges in life, and solve problems that I couldn't otherwise solve. One of the aspects of running that became important to me was the feeling of freedom it gave me. Sometimes during running all the three freedoms, from, within, and to, were in operation at that same time. Sports psychologists call this being "in the zone". Others refer to being "in the zone" as being "in flow" where you feel at one with the universe.

There are many people who have told me that they have never seen a runner with a smile on his face. That may be true but as I push harder and harder, the smile is inside. This is why I run with injuries, illness, and in bad weather. It is a chance to connect with my inner self. It becomes a form of meditation and prayer for me.

Yes, running does take a lot of work that, quite frankly, I relish. When I finish a run my whole body, mind, and soul feel alive. The only person who knows the following is my wife because it worried her. I would go out to run on the coldest day and the hottest day of the year. I did it just to see if I could. For the most part I always ran by myself for all of the reasons that I have indicated. When I ran in a race, I ran faster than when running alone. Other people's speed made me faster. We always achieve more when we are with others. Others lift our level of play!

I always competed against myself trying to match my best time. You can tell a serious runner as they ask not only the distance you have run, but also the time in which you ran it. I did reach my comeuppance in running in the 10 mile Broad Street Run. You park your car where the race ends so there is no giving up if you want to get home.

One of my best memories is running that race with a member of our faculty, Mark Luff, Hon. The organizers put the runners in a subway car in a location near their parked cars in South Philadelphia and take them via subway the ten miles to Central High School in North Philly. It seems to take forever for the subway to get there so you are thinking, "I have to run all of this way back."

It was a sunny day that was crisp and cool. As the race began I was looking at the sun over City Hall with heads in front of me bobbing up and down. I was in the back of this 30,000 plus group of runners so I saw a great many heads bobbing in front of me. In North Philadelphia where you begin, people were leaning out of windows shouting, "You're never going to make it", which added humor.

At mile eight a woman in her seventies ran up from behind me and started a conversation. She was actually speaking. I was trying to get my next breath. She told me that she had run in the very first ten mile Broad Street Run. She then said, "I will see you at the finish line, Sonny!" She took off like the road runner! Sure, I tried to catch her but to no avail. I had to laugh out loud.

## The Importance Of Sports

Sports became the barometer of competition in our community. I was athletic but not as good at sports as some of the other boys in the school. We played sports in one of three places. One was our neighborhood and another was a new sports facility that was built in our small community, The Fellowship House. It is still there today. When competing for our school, we used a field that was off site.

The town in which I lived was ingrained with all sports. It really didn't matter how bad or good one was. Sports were a platform for my friends and I to meet. I was aware that I was not as good as some of my peers were at a particular sport, but it didn't bother me. However, the older I got, the more competitive I became.

For me it was a time of innocence. We played sports for pure fun, something that has changed in our culture. Today parents scream from the sidelines of their son or daughter's little league or grade school soccer games where winning becomes the dominant reason for a game. I later became like many who favor the opportunity to win. To me, competition is an indicator that you have left the Garden of Eden, where innocence reigns; outside the Garden, it is survival of the fittest.

An example of the importance of sports can be found in an exchange that I had with my recently deceased friend, Dr. John Kelly, who became a professor and consultant at Villanova University. The way competitions were arranged in Conshohocken often put the public school students, of which I was one, against our parochial school peers like John. I felt like I competed against him all of my young life sometimes at the Fellowship House which contained a basketball court where some legendary players have played in various tournaments. There were times when I felt that this location was misnamed as the competitions had nothing to do with fellowship as much as they did with the seriousness of purpose of going to war. Once we left the court or field we became good friends again, but not a moment before. I think that must be the way of most communities, whether blue collar or not.

Years ago when I lost track of John, I was walking down a hallway in a hospital. I saw someone with a beard walking toward me with a smile on his face. It was clear that he knew who I was, but I couldn't put a face with a name until he looked at me and said, "Jim Squire, left handed jump shot." I immediately recognized John's voice, but I could not think fast enough to reply, "John Kelly, deadly three pointer!"

We embraced, caught up with what we were doing in life, discussed our families, talked about the good old days, and were reminded that perhaps sports really is a universal language. How did we both remember our signature shots after all those years that we didn't encounter each other?

This reminds me of another encounter of a similar nature. I was contacted by one of my students whose father had died suddenly of a heart attack. The Mass of Christian Burial was to be held in Philadelphia in a large Roman Catholic parish. This student was one of the premier football players in the area. He asked me to be present in the sanctuary for the service.

Upon arrival I received a cold greeting in the church vesting area. There were about a half dozen priests preparing for the service. My student came back into the area thanking me for coming and "for being on the altar". When he left, one of the priests came over to me and very angrily asked how I knew the student athlete. I told him that the student had chosen me as his advisor at EA. The priest launched into a tirade as he was the head of athletics for the Roman Catholic Archdiocese. He accused schools like mine of "skimming the great athletes off the top" from their parish schools. Finally, he asked where I grew up. When I told him I was from Conshohocken, he quickly asked, "Did you go to Conshy High?" I responded with, "Yes!" His scowl turned to a smile when he responded, "I went to St. Matt's." We were about the same age so we had to have competed against one another at some point.

This led to a trip down memory lane with the focus question being, "Did you know?" Of course I knew the people he mentioned including the Moore brothers, great athletes, who went to St. Matt's. Since the priest and I were off in one corner he invited his clergy friends to come over and meet me. "Hey, this guy's from my hometown and we probably competed against each other." There were handshakes around. I got the royal welcome and a "what do you want to do in the service?" It has always been helpful to me to have half my family be Episcopalian and the other half to be Roman Catholic.

The Thanksgiving football game played at A.A. Garthwaite Field between St. Matt's, as it was known then, and Conshohocken High was pretty much close to war with half the family given bragging rights and the other half in tears.

## On Diversity

I grew up in a community rich in diversity. There were low middle class, the poor, and a few who were affluent. One of my friends didn't sleep in a bed until he was in high school. His bed had been a pile of blankets. The population was a mix of black and white. The community was very diverse in race and religion. There were three Roman Catholic churches in our community to serve three large ethnic groups. St. Matthews was for the Irish, St. Cosmos and Damien for the Italians, and St. Mary's was for the Polish. There were churches for all the protestant denominations as well. I only knew one Jewish family. In my perception people paid no attention to religious differences. We just lived together.

Even though our community was diverse my parents could not tolerate anyone who was different from us. They were racist and my mother used pejorative terms to describe anyone who was different. When John F. Kennedy was elected President it was as though the world had come to an end. "The Pope would be running our country." This was the essence of their prejudice. This was ironic because, as I mentioned, half of our extended family was Protestant and half was Roman Catholic.

During my grade school years perceived differences between and among people did not matter to me. That would come later. When you grow up in a blue collar community and are in grade school, there is a certain sameness of people's experience. The parents are trying to get by and earn enough money to make their family as comfortable as possible. The church or family was the source of one's basic identity.

In terms of diversity issues I lived in two different worlds. One world included school and neighborhood, which embraced diversity shielded behind common socioeconomic status, and the other was the world of my home, where my parents' prejudice was a daily presence. Knowing both of these views was important to me later in life, for I had already experienced the benefits of engaging people who were different and people who were intolerant. I now see this as a gift!

It really wasn't until I left my hometown that I began to grow in my understanding and celebration of diversity by living and studying in New Haven and in Durham. They were different experiences in profound ways. Part of my awareness of the power of living in a diverse community was due to increased numbers of experiences with "others". When I lived in New Haven, race was a more central part of the public conversation, and I had much to learn. The same was true in Durham where Duke is located. Race was an important part of American discourse.

The better part of my learning came by actually meeting people who were different from me. It was then that I saw that when we drop labels, a wonderful engaging person shines through very quickly. The "other" becomes my brother or sister. This is akin to the famous refrain from the television show, <u>Mr. Roger's Neighborhood</u>, "Won't you be my neighbor?" It was a seed planted then and cultivated later by experience.

## An Encounter With The KKK

I recall a time when I couldn't see the forest for the trees. We have a home on the Chesapeake in Cecil County, Maryland. I had heard this area is a center of Klan Country but that awareness was not on top of mind on this particular day. The town nearest our home, North East, is ten miles up the road. The town has a community park with a pavilion where I was reading at one of the picnic tables. The book I had in hand was <u>Race Matters</u> by Cornel West. He is an African American scholar who is pictured prominently on the front cover. He appears to be coming right off the book cover. He was an intense guy and his captivating book is as relevant now as it was during the time that it was written.

I was engrossed in the substance of the book and became aware that there were a number of pickup trucks equipped with gun racks holding guns in the parking lot. I went back to reading until it dawned on me that there were a group of white men staring at me with looks of anger and disbelief. I had stumbled into the middle of a Klan meeting. I think they were as surprised as I was. "That white guy must be crazy!" they likely thought.

There were a couple of racial epithets spoken my way. I didn't think it would be a good time to share with them how race should matter in America. I didn't think we could even have had a conversation to agree to disagree. Discretion seemed to be the better point of valor. I quietly made my way to my car with a quick step and was relieved to be driving away. I think they were so dumbfounded that they were relieved as well.

What I have learned is that racism or any of the "isms", for that matter, are both taught and caught. Later on in this book I will explore the dynamics that cause us to act in prejudicial ways.

## What We Can Learn From Our Pets: Cultural Impact

Our culture shapes our beliefs and how we see the world around us. I saw a great cultural difference in my blue collar culture and others in our treatment of animals. This is a simple but profound way to see how culture affects action. There were many dogs in my working class community when I was growing up. I had a dog whose name was Peppy. She was pure white and looked like a Siberian husky. In our community dogs had dog houses outside. You never went to a friend's home and saw a dog living inside the home. This presented a difficult situation for me when the weather was harsh. I would want to bring Peppy inside. My mother and I had arguments about this. At times I would defy my mother and bring Peppy into the house where she would be warmer. I was ecstatic every time I was allowed to bring Peppy in from the elements. My mother nicknamed me "Doggie Jim".

Today we have a yellow lab, Sadie, who is more a part of family life than Peppy could be. I often joke with my wife that Sadie won the lottery when she got us. She is everything that you would want a companion to be. She loves three things, food, people, and running. We actually chose the home that we live in today to fit her need to run around outside in a large area. She is high energy. You are sure to find her in front of a roaring fire in the fireplace during the coldest days.

I am somewhat embarrassed to tell you a story about our electric fence. Sadie's best dog friend, Trooper, is a Vizsla, a Hungarian hunting dog. Trooper's owner also has an electric fence that is on the same frequency as ours so that they can play on each other's property. I know this is pushing the envelope regarding the opposite lifestyle of what Peppy had. Our friend, Trish Costantino, Trooper's owner, and Vicki meet regularly to walk the dogs or have play dates in our respective homes during bad weather.

It is another example of how our culture influences behavior. Keeping the dogs chained outside was the norm when I was growing up in Conshohocken. I now live on the Main Line, a mostly middle and upper class affluent area, named after a train line connecting the suburbs to Philadelphia. There are no dog houses. Dog owners or dog walkers walk dogs in our neighborhood. Our reaction to cultural norms can be to adhere to those governing our formative years or to do the opposite. I would like to think that Peppy is looking down from dog heaven and saying to me, "That is the way to treat your dog."

## On Bullying

I had the skill to move safely in the world of adolescence thanks to a neighbor, Raymond "Mushy" Mushlanka, who set up a boxing club in his garage complete with punching bag, speed bag, and weights. However, there were no ropes in his garage. It just had four walls. He would comment, "You are your most dangerous when your opponent has you against the ropes. He won't be expecting a knock-out punch." In our case it was the walls. Once the fight started there was no way to get away which is true of the boxing ring as well.

It was not the legendary Blue Horizon Fight Club in North Philadelphia, but I learned a lot from my neighbor. He was very strong and skilled. When we sparred he would always win, and I would learn another lesson about boxing and losing. It wasn't pretty. Believe it or not, there is really a lot to learn about what seems to be a primitive art form. My neighbor walked with a swagger that he had richly earned. He was that good! No one challenged him.

One of the things from my childhood that I loved was the Friday Night Fights on TV sponsored by Pabst Blue Ribbon Beer. This was a great time with my father who had stopped drinking way before this point in his life. My mother and brother were not interested in the program so it was something that my dad and I did together. I knew that my father bet on horse races. I am not sure whether he bet on the boxing matches but he seemed most interested in who was going to win. I could care less who won. I watched the fights because, for me, it was a master class in boxing. I cared about what I could learn by watching. One of my favorites was Carmen Basilio, a hard charging boxer who always took the fight to his opponent.

I didn't know at the time why Basilio was my favorite boxer. I just knew that he was always moving forward and the action never stopped and, since I was a left hander, it was great to learn that his best punch was a left hand hook. Later in life I learned that he was the most offense-oriented boxer of all time. He was nonstop action. He wasn't brave only in the ring, but he fought against the mob that controlled boxing. He would never lose a fight to receive more money. He was regarded as a man of courage.

Unlike Basilio, I didn't measure up! I didn't act on the model he provided quickly enough. I remember being afraid at this point in my life. I was afraid of the bullies in our school and embarrassed that I never took them on. The bullies that I encountered were in school and not in the neighborhood. Their behavior took the form of sitting behind me or my friends and hitting us on the head. When I turned around they would just be smiling. Whenever one of my friends was bullied, I found it easy to retaliate on their behalf. There have been recent studies that indicate bullies are insecure with low self-esteem. When I think back on bullying in my school days I realize two things: the bullies never seemed to be involved in a contact sport such as football, wrestling, or boxing where their behavior could be directly challenged, and they always had someone around them when they were bullying. They needed witnesses to their unkind acts or to come to their aid if they were losing a fight.

There were three important things in working class culture that carried over for me later in life regarding what was emphasized in boxing and how it translated to real life. You never hit someone when they are down or take advantage of another person who is vulnerable. It has to be a fair fight no matter what the fight is. Second, the championship boxers are always proactive, not reactive. They don't wait for the opponent to come to them. Third, you never sucker punch anyone. That is when you hit the person when he least expects it, catching him totally off guard. This can be accomplished by words or with a fist. Usually this occurs when someone has power over a person. People who break any of the above rules are considered to be lacking integrity.

I am sure these guidelines apply in all cultures but, from my experience, they were considered sacred in the blue collar world.

To this day I regret not taking on the bullies in my early years. I think subconsciously that is why I got involved in boxing in the first place. Any feeling of cowardice went against my need to feel courageous. That was part of the way I wanted to see myself. Failure to take on a challenge was seen as something very bad by me. It related to the other side of freedom in my life. That was the "freedom to" be in control. You will see in a moment why control was such an important character trait for me. We tend to want to control things later in life when aspects of life that are very important to us are out of our control during our younger years.

Later on in life, my development was shaped by this drive to take on the bullies of the world that started in my younger years. By not feeling that I did this enough early on, I overcompensated to make sure that no challenge went unchecked. This could be very draining at times. Some who were in my orbit thought that I looked for confrontations when leaving the situation alone would have been a better choice. Certainly my family felt that way with people that I encountered outside the home.

When I attended my first and only bullfight in Madrid, I was not as bothered by the blood and gore as I was by the fact that it wasn't a fair fight. The bull was stabbed many times by the picadors and was weakened before the bullfighter entered the ring in a very macho fashion. I was cheering for the bull since cowards look for those who they perceive to be weaker. They pick on people who they feel are at a disadvantage. I have yet to meet a courageous bully. Again to kick someone who is down is one of the things that still bother me today. There is great responsibility when you have power over another person. I want to see the justice in any action.

## *Family Life*

Family life was a nightmare for me. I shared very little of what went on in my home with friends. My mother came from a very large family with ten girls and one boy. My grandfather built the house where she and her siblings were raised. I was raised in the same home. I don't know where they put all of those people from my previous generation for the home was not large. I think my mother's siblings left home at young ages. I was shocked to learn when I went through her high school yearbook that she was regarded as a fashion statement for the school. I only saw my mother in everyday dresses during the week. She would dress up for church as a regular practice. She had a weekly ritual that included cooking, washing and ironing clothes, napping, and cleaning the house. I don't remember her smiling much let alone having "slap your knee" kind of laughter.

It seemed her life was a daily grind. She would talk with her sisters as a good many of her siblings lived nearby. My mother was a fiery figure and would back down from no one. She got into a fight with our neighbor over some issue, and she was hot and heavy in her shouting. Many years later after my father died, she went to work as a salesperson in a department store. She started to dress in the latest fashion, and began to date other men. I could see the "fashion statement" she was in high school; she was much more alive and vital. Your guess is as good as mine regarding the cause for this change. One thing remained the same. She didn't want to talk about it or share any emotion.

My father had two sisters, Ann and Grace. One became a teacher and the other an executive assistant. His two sisters were very effective people. I remember a story where it was mentioned that my father paid for Ann's college education. I never saw or heard him act in a demeaning fashion to another person. He was your basic good guy. Dad was a gregarious kind spirit who was highly regarded by his sisters. They were proud of him and what he accomplished in life. He was a meat cutter all of his working life.

My father was also a functional alcoholic. He never missed a day of work as a meat cutter, but came home most nights in a drunken state. Perhaps he was afraid of our mother who could be judgmental and brutal in her comments. She had no filters, and always spoke her mind. We always waited for him to have dinner. When he was later than usual, I would go to the local bar and implore him to come home. He always wanted "one more" so I waited until he was ready. I remember the feeling of helplessness and being out of control of something very important to me, peace at home. To this day, I still feel anger any time I am in the bar part of a restaurant that smells of stale beer, whiskey, and cigarette smoke. The conversation is loud. It can quickly take me back to those lonely walks to get dad home not knowing if I would be successful or not. It was always the mantra of "just one more".

A memory that was a formative one for me occurred on Christmas Eve when I was in elementary school. Dad didn't come home until late that night. Mom called a cousin who lived down the street to help her put together Christmas. That meant setting up the trains and decorating the tree. Where was he? I was first worried and then angry. When he finally came through the door, he was very intoxicated, more than he was most of the time.

My mother screamed at him and left the room. He had the crying jags about how hard his life was and how no one understood him. I had never seen him cry before or after that event. He made a plea to me as I was the last man standing in the kitchen. Mother, brother, and cousin had left the room. I wish I could have left the room. Facing anything and everything became a theme that I couldn't let go of. There were times when I desperately wished that I could. His tale of woe continued and the more he sobbed the angrier I became.

He was built a bit like Popeye with large muscular arms on a skinny body. I was in elementary school. I can't remember the grade. The alcohol gave me a distinct advantage since he barely knew his name. I grabbed him and threw him out of the house by maneuvering him toward the door. The smell of alcohol oozed from his pores. When I finally got him outside in the freezing cold, I screamed that he should never come back.

The next morning when we came down to see what Santa had brought, he was seated at the table in his usual spot having a cup of black coffee. I glared at him but said nothing. He offered, "I am never going to drink again!" and he never did. He would not even drink the toast at my brother's and my weddings. He didn't enter a program or seek help. He simply stopped.

That Christmas Eve became the elephant in the room. It was never mentioned again. I was surprised each night he came home sober. I knew it would not last. I was wrong.

This is when I first thought it and felt it. I wanted freedom and a particular kind of freedom at that. I wanted out! I wanted freedom from this world where I felt so little in control. When my dad was drinking and I couldn't take it anymore I would run as far and as fast from my home as I could until I was doubled over with sweat pouring down my face, even in the dead of winter. It may be why running and exercise are so important to me today.

## Middle School Years

### A Lack Of Financial Resources And A Lack Of Backup

In the middle school years I became aware that our family financial resources were severely limited. We had just enough to get by with no extra frills. There were no travels, no vacations, clothing was bought at the least expensive stores, and a simple bill of fare was served at the dinner table. Every purchase of every kind was carefully considered. I am not totally sure where I was and exactly when I became aware of this because all of my friends and extended family members, with the exception of one aunt, were in the same circumstance.

My father and I would have good conversations on our front porch during the summer months. It seemed as though whenever I heard about a new job that a person could do I would ask him, "Well, how much does that person make?" His reply would take the form of a litany. I would think of a job, never a vocation, and ask the same question. He would give me a rough answer regarding whether the salary paid a lot. We went through countless numbers of jobs! Some I dismissed outright because they didn't pay well.

Notice it had nothing to do with the quality of life associated with the work or if it involved helping others. It was all about the money!

Our lack of money made me aware that I felt I had no backup. The feeling had to be strong then for it is still with me today no matter what I do to try to resolve it. There is no way to completely get rid of it so I have accepted it and the acceptance has taken most of its power away. Alice Walker in a poem she composed in her mid 30's, <u>Sunday School, Circa 1950</u>, wrote

Who made you was
Always the question. The answer was always God.
Well, there we stood three feet high heads bowed leaning
    into bosoms.
Now I no longer ponder the catechism or brood on the Genesis
    of Life. No.
I ponder the exchange itself and salvage mostly the leaning.
    (Walker 1973)

I don't salvage the leaning. There was nothing or no one to lean on. Perhaps it was the earlier dysfunction in the family or another source of the threat that created this troubling condition. I loved to read and loved school and, as you will see later, I excelled at the highest level, but there was no talk of college. My parents had no concept of what happens at college. Only one cousin who would become my mentor had gone to college.

## High School Years

I would describe my high school years as the agony and ecstasy of human existence. High school for me was filled with amazing wonderful experiences and tragic ones that created who I am. During that time good and bad experiences were hammered out in the smithy of my soul. The good was great and the bad experiences were awful.

## *A Turning Point In My Life*

When I was a tenth grade student, I came home from school one day to see a crowd standing in the small yard of our home. They looked at me, and I could tell very quickly that whatever produced this group of bystanders was not good. Their faces were transparent with something serious peeking through their attempts to be neutral.

I passed through them quickly. I went upstairs to my parents' bedroom that seemed to be the focus and center of all of the distress. My father lay in bed agitated but not moving very much. Dr. Hargraves was next to him with his black bag at his side.

The bag seemed to contain everything necessary for healing. I grew up in a culture where we did not go to hospitals even for the most serious of conditions. People like Dr. Hargraves made house calls. Obviously, if the situation seemed beyond him, a person would be taken to the hospital in the family car. I can never remember seeing an ambulance growing up.

The doctor stood there pronouncing the verdict of what had occurred. My brother was in his own bedroom. It was then that I was introduced to what occurs when someone has a serious stroke. My dad could not move nor raise himself to a sitting position. He was dazed and mumbling incoherently.

I asked what was going on and the doctor sat me down and explained to me the meaning of a stroke. The first thing I heard was that there was no way to predict how much of his normal functioning he would regain. He would have to do rehab. Rehab was a new word for me. What was that?

My dad wasn't sent to a hospital or rehab center. That was not something we did in our community. Rehab was what other people did. My mother went about quietly providing the care he needed. I never sensed any resentment on her part.

As bad as things were for our family financially, my dad's stroke took things to a new level of need. He was a member of a union for meat cutters so there was some coverage for disability. Without these minimal benefits, there would not have been any way to literally carry on. I never heard of food stamps as a possibility. Working class people we knew didn't use those. Other people did.

We would go without before stooping to that level. There is a significant level of pride in working class America that helps people to hold onto their integrity no matter what.

Needless to say I was worried about my father and I was worried about how we would manage. This deepened my concern about backup. My brother had started college at this time. I remember him calling home one night. I asked him what he was doing. He responded that he was eating a pint of ice cream. When I hung up the phone at the end of our conversation I was angry that he had such a treat when we had few frills in our daily diet. Writing about this now feels ridiculous but watching what you have available to eat can permeate all aspects of your life.

This feeling of difference in income came back to me in a curious way when my oldest son was admitted to Princeton University. Princeton made a big deal of everyone being treated the same. The students on financial aid were known only to the admissions office in theory. In practice, everybody knew. Students on financial aid did work study. Some were assigned to the dining room to wait on those who were not in need of aid. This was classism at work! The "have nots" waited on the "haves". This is the kind of thing that drives working class people crazy. There is nothing wrong with working for your college education. Honor that! Say it! Why not add a phrase to their diversity statement that there are students here who cannot afford to attend Princeton, but they are willing to work hard at jobs here that would enable them to attend this great university?

Many politicians when they are campaigning tend to trumpet their blue collar roots that make them just like the regular blue collar people whose vote they need. Quite often they are mostly exaggerated claims. Even President Trump disputed how many millions he had received as an inheritance from his father. He claimed that it was less than people assumed and that he really was self-made.

Many around our nation have wondered how President Trump got elected. He was just as surprised as anyone that he won over someone with much more experience. The answer, in part, rests in the working class who became his base. The working class has been invisible for many years. This was their opportunity to have someone become their voice. Trump became their voice. Hillary didn't. The rest is history. Ben Bradlee conducted a study of Luzerne County in Pennsylvania as an example of a working class area that voted for President Trump. His book, <u>The Forgotten</u>, supports this point of view. (Bradlee 2018)

I like a story about John F. Kennedy during a rally in Boston when he was campaigning for his Senate seat in a blue collar neighborhood. The story may be the makings of an urban legend, but it drives home a point. As Kennedy was speaking one of the bystanders yelled, "Kennedy, you were born with a silver spoon in your mouth." Before Kennedy could respond, another bystander shouted, "John Kennedy, you didn't miss a thing!"

## *A Journey Of Courage*

So a journey began for my father during my tenth grade year. It was scary, uplifting, and incredible to learn what our human minds and bodies are capable of. My dad had to start over again like a little child. He had to stand before he could walk, and he would never run again in his life.

He had to practice writing and I watched as he did mirror writing. What the brain can do is amazing. You had to hold what he had written up to a mirror to see what it really said. His speech was slurred so he had to practice speaking while he was laying in bed. He recovered enough to write somewhat shakily and his speech returned to normal.

Since I had played sports for most of my life, I had a set of weights in our basement which my dad co-opted. I would come home from school and watch him increase the reps or weight that he was using. His whole body would glisten with perspiration. He couldn't move when he was finished so I would help him up two sets of stairs to the only bathroom in the house located on the second floor.

Day after day was filled with this ritual of practicing his speaking, his writing, his use of his arms and hands, lifting weights, and walking as he got stronger and stronger. One year after his stroke he walked down our sidewalk next to the house dragging one leg behind him with a limp. He insisted on walking all the way to his store for that first day of work.

There was a hierarchy of importance of jobs in the grocery store culture. At the top of the hierarchy was the meat cutter. That was the trade my father had learned and practiced all of his working life. We only have a few pictures of my father, and one is of him practicing his trade as a meat cutter. The photo is bloody, capturing the nature of the enterprise in its most raw state. Today this picture is displayed on the wall of our home in a collection of family photos.

After my father returned to work, the union officials and store management quickly saw that his arm and hand were not steady enough to work as a meat cutter. He was simply too shaky. As a result of his limitations, he was assigned to work as the fish man at the store, a position at the bottom of the hierarchy. But he knew the reality. He accepted that position and never complained. He did what was necessary to stay in the game of work. His limitations still required him to retire early. This early retirement was another great drain on the family finances.

When he was younger he took over as manager of the meat department when the manager was on vacation. This required him to do all of the ordering for the meat department. He did this on pages that were three feet by three feet and contained columns that identified various meat products that were ordered. He received more money when he was a manager so I asked him why he didn't become one. He had all the necessary credentials but one. He responded to me by saying that "he didn't want all that pressure and responsibility". I was surprised by his response. All I saw was that he could have made more money.

I had to deal with an ethical dilemma when Football Father and Son Night came up. On this night fathers and sons ran together onto the lighted football field before a game. He couldn't run. I didn't want him embarrassed. I didn't want to be embarrassed. The latter was the strongest of the feelings. What to do?

I knew this was bothering him as well. I waited and then suggested that one of my cousins who had been a standout on the football team some years before as a quarterback could represent my father, and that is what we did.

I watched others huddle and talk quietly and then change the subject when they saw me come near. I could hear just enough to know that they were making fun of my father with such expressions as "look how crippled he is". They called him by his nicknames, Sparky or Bud. Only his doctor called him by his real name, Walter. When others called him by nicknames it bothered me. I saw it as a way to further belittle him.

## Prayer And A Baseball Game

There were two incidents that focused some of what I was feeling at the time. My father was not very religious. In fact, he was anti-religious and would never attend church with us except on Christmas and Easter. During his days of recovering from his stroke, I would enter his room and check on him before I went to bed.

I would occasionally see him kneeling by his bedside with hands folded in prayer form and with his head down. I was brought up short one night when I asked him what he was praying for. He looked up and said, "You mostly!"

My father loved the Philadelphia Phillies baseball team. It was a common thing to see him outside on our front porch during the baseball season with his small transistor radio held close to his ear.

I decided that I would take him to a Phillies game. It would be a challenge getting him to our seats. Even though my father had returned to work, he was still very limited in his body movement and balance. I dropped him off as close to the entrance to the stadium as I possibly could. I parked the car, returned to the entrance, and escorted him to the "nose bleed" area of the stadium. He was thrilled to be there and seemed to have a quicker pace in his step. He just had to let his bad arm dangle.

I don't remember a thing that occurred in the game, but my father produced a memory that stays with me even today. One of the Phillies made a great play. The crowd roared with approval. I was still seated but my father stood up to join in the excitement of the crowd.

When he went to clap, his hands wouldn't come together in applause. He was too spastic from his stroke. His hands kept missing one another, but he was completely unaware of what he was doing. He just tried to clap. It was a sight to see. I stood and applauded, but my applause wasn't for the Phillies. It was for him. He was free! He forgot what the people might have felt or how he might be seen. It is one of the proudest moments of my life. My early high school embarrassment of him turned to a deep sense of personal pride. We never talked about what happened and I never mentioned it to anyone else. It was one of those moments that needed to be cherished and to remain without any explanation to anyone.

### School Was A Place Of Joy

My high school days were filled with great memories. I lived in two different worlds. There was the bleakness of home life. I would color it gray. There was the joy of school, memorable at so many levels. I would color it a bright green. I did my best to keep these two worlds far apart. There were lots of people who could lift my spirits. There were girl friends. There were boys and girls who were great friends. There was a small group of friends in the neighborhood who went to parochial school. I was in public school. My teachers and coaches were committed to their students and gave us the best they had.

I began taking piano lessons when I was in 5th grade. I practiced at least an hour a day. My teacher was Miss Marion Neville who lived in an apartment on the main street of our town. She was encouraging and demanding, two motivational factors that were at the heart of what I found meaningful. Thanks to her efforts and the efforts of a music teacher at the school who mentored me, I became the concert pianist for our high school. I enjoyed experiencing the growth and development of playing the piano as it was concrete. I could see improvement on a daily basis.

One of my favorite high school memories that reflected the relationships between boys and girls had to do with going to the movies on a Saturday night. We never went as couples. We went as a group.

The Riant Theatre was within walking distance from our homes. On some Saturday nights a scary movie was the offering. Of course, all of us, girls included, never wanted to be seen expressing fear.

The boys had an unspoken strategy to employ when the monster would come on the screen. We would pretend to drop our popcorn and duck behind the seat asking a neighbor, "Is it gone yet?" Then we would reappear.

Things usually broke down at the conclusion of the movie. We all walked, no strutted, as we left the theater, but there was a graveyard that stood between the theater and home. As we approached the graveyard, we ran en mass to get home as fast as we could. There were nightmares that you would think would teach us a lesson, but there we were for the next Saturday night horror movie ready to be scared to death again. We had short memories.

My close friends and I shared everything at school. Unlike some of today's students, there was no competition among us. In fact, it was just the opposite. We would help each other in any way we could. I was asked to share my Latin and Spanish translations and would readily share them with anyone who requested it. Even today one of those friends will say that I got him through the required language courses. One of our friends assisted me with math and science classes. He was just glad to be of help. It was a culture of true friendship and support. We just wanted all our friends to experience success and happiness.

## A Quest To Learn And Leave

My brother, Walt, who was two years older than me, was a source of great support. When I entered his bedroom to get help in the sciences and math, he always put down what he was working on at his desk and gave me his undivided attention. He wanted me to succeed, and I wanted the best for him.

And succeed he did. He majored in physics in college. Then he went to work at the Frankford Arsenal In Philadelphia where he was one of seven scientists who were honored for a cartridge case breakthrough. The award was the Army Research and Development

Award and was presented by Dr. Martin E. Lasser, Chief Scientist, Department of the Army.

Walt received a B.S. in Physics from West Chester University and an M.E. in Engineering from Penn State. He also completed a good amount of the coursework for a Ph.D. in Engineering from Villanova University and became a Senior Executive Fellow at Harvard University. The last years of his professional life were spent as a Senior Researcher at the Pentagon with the highest level of security clearance. His division was in the location damaged by the attack on 9/11. He initially did not know of the attack for he was deep in the Pentagon structure working on a top-secret program at the time.

After my brother's death I learned of the significant work he had accomplished regarding fluid mechanics and munitions that made a distinct difference in the lives of our troops in battle. He was a patriot. His battlefield was the planning and execution of the use of conventional munitions and anti-armor munitions within the United States Army.

In our home there was no expectation that either one of us would go to college. College was a foreign world. My father had a 6th grade education, and my mother graduated from high school in the secretarial track.

I think this is a good time to raise the question of why and how two brothers from a family, community, and school that did not place a significant value on higher education wound up pursuing so much of it.

This book is an attempt to answer that question, but I have no idea of what motivated my brother, and he had no idea of what motivated me. We never talked about such things. However, there was a certain amount of unspoken pride and respect we had for each other.

### A State College As An Entryway To Education

My brother attended West Chester University and had a good learning experience there. I was aware of his favorable experience so I decided to follow him there. Our choice was also largely based on knowing it was a school we could afford. The state system of education in all states is a valuable starting place for working class people. In addition we have a growing community college option today for people to get their foot in the door of education beyond high school. I wanted to be at Penn (The University of Pennsylvania) but it was beyond what I could afford. I knew that the financial responsibility would be mine. Unlike today there were no scholarships or financial aid that I was aware of. I never heard anything about grants or work-study options either. I would have seized those opportunities quickly.

None of my friends could remember having a college admissions officer to guide us. One friend shared with me that his college counseling consisted of a dedicated favorite language teacher, Ms. Higgins, putting a college brochure in his hands for him to read. He went on to that college based on his reading of the brochure he was given.

It is obvious that I went into a vocation that emphasized, among other things, the world of emotion. I was the family therapist when I was a child. My brother acted on his strength and interests and became a scientist concerned more with the world of function. As a child he was interested in how things work and could fix things that were broken. I recall that he built a robot and a Van de Graaff Generator for science fairs. My role was to temper the emotional stress in the home. That is why I was the one who would walk to the neighborhood bar to urge my dad to come home for dinner, a task one would assume better suited for the big brother.

When my parents learned that I was the valedictorian of my senior class, my mother did something that made me furious. She made a point of holding it up to my brother in order to make him feel that he was inferior. Likewise when my brother had done something wrong, she would tell him in my presence that he should have worked harder and been more like me. I was often furious with her for this, but I don't remember challenging her for her treatment of someone who was a great support to me. My brother knew how I felt and that seemed to be enough for him.

There is an experience from high school that should be mentioned here as it curtailed my athletic pursuits for a while during my senior year. After dinner one evening in the early fall of my senior year, I started to feel intense pain in my lower abdomen. I went to bed early and then was awakened by a more severe pain in the middle of the night. I tried to make it down a corridor to my parents' room. I could only get out a "help me" before I passed out. I regained consciousness as they were attempting to get me down the stairs to put me in the back seat of our car to go to the hospital. I don't remember how they accomplished this as my father was two years post stroke and my brother was away at college. I was taken directly into surgery. My appendix had ruptured, and I was also suffering from diverticulitis, a disease of the bowel usually found in older people. My body was full of toxins and inflammation.

When I opened my eyes after surgery. I saw my mother and father with expressions of great distress. They kept repeating as a refrain, "You are going to make it." Looking back on that moment I think they were making this statement to convince themselves of a positive outcome. I missed quite a bit of classwork, but my friends got books and assignments to me so that I could keep up with the work. I was in the hospital for an extended period of time and then was able to return home and eventually back to school. Friends matter.

I was proud of my friends although they seemed less committed than I was to getting out of the town and away from home. They did not share my deep desire for freedom from. I was president of the class as well as the class valedictorian and gave the graduation address. In addition I was voted King of the Court at our prom by my classmates, served as the concert pianist for the school, and was an editor of the yearbook. When I was going through things during our last move I found various medals, certificates, and awards given at the graduation ceremony. I didn't remember receiving those honors. I found this to be very strange. These were boxes that had remained unopened as far back as my high school graduation.

The packing process was slowed down as I read through the various awards. It is still a mystery to me that I did not remember any of them. It was a very unsettling feeling to be going through all of the memorabilia as though it was describing someone I had forgotten and was being reacquainted with. We sometimes forget our successes when we feel that we were not sufficiently challenged. It is only when I was studying at some of the most demanding educational institutions and achieved significant success that I could claim that I did have the ability to achieve at the highest level.

## The Imposter Syndrome

An example of this dynamic is seen in someone who I was counseling who could not accept the fact that she was as great a student as her grades suggested. After a stellar career in high school, she attended Swarthmore College, one of the most elite and demanding small colleges in our country. She received an A+ for all of her courses her first year there. She went to her parents and said that she didn't feel that the school was as challenging as people thought it to be so she asked her parents if she could transfer to Princeton where she thought she would be challenged more. After her year at Princeton she received an A+ in all of her courses there as well. She finally had to accept that she was a brilliant student. In psychology, we refer to this phenomenon as the "Imposter Syndrome".

## The Importance Of Friends

I have a high regard for my friends' accomplishments. They became a chemical engineer, head of a school, a history teacher, a banker, a lawyer, an entrepreneur whose family owns radio stations. The radio stations are managed by his son. Several classmates devoted their lives to careers in nursing. One has devoted her life to helping her mother through the trials and tribulations of life while working as an executive assistant. Another served several tours of duty in Vietnam as a Green Beret. A good many of my friends functioned in working class positions. I recall one friend functioning as the manager of produce at a grocery store.

The truth of the matter is that I was not the smartest kid in my class, but I was driven to always do my best. There were days when my neighborhood friends were playing a pick up game of something and I would be in my room at home doing extra math problems and translations. I could see them from my window. My strong desire was to escape the gray area of home and community. It was not to compete with my friends.

Friends make life worthwhile for they tend to love and care for us unconditionally. During my high school years my friends became a vital force in helping me to counter the issues I was dealing with at home.

My school friends made life in the classroom exciting and worthwhile. The serious girlfriends added a special dimension to what produced joy and happiness in my life. Later in life as I worked with teenagers over a long period of time, the importance of friendship was underscored for me.

Normally my relationships with friends were based in a shared purpose. Together they raised the self-esteem of the group and focused our awareness of a sense of belonging. We all felt included. This was important to all of us. The relationships I had with girls formed a powerful bond that was irrational in nature. We wanted to be together all of the time, while balancing time and emotional energy with other friends.

I had many students over the years whose parents would refer to their love interests as puppy love implying that it wasn't the real thing, that it was an immature form of love. I think the feelings of love among teenagers are more powerful than parents perceive. Many parents are anxious for their son or daughter to get over it as a passing fancy.

### Time To Step Up: Get A Job

During my high school years after my father's stroke, I decided that I should find some work to help out with the family finances. This filled my summers with varied experiences.

My first job was at Bargain City. This was an enterprise that would be similar to Walmart today. I was hired as a cashier but I wasn't very good at it. I had difficulty making the proper change for the customers because the check out line had to move so fast. I had a quota to meet. I am sure that this is still true today so keep that in mind when you are going through any line at any store. At the end of several weeks I was paying more back to Bargain City than I was making due to my inability to make proper change under the pressure to keep the line moving.

I don't go through a checkout line today without an appreciation and admiration for those who keep those belts of food constantly moving. A good many of them are able to do it with a smile. I have one check out person at our local Whole Foods Store who is about as perky, positive and engaging as a person could be. It makes my day to go through her line. Suffice it to say that my demeanor as a cashier did not match hers. Being a checker in the days before scanners and digital cash registers was above my skill level. I was a miserable failure.

My next job was at the Krylon paint factory in a nearby town. I worked at the end of a conveyor belt that moved cans of paint, many to a box, that needed to be loaded on a skid to be shipped out. I was pretty fit, but didn't anticipate the cumulative effect of loading those heavy boxes onto a skid. The conveyor belt only stopped 20 minutes for lunch. The belt ran in a continuous fashion so there was absolutely no down time. I can still picture a foreman who was a nice enough guy standing over me. The practical problem was that at the end of my shift I couldn't lift my arms. I could have done a few skids at a time with some breaks in between but not the many skids continuously that were the requirement for the job.

It reminded me of that classic episode from the I Love Lucy show in the 50s where Lucy is assigned to packing chocolates. The conveyor belt never stops and she is forced to eat as many as she can just to keep up. I found nothing funny about the never-ending stream of boxes of paint cans that came my way in that paint factory.

Dr. Richard Oermann was the superintendent of the public schools in our area. His office was based in my school. He asked to see me the week prior to my class's graduation. After congratulating me on a stellar high school career, he asked if I had a summer job. I said that things in the community were tight. My brother had found a job at a tire company delivering mail throughout the offices. That factory eventually closed a few years later.

Dr. Oermann told me that he had a job for me. He knew about my father's stroke and the challenges it presented. I could be an assistant janitor working with the full time janitor, Mr. Banks, during that summer. This was Dr. Oermann's way of giving me a "scholarship" to pay for part of college expenses. I was grateful beyond what words could express. Mr. Banks was a dignified fellow who I knew to be a good worker. The first tool Mr. Banks gave me was a putty knife. It was used to remove gum from the underside of desks and from the walkways. It was always with me. I liked painting and doing carpentry work. I didn't like cleaning the public toilets. Who does? Mr. Banks had standards and the restrooms had to sparkle.

Mr. Banks taught me one of the important ingredients of leadership. His plan for me was to work with him each day. We would meet outside the office area at 7:30 A.M. I assumed that I would end up cleaning all of the toilets, and he would take the easy jobs like cleaning windows. If you have ever had thoughts of cleaning a public restroom, you know that would not be high on your list of desired things to do so I wouldn't have blamed Mr. Banks if cleaning all of them was to be my fate.

But he surprised me. All the tasks for the assigned area to be cleaned were divided in half. He did half the restrooms in our designated area, and I did the other half. This was true for each task. One of the most important ingredients in leadership is that you shouldn't ask a person to do something you are not willing to do yourself. Keep in mind, as my boss, Mr. Banks could have required me to clean all the restroom toilets. Mr. Banks' sense of fairness motivated me to work even harder. A boss who is seen as fair is one of the greatest motivators for those who he serves and oversees.

I also had a job as a stock boy, but my brother pointed out that I had to choose a job that had more financial rewards than that job did. It was one of the few times that he indicated that I didn't challenge myself sufficiently.

Notice that none of these jobs were done to find some kind of existential meaning. One of the presidents of Haverford College, John Coleman, became a blue collar worker during his sabbatical and then wrote a book about his experience called <u>Blue Collar</u>

33

<u>Journal</u>. (Coleman 1974) The book became the basis for a TV movie. There is a huge difference between working because you need the money and working to see what that blue collar experience is like to gather research for a book. In the first case you know that you can't walk away from the job because there is no back up. In the second case you can walk away when you know that it is about writing a book and not about the need for money to support a family or to go to college.

I do believe that every American citizen should do a year of community service. I also believe that every young person should spend some time doing work that most people would not choose to do, a job where the money is the only reward. It has the potential to change your view of the world around you and create a lasting memory and impact on your life.

## Having Backup

Backup or lack thereof has been a pervasive theme in my life. It has caused distress but it has also built resilience in me. As I mentioned at the beginning, the writing of a memoir has the potential to cause us to remember things that will agree with the way that we want to be perceived. Backup was a theme for me early in life when memories are somewhat clouded and distorted but I distinctly remember an exchange I had with my mother during my last year of college. I let her know that I intended to get engaged to a person I had been dating for some years. I will never forget her words as she stared me down, "Don't think you can come running to me if you need anything. You are on your own." I went ahead with the engagement but it ended and I married someone else a few years later.

## Provincial Mother

My mother was consistent. When I was in seminary in New Haven, I let her know that I was getting married at the end of the fall term of my last year. She had said nothing about the engagement. She let me know that she and my father would not be attending the wedding. Our home was in a mill town outside of Philadelphia. I was marrying a southern girl from Raleigh, North Carolina. I assumed my mother would not be attending our wedding until she showed up on the eve of the event. Notice that my father was conspicuously absent from all the conversations or threats. I learned that my brother intervened to facilitate getting my parents to the wedding. I think this event helped me to understand something about my mother that I never saw before.

She and my father stayed at a Holiday Inn in midtown Raleigh for the wedding. She had never been in a hotel before. She made the bed before she left the room. She was unaware that the hotel had a housekeeping service. When she was told this she simply shrugged her shoulders, but others thought this lack of the basic knowledge of the world was very funny.

She was wedded to a particular set of ideas and perspectives that sprung from her particular culture. She was provincial having never traveled further than two states north of where we lived. She did not have much experience, if any, with people who were different.

Parents always affect our behavior by either our following their example or doing the opposite or something in the middle of those two extremes. Since my mother was so provincial regarding travel, I chose to do the opposite when it came to visiting new places and cultures. It was a perfect example of psychological over reach. My family and I traveled to Bermuda on two occasions when I was invited to be rector of St. Paul's, Paget for a month. We traveled to Jamaica where I was on the staff of St. James' Parish, Montego Bay for a month as well. We have been to Greece and the Greek Islands, Russia, Israel, Rome, Spain, England, Costa Rica, Italy, France, Ireland, and a number of Caribbean islands. If that is not psychological over reach regarding travel, I don't know what is.

I wonder what she would think today of the day several years ago when I blessed the marriage of my gay son and his partner who is black. Would she love him like our whole family does because he is kind, ethical, sensitive, and creative? He raised himself from a culture that didn't celebrate ballet to become the first black soloist with the Pennsylvania Ballet. Talk about grit. Are cultural biases like my mother's too large to overcome? I don't know. I would like to think not. How did the family of my son's partner regard this relationship and us being white? Were there any lingering biases there? How did both families process the fact that they were both gay?

As I was writing this section one of my sons called to just see how I was doing. I told him that I was writing about the phenomenon of the need for backup. I told him that I didn't feel I had it in my life. I wanted to underscore that he had backup in his life. We exchanged "I love you(s)", as always. We tend to provide for our children what we didn't have as we were growing up.

## *Backup Defined*

Backup is about money, support, and love or respect for another. People in a working class culture always have money on their minds. The thought of money is never far away. When you have money as backup you never have to think about it. It is like the air you breathe. It is life giving and you have the luxury of never having to think about it for much of the time. It is a given in your life. For working class people money is the shadow that follows behind you wherever you go. It is always on your mind and you never take for granted that it will always be available to you.

Backup or lack thereof and a conviction regarding my beliefs are key drivers in my life. Please don't ever say to someone who has come from nothing or little that money doesn't matter. It does. But it matters in a very particular way. It gives you choices.

Consider the Hedonic Effect, a phenomenon that describes an inclination of people to return quickly to a level of happiness despite major positive or negative circumstances. This means that money will not yield lasting happiness. It does, however, give you choices. This can be a two edged sword. Barry Schwartz, retired professor of Social Theory and Social Action in the Psychology Department at Swarthmore College, writes in his book, The Paradox Of Choice: When More Is Less, (Schwartz, 2005) that sometimes we have too many choices and that paralyzes our decision making. We need a balance.

## *Reflection*

Do you feel you have backup in your life? Who is that for you? What is that for you?

Have you had an experience where you have prejudged a person but, after meeting him or her, discovered that you changed your opinion? Did they go from being the "other" to being more like your "neighbor"?

How has the culture in which you have grown up shaped who you are today for the good or the bad?

What is your attitude toward money? Do you feel you had enough in the past? Do you feel that you have enough in the present? As you look to the future do you feel confident your money will support your future dreams and wishes?

What events do you look back on from your younger years that have become seminal points for who you are today? Think of situations that were negative and situations that were positive.

If you have siblings how would you categorize your sibling relationships? Do they affect how you treat others today? In your early family life was there a role you played that was different from your sibling(s)?

Can you identify parts of your life (early life or otherwise) where you have taken an experience and allowed it to become part of your positive growth? Did this result in your being helpful to others?

What were the high points and low points of your high school days? Did the agony and ecstasy of this key developmental time impact who you are today? If so, how?

Was there any experience in your high school days that helped you to develop grit? Is that grit still with you today?

Remembering that parents are always the reference point for our identity, what was the nature of your relationship with your parents? In what way do you have characteristics of your mother? Father? or both? Have you ever felt they had certain characteristics that you never wanted to see in yourself?

What was the shared purpose that brought you and your high school friends together? Do you feel your friendships since then have been built on shared experiences as well?

Were there unwritten rules in your friendships then? How about today? Does your moral code, developed during your adolescent years, hold true for you today? If it is different, what ways are different from what you adhered to as an adolescent?

What are the parts of your life experience that help you connect well with others?

Have you ever had a job that challenged your mind, body, and spirit?

Have you worked hard because it was necessary to earn the money or was the hard work just a way to have a different experience? Do you see what you are doing or what you want to do in life as a vocation or do you regard it as something just to earn money?

# CHAPTER 2: COMING OF AGE

## College Days

As noted, I knew that I had to be responsible for a significant part of room, board, and tuition for college. It was a challenge to put the funds together. I would have preferred to attend Penn, but the sheer amount of money that I would have had to pay for loans after graduation scared me. Since there had been no expectation that my brother or I would attend college, funds were not saved for the college experience. My parents contributed as much as they could afford to our college education. They did this willingly even though they had no grasp of the significance of a college education. The value system in blue collar communities focuses on what you can do with your hands to earn a living, not what you can do with your mind.

With no expectations, the bar was set low. The college experience felt like a next step for me. It was my first step in the transition between "freedom from" and "freedom to". I poured myself into the academic life and participated very little in extracurricular affairs. My focus was on academic performance.

## A Brush With The Law And A Bully

There were several pivotal events in college that began to shape my life. The first such event was my suspension from college for a semester due to a close encounter with the law. I was in a bar with friends during one of our college breaks, when it was raided by the LCB (the Liquor Control Board), the entity responsible for catching underage drinkers across the state in bars that served minors.

I was there with my friends who were drinking when the bar was raided. No matter what I was drinking it was still illegal for me to be in the bar as I was not 21. The irony was that I was not drinking an alcoholic beverage. I was drinking a coke. That was not so much a matter of good choice for my age as much as it was our family's history of alcoholism. The impact of alcohol on a family was very real for me.

The LCB at that time was loaded with agents who were on a power trip and loved capturing college age students. They knew they could do anything during the raid and the rest of us were helpless. This is an example that absolute power has the potential to corrupt absolutely. And it did.

One of the agents was very aggressive in searching one of the underage coeds who was caught. She was crying while mumbling something about what she would do if her parents found out. The agent's hands were in every place that they shouldn't have been as he exercised his power with a broad smile on his face. In today's language the agent was sexually harassing the student. He was the very embodiment of a bully. I got between the two, pushed him away with great anger, and was arrested for that as well. I remained between them. The arrest had the potential to make me a legend on campus for all the wrong reasons. My friends on my dorm hall used this opportunity to repeatedly play a song that was popular at the time with the refrain, "I fought the law and the law won."

I was called to the office of the Dean of Students who lived in our dorm with his wife. He was probably the most feared man on campus. He had played football at Penn State and had been the football coach at my college. He was old school and tough as nails.

When I went to his office, I was scared to the point of shaking. He dressed me down thoroughly and then stopped. He got a smile on his face and said that he had heard what happened including the details of my involvement in the altercation with the LCB agent. He said, "I would have done the same thing, but I still have to suspend you for a semester." The suspension meant that I was free to do everything that I normally would do, but any additional offense during the term would mean that I would be expelled. All the students involved were worried about what their parents would say. I was not. My parents said what I expected, nothing. The whole culture of higher education was beyond their knowledge or experience. This further communicated that I was on my own.

With regard to my parents, I learned a very valuable lesson during these college years. Up to that point I had spent a great deal of time focusing on my parents inadequacies and not enough time focusing on their strengths. There is an aphorism, "the older we get the smarter our parents seem to be." I finally reached a point where I saw them as two people doing their best with what they had. This certainly wasn't unconditional positive regard from them, but it was the best they had to offer.

## Emotionalism And Functionalism

Later in life when doing graduate work in psychology and family systems, I was able to see the psychological issues that were involved in my family dynamics. When counseling people, I sometimes think of two different systems that operate in most families. One system is referred to as emotionalism and the other as functionalism.

Emotionalism is when parents emphasize emotion in their roles. In this setting a child returning from school would first be asked how their day went and how they were feeling. This system emphasizes empathy and the importance of empowering relationships in life. Nurturing would be at the head of the list of important characteristics to have. As a gender issue, we usually think of this as a mother's role.

Functionalism, on the other hand, focuses on the question, "What did you do in school today?" It focuses attention on various roles parents play, such as breadwinner or homemaker.

Today many families attempt to have the parents or partners share roles so that earning the income isn't left to one while homemaking is the sole domain of the other.

In my case, I was confused since my father was based in both functionalism and emotionalism. He earned the paycheck but also was emotionally available to my brother and me.

My mother, on the other hand, focused on functionalism. Her focus was on accomplishing the household duties with emotionalism playing almost no role in her parenting. For example, if I became injured playing a sport or boxing next door at the fight club, she would more likely ask, "Did you win?" and not "How are you?"

There is nothing wrong with any of these arrangements, but it was important for me to figure it out. I wish I had been aware of these insights when I was growing up. Perhaps these insights will be helpful to you, the reader. The ideal would be to have some understanding of the balance of emotionalism and functionalism in the family that would lead to clear understanding of roles. All families have overt rules, a situation that leads to the family members having a clear idea of what can be done or said. All families also have covert rules that are not formalized resulting in a tacit understanding of what can or cannot be said or done.

My college years were a tough time as the Vietnam War was at its peak. To make the draft equitable, all men eighteen and older were given a number in a lottery system. If your number came up, you were compelled to report for service. This happened to several of my friends. You can imagine how unsettling this was for us all.

### The Beginning Of A Spiritual Journey

During my college days, I began a spiritual journey not a religious one. There is a saying, "religion is for those who are afraid of going to hell and spirituality is for those who have already been there." A lot of my spiritual development came about because of some tough times. Having no backup was part of what created rich soil that was ripe for my spiritual journey to begin.

There have been many stories about people who went through the hard times of the Great Depression and later in life became very financially successful. In spite of their success, they kept their cupboards stocked full with food. They kept much more than they needed. When interviewed they would state that life was a slippery slope, one bad decision or action would put them back into the days of the Depression. Those days never left them. Sounds crazy, but I understood fully what that meant.

I have a friend who is very successful in the world of finance. He grew up in a family that went from hardship to hardship. He is a self made man. He has a great family now, but they have to vacation on their own. He cannot leave his business even though he knows that the business could go on without him for the duration of a vacation. His family doesn't like this characteristic, but they know from where he has come, so they accept the situation for what it is. His behavior seems irrational until you hear his life story.

He sought me out for counseling about the issue. He knew something of my past and looked at me and asked, "You get it, don't you?" I did and harbored the same feelings that he had even though I had not been through the same conditions of impoverishment he had. Just knowing that someone else could understand his story was enough for him to make small inroads into the vacation issue.

### The School Of Hard Knocks: Valuable Lessons

When I was in college I put together several jobs to cover the cost of my education including working as a mailman one Christmas break during a snowstorm. None of the jobs changed me as much as my job at the Alan Wood Steel Company. My brother had worked there to pay for his college education. From his experience I knew the steel mill would pay me the money I needed. My brother was a slagger in the open hearth. It was, in my opinion, the most difficult job in the plant. He had to keep shoveling the ash around the open hearth or pit of fire where the iron was in process to become steel. It was hot dirty work! There were days when he would be beet red from the heat.

I still have my badge from that mill. It sits in the top drawer of my dresser to remind me that I can do anything I have to do in order to get by and reach a goal. It is included in the photo section of this book. It reminds me to never give up! The badge contains a picture of me with neck flexed, wearing black glasses that are ironically back in fashion today with the number 368 below the photo. The badge is encased in steel with coal dust embedded in it. Some people don't recognize me in that picture.

I was part of a small group of college students employed at the mill. The regular workers called me the "professor" because I seemed educated to them. The steel mill experience opened a whole new world for me. I can't say that the regular workers were a source of great support as they had a lottery to predict the first college kid who would pass out on hot days. It was summer and I was working in the coke plant. Coke is the fuel used in the creation of steel. In the coke plant ovens burned coal at high temperatures to convert the coal to coke. There is no way to describe the heat and the smell of burning sulfur. The coke ovens were one major part of the coke production and the other major part was the coal handler.

I hoped I would be assigned to work in the coal handler and not the ovens. They are both evils of a different kind. The conditions in the steel mill were representative of the challenging working conditions operating at the turn of the 20th century. Now workers couldn't possibly be put through what we went through back then. The work in the coal handler was rigorous and different from what a worker would experience across the river where the steel was being made and shipped.

The coal handler is a huge device that wraps its arms around a train coal car and turns the coal car over, unloading the coal and dumping it so that the coal goes down a huge funnel below. The coal is poured onto belts below ground to begin its journey on several different belts that lead upward to the coke ovens. The housing for the belts are several stories high with rollers to facilitate movement. I spent a good deal of my day underground since the coal hitting the belts as it was dumped from the coal car was a theoretical assumption. In reality it spilled off the belts onto the floor on either side of the belt. My job was to shovel the coal back onto the belt in order to keep the pathway clear.

There was coal dust everywhere. There were times throughout the day where you couldn't see your hand in front of you and getting the next breath in air full of coal dust was a challenge. At one level, I think that this must be what coal miners experience.

One of the requirements for the coal handler was the ability to work a ten hour shift five days a week. The coal never stops being dumped onto the belt so workers had to take breaks and eat lunch on their own time. It was a matter of pay me now or pay me later because the coal never stopped falling off the belt.

Working fifty hours a week did not leave much time for anything other than working, eating, and sleeping. When I went to bed I can remember laying there feeling as though every muscle in my body was on fire. When I blew my nose black mucus would appear in the handkerchief. My sputum was black in color. I could smell the coke and sulfur gasses in my nostrils even when I was away from the plant. I could never get away from the job for it seemed to fill every pore of my body.

I had a "spell man" for my job. This meant that on my days off, he would come in and keep the work from getting ahead of me. Often when I returned after two days off I was knee deep in coal and coal dust because the spell man did nothing but hide and have a mini-vacation. The only way you could measure a person's work was how much coal was still on the floor. Co-workers just chose to look aside in my absence. I hadn't known that my spell man was one of the favored ones in the union. It didn't stop me from confronting him as I felt I had nothing to lose. After the confrontation he stopped avoiding his responsibility. I didn't even need what Mushy Mushlanka taught me. After that confrontation I would return from a day off to floors under the belt that were mostly clean of coal and coal dust.

In the steel mill we did not have ready access to hand washing facilities so we would gather in a metal shed, our bodies covered with coal dust, and eat voraciously like animals. I don't think I could ever eat a Lebanon Bologna sandwich with cheese and mustard and a chocolate Tastykake without being transported back to the corrugated metal shed where we gathered to eat. I was the only college guy assigned to this area so I got to know the regular employees very well. I learned a great deal from them about what is needed to get food and shelter for your family. They were the embodiment of working class culture.

One day I didn't have a ride home so my father had to pick me up at the coke plant after work. I had not had time to shower and clean up in the mill after work. This particular night I had an engagement so there was just time for getting home, showering quickly, and then out for the evening. These occasions were rare as I spent the summer working, sleeping, and eating. My father was used to seeing me come home from work clean. When he saw me emerge through the exit, I could see tears in his eyes. I looked like someone straight from a politically incorrect minstrel show. I was covered in black from head to toe with only the whites of my eyes and teeth showing. I could see the emotion in his eyes and feel what he was feeling, regret and sadness for lack of backup. I quickly made light of my appearance and said simply, "I got this thing. Don't worry!"

After my father's reaction, I wished that I had spared him seeing me covered with soot, a reflection of the hard and dirty work I was forced to do in order to ensure my college education. I never asked him to pick me up again.

We were paid well for work in the steel mill because it was mandated that even the summer workers had to be part of the steel workers union. It was a tough union that constantly made demands on management. If you worked one hour, you got paid for forty. The benefits included healthcare insurance and a mini-sabbatical every five years.

I learned a lot about the gang culture of a mill. The gangs were referred to as the Italian mafia and the Irish mafia. We were paid in cash on Fridays. The Brinks truck arrived and workers would line up to receive their pay. We formed a long line to get the hard cash from one of the guards on the truck.

When you got to the front of the line, the Brinks man would ask your number, not your name. I would look him in the eye and say, "#368." His face remained expressionless as he handed over the money. When I thought about it, you never get your number called today except if you are on a sports team. On the playing field your number is called to highlight an outstanding play. But at the mill, identification by number was just another way you became invisible in the ranks of many.

When I first arrived at the coal handler, I met the Baron whose job it was to grease the rollers under the belts transporting coal to the ovens. Later that day The Baron handed me his grease gun and said, "Look kid, you have to go up there anyway to shovel the coal, do me a favor and grease the wheels." When I looked at him with controlled anger, as though he had three heads, a regular worker pulled me aside and said, "Keep your life simple. Just do it." I did as he commanded with a reluctant attitude and he never asked me to do it again. I noticed later that he paid other people to do his job for him. He never did any work that I saw.

On payday the Baron was usually standing in the parking lot across from the Brinks truck, already showered and changed. He was a loan shark. The people who had taken a loan from him knew that it was time to pay up. Sometimes all of a worker's hard earned cash had to be turned over to the Baron. I wondered how those families made it through the next week.

On one occasion when I was walking across the gravel lot across from the coke plant, the Baron was going to his car. A car backfired and I watched the Baron do a swan dive over the hood of a parked car thinking the sound was a gunshot. He didn't think it was funny, but I bent over laughing. Clearly the Baron had made enemies.

As I look back on my days in the coal handler, I still wonder how I did what I did for I have a fear of heights as it relates to enclosed spaces and there were plenty of somewhat enclosed spaces in the corrugated metal that housed the belts. There were also open spaces at high levels where you could see all the way down to the ground.

There were plenty of fellow workers who took time to tell me the facts of life regarding how to hang tough and make it in the world. Their litany included everything that our culture requires of a "real man". I was advised to avoid showing any emotion no matter how hard the job was and by all means I was never to show fear. The underlying premise was that only the strong survive. I took it all in. Working class people feel life is not fair. They believe the deck is stacked against them. The steel workers were very quick to point this out. My response then and now was, "it is what it is." The experience definitely made an impression on me and shaped me in a significant way. I remain grateful to this day to an African American worker who took me under his wing to instruct me in the ways of the world.

I only knew two things about him. He had a small child who was a boy, and he lived in the poorest section of Conshohocken. There was a bench outside of the lunch shed where this gentleman taught me the ways of the world. He would pace back and forth with his hands behind his back as he bent over. He looked like a coach on the sideline of an athletic field. He talked about the racism he had experienced that underscored that the world was not a friendly place. He had chapter and verse of his own life to support his point of view. He emphasized the value of hard work and guarding against people taking advantage of you. He would become animated in this discourse. His words could not keep up with what he was thinking so he seemed to stutter at times as he expressed his convictions. I valued the lessons he taught me and incorporated them with what I learned at the various institutions of higher learning that I attended.

During the month of August one summer, the coke plant was closed for repairs so the small group of college kids was shipped to the other side of the Schuylkill River where the cold rolling mill was located. This is where the finished steel was banded into coiled rolls to be shipped. It was also where the most money could be made since there was an hour per hour bonus. Any steel that was banded together beyond the day's quota for shipping would result in a share of the profits returned to the workers. The work there was a total team effort.

There was a moment of cognitive dissonance when we arrived in filthy clothing from the coke plant to be greeted by workers in white shirts and khaki pants. It was an interesting meet and greet. They took all of us behind a restroom area located in the center of the factory floor. They made it very clear that they were there to provide support for their families and not to earn money for a college education. Respect for a college education was not high on their list. If we slowed them up in any way that would reduce their bonus, they would make our lives more than interesting. Suffice it to say that we worked harder than we thought possible to keep up with these seasoned people. Fear is a tremendous motivator. They were legitimate tough guys.

Later in life I had a small world experience as I was blessing the marriage of a couple on the north shore of Massachusetts. At the reception dinner I sat next to a member of the Wood family who had owned the steel company. The company had to fold because of the demands of the union. It left this owner resentful of the union's role in everything that occurred leading to the mill closure.

Shortly after I graduated from college, a friend told me about a job in the city. I went to work at the Nice Ball Bearing plant. It was a way for me to generate income before starting graduate school and hopefully earning income as a substitute teacher in the Philadelphia Public School System in the fall. Ball bearings are balls of metal that allow movement with little or no friction. I had never used a commercial lathe and in this job I was surrounded by three of them. The supervisors told me that they would teach me how to use them. I was required to move from one lathe to the other throughout the day creating a quota that was the expectation for each workday. The only break was at lunch.

I lacked the skills of the other workers so it was a challenge for me to produce the quality of ball bearings set by the factory. I would eat lunch with people who had been doing this all their life. I don't know how they did it. It was monotonous and boring. I am sure today there is an automated process that can produce the product better than any person. I could not shake the feeling that I brought down the standards of the factory. Quite frankly I felt guilty about that and had nightmares about my perceived failure.

My life up to this point was focused on "freedom from". The drive was to get away from my home and a community that seemed to have no future. Now my focus was more on the "freedom to" rolling around in my soul. Now my quest was to define my future away from the family and community.

## A Town In Transition

The various companies were closing at a rapid pace in Conshohocken. This included the steel mill, a tire company, a wire company, and a chemical company that were major employers of this blue collar community. I have been told that people stood at the closed entrance gates in complete disbelief that such a thing had happened. They did not see the connection between union demands and a company's ability to meet them. People were worried about how to support their families. Today Conshohocken has gone through an unbelievable transformation with new office buildings and apartments. It has become a commuter town as well for the city of Philadelphia. It is a place to be. One builder of these apartments, Brian O'Neill, was a member of the Board of Trustees of The Episcopal Academy. He is one of the largest developers on the east coast and has been recognized by President Bush for taking "brown" areas and developing them into sites for housing.

One of his apartment buildings in Conshohocken had a terrible fire. I contacted Brian at seven on a Saturday morning to see how he was doing as he was at the site of the fire. He was more concerned with the people than he was with the burning building. He is a tough guy with a big heart. When I concluded my conversation with him, I thought about the irony of someone who had fled the town talking to someone who was literally rebuilding it.

Brian did not attend college. I watched him on a YouTube video when he was meeting with the Conshohocken Borough Council about acquiring land for a building site. He was respectful as he negotiated the deal for the property. The council members were challenging in the negotiation. He never lost his patience. I knew that at the end of that meeting he would accomplish his goal, and he did. He was a key person in the building of the new campus for our school. Brian is a tough guy, but I know him as someone who cares deeply about people. He has a heart of gold. When one of our students died, I did the committal service at a nearby cemetery following the Mass of Christian Burial. I blessed the body before it was put inside of a mausoleum. It was a difficult time for everyone. It was a bitter cold day. I turned my head to the left. There was Brian standing next to me having a ministry of presence for this grieving family. He gave a small smile when we made eye contact.

Conshohocken is thriving today.

### Call To Ministry

I think everyone who is called to the ordained ministry has a different experience. I can only speak from my own perspective and experience. Let me make clear that the journey to be a priest is one of the most challenging processes there is. I know parents that won't let their children become either doctors or clergy as they want to protect them from the rigors that are involved in those professions. So at one level I experienced the call to ministry as an irrational decision. It didn't make sense. For me the decision to enter the ministry was influenced by two people, each for a different reason, for whom I had a high regard.

My cousin, Noble Smith, was the first person in our extended family to go to college. He was a center on our high school football team and catcher on the baseball team. He went to a local liberal arts college on an athletic scholarship and then could not continue to play because of injuries to his knees.

He was popular. He was athletic. He was quick to laugh and people just loved to be around him. When he was in college he was called to be an Episcopal priest. It sounds trite to say but he was a good person. He was sensitive to the needs of others. He was the cousin who came to help my mother put together the Christmas gifts and decorate the tree when my father was out drinking. There was something different about this cousin. He was flamboyant, rode an orange motorcycle, and was cool.

I always looked forward to having him drop by our house to share what was going on in his life. He really was one of those larger than life people who periodically come into our lives and enrich them. What he was doing was always interesting. He was a very resilient person. Nothing stopped him from achieving his goals.

When Noble lost his college athletic scholarship due to injuries, he worked three jobs to pay for his education. I remember one summer night when he was dropped off by a cab in front of his house located down the street from where I lived. A few men had to help him to get out of the car and into his house because he was suffering from heat exhaustion. He recovered and went right back to his three jobs.

Noble and I would sit and talk during those summer nights. He shared with me his ambitions and how he thought the ministry was a way to accomplish everything he felt called to do. My cousin became my mentor. I couldn't think of anyone who I admired more. His goals were to share his faith with others and to develop a lively faith community after his ordination. He achieved this goal making his first and only parish into a model for how deepening one's faith can be a powerful force in our lives. His church became a large community of dedicated Christians under his leadership. Central to what he taught me, by his example, is that faith is personal and interpersonal. In the Letter of James in the New Testament it is succinctly stated, "Faith without works is dead." (James 2:14)

Noble later became a professional baseball umpire as he continued to lead his congregation. He worked the third base line and called Pete Rose out a few times. I asked him one night to share his secret to accomplishing all that he did.

He looked me in the eye when I raised the question and said, "We all have different gifts and abilities. We all are capable of having a great attitude. But there is always one thing required for success." I was hanging on his every word. He said, "Never let anyone outwork you." To this day his words still move around within me and I try to give 100 percent to everything I do. He planted a seed in my life that took some time to take root. Over time he awakened the spirituality that was dormant within me until this calling became real in my own life.

I gave the following address on September 7, 1990 to celebrate the life of Noble Smith. I hope you can see more clearly who Noble was and why he had such a huge impact on who I became. My goal was to have his legacy live on in me.

As a nation we seem to long for heroes or leaders such as were found in the days of old. On June 21st my hero who had the greatest impact on my life died after a two years struggle with cancer. He was my cousin. His name is the Reverend Dr. Noble M. Smith. For 31 years he served as Rector of Historic Trinity Parish in Northeast Philadelphia.

He was 56 years old when he died. I would like to share a bit about him and about his memorial service I attended on June 25th for in the words of Bishop Bartlett, "We need to find more people like Noble and to encourage others to learn from his life." Three bishops presided at the service that was held on a crisp clear day. It was good that the day was crisp and clear for his colonial church seated only a hundred. Seven hundred were present most standing outside listening to the words of the liturgy being broadcast. What can we learn from this life lived that elicited such a response from all sorts and conditions of people?

Noble grew up just four houses away from my home in Conshohocken which is now a Yuppie community but then it was strictly blue collar, religiously and ethnically diverse. The primary transmitter of values was what you learned on the street. During my younger years my father was a functional alcoholic meaning that he could always hold down a job in spite of his illness. Life in our family was therefore unpredictable. You never knew when dad was going to come home and you never knew what state he would be in. A good bit of my perspective of the world at that time was looking at life through a barstool.

One of my earliest memories is hiding on the stairs on Christmas Eve watching Noble who was 16 or 17 put together the secular part of Christmas as dad would not be of any help when he was intoxicated. Noble wrapped the presents, put up the tree, and set up the trains. I would watch his efforts from my vantage point on the stairs. This would take hours, and the next day he would come into the home before he would open his own presents to see what Santa had brought us. He would ooh and ah and bring joy to a strained situation. He was what you would call your basic good person.

He worked three jobs to put himself through Ursinus College. I clearly remember seeing him literally being carried into his home by friends because he was exhausted. He never gave up on anything that he did. The cancer that took his life in two years was supposed to kill him in six months. He worked as a parish priest while being dosed with portable chemotherapy until his last days. When he was in college and working during the summer at these various jobs, I would wait for him to come down the street in the late evening hours. I would force myself to stay awake because he would tell me about his day, ask about mine, and "give me a piece of his mind" as he put it. As I look back on it his words were hard truths such as "you only get out of something what you put into it". "Never give in. Never back down." He was a product of a community where work was sacred.

Noble once said, "You know all your life you are going to meet people smarter than you. That's a given. But nobody should outwork you. There is no excuse for that." That statement was how he lived his life.

Noble was one of the toughest people I have ever met. He was kind, considerate, and loved and respected everyone, but a tougher competitor in athletics you'd never want to meet. He was the center on his high school championship football team and at college. A set of bad knees prevented him from entering the pros. He was also the catcher on his high school and college baseball teams.

One of his friends at his memorial service said that those rules learned in sports as a young man were a key to his leadership ability. The center handles the ball on every play but passes it on to someone else to get the glory. The greatest pitcher in the world is only as good as the catcher who is on the receiving end. The greatest leader is only as good as the person who can implement the ideas.

Another friend at his memorial service reflected that if you worked with Noble, you might get roughed up a little for he was, as we all are, a product of our upbringing. When he said "yes" he meant "yes". When he said "no" he meant "no". "Maybe" was not in his vocabulary. Noble was also a major league baseball umpire. Bishop Allen Bartlett told the story that one day when Noble was umpiring, the fiery Pete Rose slid into third base with great fury knocking the third baseman out cold. Noble called him out, and Pete started for Noble. Noble never waited for life to happen to him so he went right for Pete. Pete then put his nose on Noble's and said, "Nice call ump!"

Noble was decisive and direct. There was nothing political about him. He said what he felt and let the chips fall where they may. During Noble's memorial service a priest sitting next to me who was a seminary classmate of Noble's said, "Did you know that this great priest whose life we are celebrating today was expelled from seminary?" I said that I knew that there was an incident, but I never knew what it was. Evidently a professor asked all the students to evaluate his course. Noble wrote that the course was worthless and was expelled. Noble was asked several times to change his evaluation to gain readmission, but he would not.

The seminary was having great trouble with this particular faculty member so Noble was reinstated and the faculty member was let go. Honesty and integrity were hallmarks of his life.

Noble lived the Gospel twenty-four hours a day, seven days a week. He chose to focus much of his ministry with youth and with the aging. He talked about the Gospel on summer nights as we sat on cement steps. He said, "It is the only thing that makes sense to me." Hence the Gospel became the only thing that made sense to me.

This man who was buried with a liturgy fit for a king was honored in that fashion for he always saw himself as a servant to others. He was humble and self effacing. In one of our last conversations he said, "I wish I would have done something with my life. I wish I would have helped others more."

This coming from a man whose life could cause a Bishop to ask God that we have more like him. His parents couldn't have named him better...for Noble...aptly describes this servant of the living Lord. Amen

Noble was a gift to me. He was back up of a particular sort as he knew my needs and aspirations better than I did. As noted there are times when the important things in life are caught and sometimes they are taught. But to have the essential ingredients to living a life with purpose come in both forms of being caught and taught was a powerful piece of motivation and inspiration for me. I can still hear his laugh as he is in the midst of people who he is helping.

My children would become part of this legacy as I would ask them, until it became too annoying, "Are you feeling the fire? Whatever you want to do, give it your all. Mediocrity is unacceptable." If I am having a challenging day, they will give it right back to me, "Dad, are you feeling the fire?"

## A Second Mentor

I had a second mentor who was never aware of how he influenced me. He was a clergyman and the father of a girl to whom I was once engaged. I spent as much time with him as I spent with my own family and friends. He was consistently good, spiritual, and authentic. What you saw was what you got. His life cast a spell over me, ingraining the importance of spirituality and of putting others before self.

His family home was the opposite of my own. He created an environment of acceptance. He was not judgmental. He and his wife created a peaceable kingdom. I was aware that he could have been successful in any occupation but he chose ministry to others as the most important thing that he could do. He was a Penn grad. We never engaged in long discussions the way I did with my cousin but his spirituality was contagious.

The first step in acting on a calling to the ministry in the Episcopal Church is to get permission from your bishop to enter the ordination process. My bishop, Bishop Robert Dewitt, opposed the war in Vietnam, championed women's causes, and spoke out on issues of racism. I am thankful he championed these issues. But he was clueless when it came to the issue of classism.

## Meeting The Bishop

When I first met with Bishop DeWitt, I remember him rubbing his eyes a bit as though he was thinking hard about whether I should enter the ordination process. Although I had no prior history with him, I assumed he had prepared for our interview by reading about my background. Obviously he had not for he looked up and said, "I don't think you are ready. You need some real life experience. You need to experience people who have had it tough."

He could have said anything but that as his reason for rejecting me. I was stunned. His response indicated that he didn't know a thing about me. I wondered what kind of an experience he was encouraging me to have based on his own life and his interpretation of that phrase, "more real life experience".

I left his office and called my cousin, Noble. To say that he was furious would be a major understatement. He said, "If anything, you have had too much real world experience." The Bishop had said that I needed to see how the other half lived. This is code for someone who has had it rough. I had no recourse other than to redirect my path in a quest to determine how the other half lived and, for that matter, who they were in the Bishop's mind. The Bishop could not be swayed by my cousin's frontal attack, his effort to convince the bishop that he was making a big mistake.

### Finding The Other Half When That Other Half Is Me

I majored in biology in college so this roadblock was an opportunity to enroll in a local university. At Temple University's Conwell School of Theology I took courses in theology, biblical study and history of religion to get a start on the seminary education I hoped to undertake.

I also applied to be a substitute teacher in the Philadelphia Public School System. If you know anything about education and teaching you know that the substitute teacher is like a sitting duck. I found myself during the days when I wasn't in class in graduate school studying religion, working as a substitute teacher in some great schools but also in some schools that were challenges for any teacher.

At a school in one of the toughest parts of the city I was told to report to the top floor and wait for instructions. Once there the principal came up and told me what to expect from my day. The students on this open floor were unable to learn in a traditional classroom or they had behavior issues. They were on the verge of expulsion.

The principal asked if I could handle this situation and I told him it would not be a problem. The students walked around like they were hanging out on a street corner which reminded me of some of my experiences when I was their age. I felt comfortable there as, at one level, I was used to this context of a street corner structure. When you grow up where I grew up, you also realize that the number one virtue is loyalty to the group with no squealing on anyone. I quickly went to my "freedom from" mindset of being a kid their age and went from group to group to see what they were interested in learning that day. They thought I was crazy. They were bright kids shaped by the street culture that formed their home. The students did not take their learning seriously. They told me that most substitute teachers hang outside the door just to make sure they didn't hurt one another. I didn't fit their view of the adult world. Today we learn.

One of my memories of this substitute teaching goes back to my experience with unions in the steel mill and with my father. The head of the teachers' union was an interesting guy who threw together his lesson plans for his students on the fly. He was more interested in the politics of the union than what was occurring in the classroom. He was focused on what the teachers could get rather than what they should be giving to the students. This attitude created mixed emotions in me. On the one hand I don't know what my family would have done without the union's intervention when my father had his stroke. On the other hand, I had first hand experience with unions out to get what was best for the union members, not what was best for the management of the plant or, in this case, what was best for the students. Whenever there are strikes, it really seems to always come down to money wrapped in other ancillary claims.

I was still looking for this "other half" that I needed to experience! I knew, though, that these kids were the "other half". They were my own kind. Kids can tell in a heartbeat if you are comfortable with them or not so my upbringing paid off in a big way. I didn't feel afraid or anxious. The students opened up to me.

## Broken Engagement

In the fall as I was entering my graduate study at Temple University, my engagement was broken after a six year relationship with my fiancée. I did what I always do in that kind of situation. I threw myself into my work and prayed. I dated other women during that year and I began to notice that I was attracted to strong women. I recall finding out that my former fiancée was to be married at the end of that academic year. On the evening she was married, I remember sitting on the front steps of a row home down from where I lived. If I looked one way, I could see the billowing smoke coming from the mill. If I looked the other way, I was literally looking into a dead end street. Both were symbolic of an important crossroads in my life.

## A Return Meeting With The Bishop

After completing the year of graduate work at Temple University and working as a substitute teacher, I met again with the Bishop who had initially refused my request to enter the ordination process. He looked at me and said, "You're back here again!" He really knew how to make a guy feel special. He said, "You will probably be back next year if I fail to accept you again." I replied, "I would be back." He reluctantly gave me the opportunity to apply to three schools in the Northeast to continue in theological studies with the goal of being ordained into the Episcopal Priesthood.

You cannot begin the process to ordination in the Episcopal Church until you have approval from your bishop. The process to become an Episcopal priest is a rigorous one. I would put it up against any profession. There are meetings with career development counselors to identify personality traits that would be helpful and those that would not. There are meetings with a psychiatrist and medical doctors to assess your mental and physical health. There is an academic standard to be met to enter into a seminary such as Berkeley at Yale where I attended. There are various meetings with the Commission on Ministry, an organization consisting of laity and clergy tasked with discerning whether candidates are qualified to take on the challenges of the ordination process and to ensure candidates follow appropriate canon law, the canon laws that govern the Episcopal Church.

I was a member of this committee later in life and said on occasion, "Jesus on a good day could pass all the requirements." It was necessarily rigorous as a process, but there were times when interviewing candidates that I thought it was a bit too rigorous. Did we lose people because they didn't fit the ideal of what the process was designed to accomplish? I think the answer is yes. I wanted to make the process more pastoral in nature and less like a fraternity or sorority hazing.

During the 60s there was not significant focus on class as an issue. Other issues at that time became the focal points of discussion. The Vietnam War was raging. Race and gender were the issues dominant in conversations and the national dialogue at the time. Certainly there were books and dialogue regarding the working class, but I would not say that it was central to political activity. The blue collar worker was lost in the shuffle.

I was in the midst of final exams in my graduate program at Temple when quite by happenstance I met Vicki, my wife of forty-nine years now. This book is dedicated to her.

### Love At First Sight

At the time I met Vicki I didn't think I was a love at first sight romantic, but I have no other way describe it. There she was gorgeous in an orange dress, golden hair, tanned, and speaking with a deep southern accent. She is just over five feet tall, a full foot shorter than me. I still can touch the intimacy of that moment. That evening I went with her to show her slides from a mission trip she had taken to Panama with her church group.

The timing of our meeting and the geographical distance couldn't have been worse. She lived in Raleigh and was serving as secretary of her class at North Carolina State University. At the end of that summer I would be heading to New Haven, CT to begin a new adventure at the Berkeley Divinity School at Yale. Raleigh and New Haven are separated by thirteen hours of driving or two hours of flying.

I made weekend trips that summer from Philadelphia to Raleigh. My friends thought I had lost my mind. They were right. Vicki's parents welcomed me into their home during those weekend visits.

Vicki's mother, a welcoming presence, was quick to laugh. Her father was the reincarnation of Ernest Hemingway. He owned a used truck company and loved flying his small plane to nearby towns to conduct his business. He served in the Army Air Corps during World War II. He enjoyed fishing and hunting. He bought Vicki's mother a pink mustang, the only one in Raleigh. It was symbolic of his one of a kind personality.

I told, not asked, Vicki that I planned to marry her very early in our relationship. That is how crazy I was about her. She had the gifts of presence, strength, and the ability to love fiercely. She was quick to let me know that marriage to me was not going to happen as she had no plans to marry someone who was tall. I am six feet one inch tall. She also had no intention of marrying a clergyman with the bizarre hours that go along with that vocation.

Keep in mind that she was a very popular student on the North Carolina State University campus where the ratio of men to women was eight to one. As I mentioned she was elected secretary of her class. On top of that I was a Yankee! I like challenges, but most sane men would have walked away and let this one go. I was not sane, as my friends pointed out to me.

We spent wonderful weekends together that summer when I could get to Raleigh. I would leave on a Friday night from Philadelphia and return on Sunday night to be at work on Monday. The eight hour drive was not a deterrent. I often kid my wife that we got along so well that summer because I couldn't understand half of what she said with that thick southern accent of hers. To this day she can be on the phone with a sorority sister or family member who still live in Raleigh and that accent can return in a blink of an eye.

My mother was a very strong woman who set the pattern for me to be attracted to a different kind of strong women. I look back on the women I have hired or have been close to as colleagues and find that strength is a common theme. The description that southern women are like a steel fist in a velvet glove is true.

### The South As A Different Cultural Experience

As I began spending time in the South with Vicki I experienced a culture different from the one in which I grew up. I found there is credence in what I had read about southern culture. It exudes a warmer spirit and a low key approach to life.

Three anecdotes demonstrate the southern culture I experienced directly. First, when Vicki told her sorority sisters she was dating someone from the North, they gave her a hard time. So I had to win her over along with her sorority sisters. I am pleased to say that I am now an unofficial honorary member of Sigma Kappa Sorority. These women represent the best of sorority life. They keep in touch to support one another and plan frequent times to get together. All three schools in the research triangle area, North Carolina State, The University of North Carolina and Duke are represented by undergraduate and graduate degrees earned by her sorority sisters and their spouses. I had never experienced anything like their school spirit for sports and institutions before I arrived there. These people are crazy about their teams and schools!

When I first worshipped at Christ Episcopal Church in Raleigh, the oldest Episcopal Church in that city, I walked through the front door to encounter a plaque that read, "To Our Brave Soldiers Who Fought The Enemy in the Great War." Enemy was capitalized in bold letters. They were talking about me as a Northerner.

I went to the local supermarket to buy groceries and was part of a long line of patrons who were waiting to check out. When it was my turn the cashier noticed that I had failed to pick up the second item of a buy one get one free offer. She calmly said, "We will wait for you. Go get it." As a Philly native, I paused as I was thinking that would not be the custom in my grocery store up north where going to the store can be like going to war. So I looked back at the people waiting in the long line and all said, "No problem! We'll wait." If I were back in Philly I would have been accosted verbally or physically in a just a few steps.

### *Life At Berkeley At Yale*

The fall after I met Vicki I began my seminary education at Berkeley at Yale in New Haven. I was scared but also excited about the learning that would be ahead. The climate of the school was a culture shock for me. Some of the people in the school were very affluent. The turmoil, demonstrations, and protests of the sixties were a vital part of the school community. Blue collar neighborhoods like mine did not have protesting. We had something called work.

I was criticized by some of my fellow students for not having enough of a revolutionary spirit. These were heady times with the Bobby Seale and the Black Panther Trial at the New Haven Courthouse. Protesters had overrun Columbia University and taken the administration offices hostage. Woodstock was in the air.

I noticed that a good many of these protesters had back up. They could always go home or get money from their parents. They were intoxicated by the thrill of being on the front lines of change.

This was driven home to me in a rather vivid way. When I arrived at Berkeley I became good friends with Tim Blauvelt. He was a great distance runner, was from Harlem, and had attended Wesleyan University. We received the same assignment for field work.

Most of the seminary students were sent to inner city churches in New Haven or other close by urban areas. They were ecstatic about their assignments. The purpose was to put the students into an environment that was very unlike where they grew up. That phrase "to learn how the other half lived" was very much in the air.

## Time At Darien

Tim and I were assigned to St. Luke's Church in Darien. I had no idea of what our Sunday experience would be. I had never even heard of the town before. I soon learned that Darien, Connecticut is one of the most affluent suburbs in America. It is a bedroom community for the rich and famous of New York City.

Over the course of our time there we observed a central theme of human existence. Everyone has some struggle in his life. When you enter into relationships with others the barriers come down and you find that you have more in common than you expected given your differences in background and station in life. There is an expression that comes from a book title, "the rich are different." They aren't.

We are all made from the same human clay. Tim and I were in the middle of many challenging situations. They ran the gamut from keeping up with the Joneses, to infidelity, to absentee parents, to rebellious adolescents, to forms of abuse. But most people we met were just like Tim and me in that they were trying to do their best with what they had, nurturing others as best they could. They had a great moral code to guide their actions.

## Working Class And The 60s

It finally dawned on my fellow students that maybe I was not revolutionary enough to meet their standard of revolutionary fervor because their revolution was, in part, to free people like me, the disenfranchised of our nation. The working class was lost in the shuffle. However, as I mentioned, the movement was more about race and gender than it was about class. An unpopular war was raging. While my peers were in the streets, I was in the library doing what I had always done. I worked hard to learn so that I could embrace that "freedom to" part of me and became a person of prayer.

I learned the clothing of the revolutionaries would sometimes cost more than what I was wearing. It cost money to look poor. This remains true today.

## A Great Learning Experience With Outstanding People

For me Berkeley at Yale was like another world of learning. I loved the courses I took, kept my head down, and tried to do my best in the world of academics. I believe faith is caught as well as taught and the same is true for great teaching and learning. I was blessed to have some of the best teachers and mentors, better than I could have hoped for.

I will highlight five exceptional people to give you a sense of the thrill of learning in the Berkeley at Yale community.

My first class was especially memorable for me. It was held in a classroom on Prospect Avenue, a central traffic artery in New Haven. As the class began The Reverend Dr. Edward Rochie Hardy, Professor of Church History, entered the room. He was an imposing person, tall with a real presence about him.

Dr. Hardy was New York City's most famous child prodigy. He was only 26 when he received his 5th academic degree. He matriculated at NYU at the age of 5. At 10 he passed Harvard's entrance examinations but waited until he was 12 to enter Columbia University. He was familiar with 12 different languages and translated ancient texts that would baffle the scientists. He was an academic force of nature.

As the class began he handed out the course syllabus. The list of books required for the course was daunting. He then held up a book that was the central text for the course. It had a light blue cover with maroon wording and was several inches thick, the text in the smallest of print. It was a hefty volume, <u>A History of Christianity</u>, by Kenneth Scott Latourette. Dr. Hardy simply said, "Gentlemen, I expect you to know everything that is in this text and the other assigned readings. My lectures are going to be about everything that is not contained in them. You are responsible for both."

Dr. Hardy taught the historical connections behind the scenes of all the major topics in church history. He did so without referring to any notes. He was eccentric. When someone would blow their car horn on the busy street outside the classroom he would turn toward the window, take out his white handkerchief, and wave in that direction. He was a character who was well known by the New Haven police since he zoomed around town with his huge figure crammed into a baby blue Volkswagen beetle.

Dr. Werner Rode was a world famous professor of Phenomenology, Existentialism, and Faith. He had a rich French accent and moved us through complex ideas, connecting thoughts together in a way that reading a book could not. His insights and wisdom were essential to the learning process. With his guidance our class soared to new heights of understanding. He cut a dashing figure looking like someone who would be equally at home in Paris, London, and Berlin as well as in New Haven.

I took a course in homiletics, the art of preaching, with Dr. Percy Urban. His son, Dr. Linwood Urban, then Chair of the Religion Department at Swarthmore College, would be the person who encouraged me to apply for the position of Chaplain at the Episcopal Academy. It is a small world.

Dr. Percy Urban was a fiery force. He held the class in his home and we sat around his large dinner table for our sessions. He was a chain smoker, coughing and wheezing frequently throughout the class. At times it took him some time to catch his breath because of his animated style. His wife would appear just at the right time to replace the full ashtray with a new empty one. Dr. Urban was short in stature and he presided over the class while leaning over the table. He would bang the table with his fist to make a point as he was reviewing each of the sermons my classmates and I prepared for his class. It is an understatement to say that no one could lose focus in this class for even a moment.

He would call us each by name and then give his commentary on the work we had done. During one very memorable class for me he became even more animated than usual, leaned far over the table puffing away on his cigarette, and proclaimed, "Mr. Squire, you are a gifted writer, but sometimes you get too cute with your metaphors. Change that or you will get yourself in trouble." Bang! His fist came down hard on the table. Our books bounced about on the table as if the table were a trampoline.

Dr. Urban was not interested in grammar or style. He wanted us to be able to speak words that would touch the hearts of others. He never stated this directly as he taught, but that is what all of us in the class caught.

Dr. Richard Kalter was beyond brilliant. He facilitated his students in identifying central themes and connections regarding anything we were studying, including the philosophy of religion. He requested that his students call him Richard. He was the embodiment of the intellectual. He could lose himself in discussing the value of the important connections between mind and spirit. Richard's hair was long and unkempt. He wore wire-rimmed glasses and occasionally would push them down his nose and look over them when he was teaching. I can think of few people who could be as engrossed in thought as Richard could be.

Richard decided to come to our wedding in Raleigh where things were more conservative than in New Haven. His relationships with people and his faith were very important to him so he put his fears and discomfort aside and traveled to Raleigh for our wedding. He would kid Vicki and me about feeling as though he was heading into enemy territory. I am sure some of the people in the South were not ready for him as he seemed to be a foreigner in a strange land, and in many ways he was. As I indicated, people came first and his fears and discomfort second. Vicki and I were thrilled to have him with us for our big day.

One of my favorite people at Berkeley at Yale was Miss Betsy Rafferty. She was right out of central casting. If you have seen <u>Downton Abbey</u>, she was like the two elderly dames who play such a central role in that television production. She was a very sophisticated and proper person.

The unmarried members of our school community had their meals in the refectory. At times we had the married members of our school at lunch. Miss Rafferty was always present for dinner. And what a dinner it was! The food was terrific. I was a waiter to help pay for school and to have some spending money. Waiters sat at the end of the table. We lit the candles on the table, a blessing was said, and a bell was rung. Then we would be off to the kitchen to bring the dinner out on large trays. All the waiters wore starched white jackets. We marched the food and dirty trays in and out of the kitchen. Miss Rafferty taught the proper way to serve food to others. The dinners were always soup to nuts. Proper etiquette was emphasized

Miss Rafferty's table selection was random. There was no assigned seating for the students so we never knew when to expect her at our table. She was there to teach us how to be gentlemen. The nights she didn't come to dinner, the ambiance at the table was very different. It was like a fraternity house dinner gone south so her function was very much needed. She was a powerful presence and respected by all. Whenever Miss Rafferty was present everyone would be on their very best behavior expressing the punctilio of the most civil people of the time. Once again we see demonstrated that important aspects of life and life's journey are just as often caught as they are taught. We were catching a lot of the very best behavior of our time. Manners were a virtue as seen through Miss Rafferty's eyes, something that our present culture too often forgets.

I received some criticism along the way in New Haven. I filled the walls of my room with Vince Lombardi quotes like "Winners never quit and quitters never win". The saying made famous by

Notre Dame, "Play like a champion today", was also prominently displayed. A lot of people thought I came from another planet and I guess, at one level, I did. The planet was working class America that was invisible on the American landscape at that time in history, and in my opinion still is today.

## A Lesson Learned About Race

Since I was dating a southern girl, I thought it would be great to have a Confederate Flag in my room. I hung it on a wall. For me it stood for love and great memories. I had a lot of lessons to learn about race and gender issues. One night I was visited by one of my African American schoolmates. I knew that this fellow and I were on the same side on most issues so I was struck by the fact that he wanted to know why the flag was hanging there. I told him.

He took some time to tell me what it meant to him. He was clear and direct in sharing his point of view and I knew he had my best interest at heart so I listened carefully to his perspective. When he left the room, I took down the flag, folded it and put it in a drawer. This issue of that flag and the memories it represents is still a hot topic today. I am grateful to my friend for helping me understand a different way of perceiving it.

I loved studying at the Yale Beineke Rare Book Library. The building is very modern with thin translucent marble serving as windows. For some reason I felt this was a place that filled my spirit with a willingness to take in all that was holy and good. It was my sacred space. This was another reason my friends thought that I came from another planet.

## Beginning At Duke University Medical Center

During this first year at Berkeley Vicki and I continued correspondence and phone conversations with one another. Then something wonderful happened. I was accepted at Duke Medical Center to do a twelve week program in pastoral counseling during the coming summer. I would be an intern there in pastoral counseling. This involved counseling patients on the various hospital wards, creating verbatims of conversations I had with patients, and having these exchanges analyzed by supervisors. We were also required to do group therapy with our colleagues in the program. These group therapy sessions occurred several times a week. It was a very intense experience and I loved every minute of it.

I never thought my experiences with my mother would help me in any way as I was going through life, but they did during this program. Part of group work is to identify and name behaviors in others that you find unhelpful. The theory is that once a person knows they are coming across in the wrong way, they will cease that form of behavior. The group experience is hard hitting. It sometimes came under the heading of a movement that was nationwide at the time called sensitivity training. There were sessions where one or two members of the group would leave in tears feeling devastated as a hard truth came their way.

The group work was enlightening to me. For one thing I became aware of how truly competitive I really am and I had to claim that, but I quickly became aware also that my mother could have invented sensitivity training without even realizing it. She had no filters. She told you exactly what she was feeling at the time. She could be brutal but, at times, show interest in how I was doing. It was not part of my mother's makeup to use the Carl Rogers' approach. Carl Rogers was a psychologist who invented Client Centered Therapy wherein therapists frequently ask, "How did that statement make you feel?" My mother didn't care how her honest expression affected other people.

This attitude of honest expression is part of the science of group dynamics so I felt very much at home. This was my life when I was young and still was at that point in time.

There is a story, maybe an urban legend, that a seminarian completed his sensitivity training and when he went home, he couldn't wait to see his bishop to tell him what he thought of him. He did just that and the outcome was not positive. As the story goes, the bishop thanked him and said, "In the interest of candor, let me tell you that I am no longer your bishop and you should find another one." Total honesty has its place, but not all the time.

During that summer when I was not on call at Duke University Hospital on a weekend, I spent the weekends in Raleigh with Vicki. Those days were magical. There is no other word for them. At the end of the summer I left Raleigh, stopped in Philadelphia to have some conversation with my parents and then continued on to New Haven. My mother tolerated our time together. My father wanted me to spend the night, but I continued on to New Haven after having dinner with them.

## The Last Year In New Haven

### Engagement

Vicki and I became engaged during that fall, my last year at Berkeley. We planned to be married on December 20th. Once when I asked her why she married me, she began by saying, "You were persistent!" After some laughter, I am glad that some other characteristics followed that first line.

We stayed in phone conversation throughout the fall. Vicki flew to New York for the Thanksgiving vacation. I drove to New York to pick her up in my almost new tan VW beetle. We headed back to New Haven in a driving rainstorm. As we approached the bridge over the Housatonic River in Connecticut, all the lights were out on the bridge and we couldn't see far ahead.

Before I realized it we came upon cars that had been turned around in slippery conditions and were facing us in our lane. We hit a car head on before I could stop. Our car veered over to the railing and landed up on the railing of the bridge looking down at the river. We carefully balanced ourselves in the car trying our best to lean as far back as we could so that we would not topple over into the roaring river below.

An ambulance, fire trucks, and tow trucks arrived. The car was put back onto the road. We were able to have it towed to New Haven to a garage. The car could be repaired. There were few parts on our bodies that were not battered or bruised. We were lucky and we knew it.

A professor, The Rev. Dr. John Romig Johnson, invited Vicki and me to join his family for Thanksgiving dinner. I called my home in Philadelphia to give my family holiday greetings, but my mother refused to speak with me. She didn't approve of the pending marriage, but my father got on the phone and asked how Vicki and I were doing and whether we needed anything. I told him how much I appreciated his offer, but made it clear that we were fine. I did not tell him about the near fatal automobile accident on the bridge. He wasn't sure if my mother would agree to attend the wedding, but he would try to be there.

## The Wedding And Canonical Exams

Vicki and I were married in her hometown of Raleigh, North Carolina on December 20th of 1969. My mother, father, brother and his wife as well as seminarian friends, my rector from my home parish, and a professor from Berkeley at Yale were present for our wedding. Initially my mother refused to come, but my brother convinced her to do so. As I have mentioned, my mother was very provincial having only traveled to just a few states north of Pennsylvania to visit with relatives. My family stayed at the Holiday Inn in downtown Raleigh.

After we had sent out our wedding invitations, I learned from my Diocese that my canonical exams would be on the three days following Christmas of that year. The exams were never scheduled far in advance. If you had plans, the canonical exams had to come first. Canonical exams are like bar exams. My exams were scheduled on three consecutive eight hour days. They included examinations in all areas of study covered in seminary such as history, the Bible, ethics, theology, pastoral care, and the origin and history of worship. The exams are challenging, but I was able to pass them the first time around. That whole period of time is a bit of a blur because within a week's time I was married, went on a three day honeymoon to Williamsburg, Virginia, spent Christmas with my new in laws, and successfully completed my canonical exams.

## *Final Months At Yale*

After the first of the year, Vicki and I returned to New Haven. She took courses at a local college so that she could continue to work toward her undergraduate degree. I had promised her family that she would finish college since our marriage resulted in her leaving North Carolina State University in the middle of her junior year. We had to deal with a bit of reverse prejudice experienced during a course she took in public speaking. The professor told her she would fail the course unless she could lose her southern accent.

Just before graduation from seminary I was accepted into a highly selective graduate program in pastoral counseling at Duke University. An internship in counseling at the medical center was an integral part of the program as well as a requirement to get another graduate degree. I received the Jarvis Traveling Fellowship to Duke from Berkeley at Yale as well as some financial assistance from the Diocese of Pennsylvania. This was great news for me and for Vicki because this meant that she could be a fulltime student, putting her back on track to graduate with her class at North Carolina State University.

## *An Eye Opening Dinner*

Just before graduation my bishop who rejected me initially due to his judgment that I lacked real world experience invited all senior seminarians from the diocese back to Philadelphia for a dinner at his home. It was an eye opening experience. I went to his address in Ambler, Pennsylvania and turned onto the drive to his home. It was a long drive as I passed the tennis courts on my left, saw the swimming pool on my right, and the horses and stable behind the manse. He greeted us in bare feet and wearing a T-shirt, reflecting the image he wanted to project. His home represented major back up.

I want you to imagine what it was like for me to make that drive up to his home after being turned down for not knowing how the other half lived or having enough real world experience and challenges.

## Bishop Ogilby And Bishop Bartlett

Two bishops who embodied authenticity and spirituality followed Bishop DeWitt. Lyman Ogilby and Allen Bartlett became good friends of mine. Lyman is now deceased but in his retirement he assisted as bishop in dioceses that were in need of this function. In his retirement Allen continues his peacekeeping work in the Middle East focusing on the plight of the Palestinians.

One of the things I have picked up working with young people for 38 years is an intolerance of phonies and people who live inauthentic lives. As I have mentioned Bishop DeWitt was a staunch advocate of the poor and women's rights. He also was part of the anti-war effort and stood out against our presence in Vietnam. I have great admiration for the work he did in those areas of social justice. However, he had no idea, in my opinion, of the issues of classism that were pervasive in our culture and still exist today. He retired to Isle au Haut off the coast of Maine.

## Days At Duke University And Duke University Hospital

Immediately after my graduation from Berkeley we left for North Carolina and drove through the night to our apartment in Raleigh so that we could both start classes the following Monday. North Carolina State University is in Raleigh so I commuted to Durham each day to my classes and training at Duke. I spent my on call nights at the hospital.

We enjoyed a very busy life as both of us were taking very demanding courses and I had the clinical internship on top of the course work. Vicki took organic chemistry during the summer session and ran up a bill with all the glassware she broke during labs.

She was a superstar student taking a difficult major in biology. This year was one of the best years of my academic life. It was an intense program that brought together wonderful colleagues with whom I would spend the year. It was also a program that was not for the faint of heart.

Duke University Medical Center was seen as the premier place in the South for treatment of challenging medical diagnoses. Patients did not go there for routine procedures such as tonsillectomies. The program presented me with an opportunity to counsel people with serious concerns of mind, body, and spirit. Duke was one of the largest hospitals in the world at that time. I recently returned to tour the campus. The hospital has expanded greatly since my time there.

Many cutting edge medical practices were part of the patient experience. These patients needed the very best counseling support whether it was on the psychiatric unit, medical care unit, or in the emergency room. I also provided counseling to the medical staff. From my counseling experiences with critically ill black women I observed a theme. I shared my insights in a paper I submitted titled The Existential Nature of Intentional Time in Black Women With Serious Illnesses. After years of being packed away in the recesses of my mind, it would resurface as a central premise for my book, Watch Your Time.

My goal during on call rotations when sleep was at a premium was to present myself with a welcoming energy. What made the program rigorous was the challenging coursework we were involved in while working in the hospital. Some of my colleagues referred to it as an intellectual marine boot camp.

I am reminded of advice I received from one of my children's doctors years later in my life. After being up for most of the night he said to me the next morning, "You need to look your best to communicate that you are ready to help, rather than to look as though you are tired and weary. If you are looking for a profession where people feel sorry for you, you have chosen the wrong one."

One of the things I learned during this program was how to multitask when in the middle of several high pressure situations. I learned that this was the world in which I am most comfortable. I thrived in that arena. Some people are great at addressing challenges at a slow pace. Others need to be in the middle of things. I was in the latter group. This became true of my 45 years of active ministry. This was another gift from my mother. I have always been comfortable in the middle of conflict. Life at home was a template for creating that comfort in the midst of conflict.

Our graduations from Duke and North Carolina State University were on the same day. Vicki would graduate with her class. I had kept my promise to her family and attended her graduation along with her family. I had my diploma from Duke mailed to me.

After Duke I continued supervision of my work in counseling to get to the next level of accreditation with the American Association of Pastoral Counselors. I did this at Delaware State Hospital with a terrific supervisor, Dick Flowers, one of the most astute teachers in the field.

### Epilogue: The Death Of My Mother

I wrote the following meditation after my mother's death. My words demonstrate my mother's emphasis on functionalism.

> My mother died on June 14, 1976. I learned much about life, about the Christian message, and about my self on June 13th, the day before she died. There are occasions in life that demand that I stop and take stock of where I am. This represents one of them. I was called to a nearby Roman Catholic hospital. The caller beckoned me simply with the words, "Come quickly. Your mother is critically ill." I waited in the critical care waiting room. Hanging on the wall opposite my chair and slouched body hung a crucifix, a wood cut of the broken body of Christ. Beyond the wall was a person with whom I had struggled as a child, adolescent, and adult.
>
> Mothers have important meaning to all of us. A friend wrote me a note composed on a plane shortly after she became aware of my loss. Part of what she said is, "I was in my early 50s when my mother died, but even now I think about her every day. I just recently said it was my mother's birthday today. She was 105 years old. So mothers are special people in many ways." My friend closed by saying, "My mother was very funny and did her own thing and wore slacks long before fashion indicated."

On the day before my mother died, I walked into the room to see her. She didn't say, "Hello! Glad to see you!" or any other expression that most of us would interpret as a standard greeting. She looked up at the clock before her, noticed the noon hour and asked, "Have you had your lunch yet?" I was furious. You don't ask someone as independent as I am if they have had their lunch.

I informed her that I hadn't, but that there was a nice coffee shop downstairs. I said that I would get a bite there very soon. She started to say something, but it began to sound like an apology that she couldn't get lunch for me or that she hadn't had the foresight to have something prepared for me in the Special Care Unit. I cut this exchange off and shifted things back to her. I can think of nothing as terrifying as experiencing that awful emptiness of wondering where, how, and in what form your next breath would come. Her lungs were failing. She was slowly drowning. That was her world.

When I left I got the number of the doctor's service to talk with him directly. This was out of a concern for my mother's life as well as for my own need to show the world once again how tough, take charge, and in control I really am.

I went back to the waiting room, back to that Christ on the cross hanging on the wall. Alone. The cross was not a sign, a symbol, or even an instrument of peace for me. It was a challenge. This time I purposely sat across from the hanging form. Since I was raised in the streets of a mill town, the feeling was a familiar one, like squaring off with an opponent just before we lashed out at each other, no holds barred, until a bloody end.

The cross of Christ didn't want to fight. I felt silly. What a contrast. Me sitting on the edge of my seat ready to take on anything and anyone who came along feeling angry, lost, and alone. Across from me was a broken man hanging, palms turned toward me, saying, "Come, I'm not going to hurt you."

I knew the struggle, only I was used to being on the other side. I was used to being priest and helper, and not one who easily asks for help. I was playing the game that had been played on me so many times. O. Hobart Mowrer describes this game best when he described my work with others who are struggling.

He said, "It is as though the patient and the therapist have sat down to play a game of cards. The hands are dealt out. The patient holds his cards close to his vest, inspecting them carefully. After some deliberation, he selects a card for his first play. He watches the therapist carefully for a response to this first attempt at strategy to find out if he has made the right play. Now it is the therapist's turn to play. Much to the patient's amazement, the therapist begins by laying his cards on the table face up, ready to encounter the patient transparently and without guile. It often takes a long while before the patient is willing to do the same." (Kopp 1972)

There was that wooden Christ...palms out... cards on the table, face up. There I was...tough... cards close to my vest, the bruises and the pain of that part of me that is an urchin...that is alone.

The cross began to speak within me. I thought of my wife and my children.

I thought of people who I had spent the week before with...battered, broken, and bruised.

I thought of a friend who signed a letter..."thank you good person"...which lit a spark that I had snuffed out in my own moments of self destruction.

I prayed to be open to that Spirit that hung before me and began to recall phrases shared by one

78

who came to me when I was in the more familiar position of helper and not one in need.

The phrases came back. First they were just snatches and forms. I was amazed at how much I could remember from a once memorized verse.

Between the Christ on the wall and the street urchin were Alice walker's words from her poem, <u>Sunday School Circa 1950</u>.

Who made you was always
The question
The answer was always God.
Well, there we stood
Three feet high
Heads bowed
Leaning into
Bosums.
Now I no longer recall the catechisms
Or brood on the genesis of life.
No.
I ponder the exchange itself
And Salvage mostly the leaning.

I ponder the exchange itself and salvage mostly the leaning. (Walker 1973)

I look up through the hanging cross to the person who lay helpless behind the wall.

Who made you?
Have you had your lunch yet?
Her last words to me.
No, I can take care of myself.

My eyes came back to the cross...at first blurred...as if they had tried to see too much...out of focus at crossing too much time...too much death...

the cross...the broken person...the outstretched palms...the ultimate vulnerability...the words...

"Come I am not going to hurt you."

I ponder this exchange itself and now salvage mostly my leaning.

## Reflections

When was the last time you stood up for someone else knowing that you would pay a high price?

What governs your life? Are you more functional or emotional or a balance of both?

Is there something that can transport you back to challenging times?

Have you ever protected your parents from the hard times you were experiencing?

What has influenced your spiritual life the most?

Who is or was a mentor for you?

How would you describe the cultural influences in your life?

What teacher from your past do you value the most?

Choose one word to describe yourself.

# *CHAPTER 3: THE TURNING POINT*

## *The Swarthmore Years*

After completion of my graduate degree from Duke, I received a call to be the Assistant Rector of Trinity Church in Swarthmore, PA. Swarthmore is an idyllic small college town and the parish is located within walking distance of the college. The percentage of graduates of Swarthmore College who return to their college community to live is one of the highest in the nation. The community is bucolic. There are great town and gown relationships. The currency is ideas. When we moved there, the town was filled with architects, writers for the *New York Times*, the author of the best selling book, The Selling of the President, musicians, publishers, and people pursuing unconventional quests. Professors and staff from the college were active in the community spreading the influence of one of the best small liberal arts colleges in the nation.

I have often referred to our seven years there as a swing through an intellectual jungle gym, and I loved every minute of it. When we were invited to a party, topics such as sports or the entertainment industry were not part of the discussions. Current affairs and world political issues were front and center.

I worked with a terrific staff. This parish was seen as one of the most socially active places in the Philadelphia area. In Swarthmore there is a real connection between what people do on behalf of others and the lifestyle they live.

I want you to imagine what it was like to climb into the pulpit on a Sunday morning and preach to the assembled group described above. People offered comments on every sermon. This was expected in a community of give and take. I am reminded of the truth that I learned regarding feedback, "The time to worry is when people aren't giving you feedback, for that is an indication that they have given up on you." (Pausch 2008) More importantly, despite criticism, I knew that people were on my side and had my best interests at heart. They were also quick to praise.

The heart of my ministry in that community was guiding families through many tragedies. During my seven years in Swarthmore some of those tragedies were my own. Two of my children were born then and my daughter was diagnosed with a rare form of leukemia while we were in Swarthmore. Both of my parents died when I was in my twenties during that period of time. My father died in 1974, and my mother died in 1978. My father died at home. I do not know his cause of death or, at least, was never told. My mother died in a hospital. Her diagnosis was pulmonary failure, but the cause of that failure was never determined. Prior to my mother's hospitalization, any treatments my family received were done in a doctor's office or at home. There were no trips to the hospital for any form of testing.

Later in my life, I was on an airplane when my seatmate asked me when my parents died. It was a conversation about family life. When I told her I was in my 20s when both parents died, she responded, "Oh, you are an orphan in the universe."

I noticed a significant change in my mother after the death of my father. My mother seemed to come to life. She was much more active and engaging. She laughed more and had a smile on her face. She went to work as a salesperson in a department store and returned to her high school days of dressing in the latest fashions. I was delighted with this change. When Thaddeus was born, she took great joy in taking care of him and seemed to mellow out. She had several good years of these changes. Toward the end of her life my mother needed nursing care. Most of her care was provided by Vicki. That was somewhat ironic given the hard time that she gave us before our marriage. Vicki was able to move beyond all of that and took the higher road of providing her with excellent care.

On a good news note, Vicki and I had the joy of welcoming first Thaddeus and then Joanna into our lives while in Swarthmore. Thad was born as an old wise man.

Our second child, Joanna, was not easy. She was interested in many different things and was also a true joy, but she had the gift of being stubborn and having to have things her own way. When there was a special occasion at the church, Vicki would lay Joanna's church clothes out for her and Joanna would later appear wearing something more appropriate for a hike in the woods.

Our lives were greatly enriched with time spent enjoying our young family. For me, it was great to see my wife enjoying her role as mother of our children. There is nothing better.

Both children would play on the floor together, rough housing with me. Thad would declare, "glasses off," as his cue for me to remove my glasses and get on the floor with them. Both loved to read and be read to. One day while playing with Joanna, I notice the bruising on her body, the symptom that led us to our ultimate health care challenge and tragedy. I will share her story later in this narrative.

### Founding A Counseling Center

While serving at Trinity Church in Swarthmore, I was part of a group that founded a counseling center on the outskirts of Chester, Pennsylvania. Chester is one of the poorest cities in the nation. The residents were in dire need of the care we could provide. I was a member of the founding board and a counselor at the center.

Two incidents highlight how the counseling center served those who had fallen through the mental health safety net.

Our counseling rooms were not equipped with phones to contact others if help was needed. This was a terrible oversight on our part. One of our counselors was working with a client when loud noises and the sound of furniture being moved could be heard coming from his office. After the client had left in a fury, I helped the therapist up off the ground and asked, "What happened?" The therapist was so client-centered that the only concern he had was trying to figure out what the client was trying to say before he became overwhelmed by his anger.

The initial goal in a counseling relationship is to get a sense of the client by taking their history. I began work with a new client who had a complicated and tragic history. She lived in Chester, had children but no husband, and was affiliated with a local gang. She was strikingly beautiful with an exotic appearance and she always came to the sessions wearing a black cape over her clothing. I could not see her hands.

I thought we were making good progress on the issues she brought to counseling, but in one of the early sessions something happened that frightened her. You have probably seen horror movies in your life, but there is nothing as scary as watching someone become psychotic. Some refer to it as descending into madness.

Psychosis can be triggered by something that scares the client. I was taught in training to make myself smaller in situations where the client becomes threatening so that you don't add to their fright. This is a very counter-intuitive action because our first instinct is self-protection.

I am over six feet tall so the best way to make myself look smaller is to sit on the floor in an attempt to reduce the client's fears. She walked around me several times. I had only one question, "What did she have under that black cape?" She left the room and I never found out. But she had young children at home so I called the local mental health facility. The laws regarding hospitalization of patients who need that structure and intense counseling are limiting. The laws require consideration of just two questions, "Has the client hurt you? Has the client hurt herself?" If the answers are "No" then the reply is, "Sorry, there is nothing we can do."

I called the police and asked them to go to the home. I indicated that they needed to be careful because she would surely see them as threatening. She was taken into custody and the children were turned over to social services.

It took me awhile to get the image of that person who became psychotic out of my mind. I was afraid. In an urban setting, counseling issues tend to be more sociopathic and homicidal in nature. Your garden variety neuroses appear more in the suburban realm of mental health.

## Tragedy And Heartbreak

A painful personal tragedy occurred during a time period that bridged my time in Swarthmore and the beginning of my ministry at the Episcopal Academy. Rabbi Harold Kushner wrote in <u>When Bad Things Happen To Good People</u>, "Tragedy doesn't have a ticket into your life. It has a box seat". (Kushner 1981) That expression means everyone will experience it. It is not a matter of if. It is a matter of when.

It was Good Friday in 1978 when my world changed. It would never be the same again. After our three-year-old daughter, Joanna had experienced several vague illnesses, some low grade fevers, and general fatigue, Vicki and I began to notice bruising on many parts of her body. Initial evaluation by her pediatrician revealed some abnormalities in her blood work so we were instructed to take her to a hospital lab for more specialized testing. That afternoon we received the call to bring her to the hospital for admission. A bone marrow biopsy was scheduled.

The next day we were taken to a room to meet with a team of doctors. We were told that Joanna had leukemia. She was transferred to the Children's Hospital of Philadelphia (CHOP) to begin treatment. Further analysis of her bone marrow revealed the diagnosis of histiocytic leukemia, an extremely rare form of the cancer, that is very aggressive and usually fatal. The year Joanna was diagnosed there were only thirty-three cases of her form of cancer in the United States. Even today there are no successful treatment options for this disease. Chemotherapy was the only treatment option but we were told the chances for response to the treatment were very slim.

Needless to say fervent prayer began along with the chemotherapy and continued throughout her treatment. The side effects of the chemotherapy were devastating. I recall Joanna had difficulty with eating, speaking, and drinking due to painful mouth sores. The most heart-wrenching thing was to watch her going through her treatment while she did not understand what was going on. The doctors, nurses, Vicki, and I tried our best to help her understand that the treatment and the side effects were going to make her better.

This was a tough sell to a three-year-old undergoing chemotherapy of the most rigorous kind. The doctors had communicated little hope for a cure. There is an important word that you need to hear in moments like these. That word is hope. Some of the worst words in the English language are "there is nothing else that can be done." Hope was not offered to us.

Putting my head down and pushing forward was not making a difference in the outcome for Joanna. I was totally out of control in this situation. We prayed and had prayer groups praying for her recovery.

Following is a sermon that I wrote after we learned of Joanna's diagnosis.

On a visit this past week to my daughter who is a patient on the Oncology Unit of Children's Hospital, I was greeted by an angry middle-aged woman before I could enter the door of Joanna's room. I was wearing my clerical collar, something that I tried never to do when visiting because I want to be seen primarily as Joanna's father and nothing else. But schedules didn't always allow me to get into coat and tie as was the case on this particular day.

The woman who greeted me held me tightly by the arm and asked if I was an Episcopal priest. I was anxious to get past her to see how Joanna was doing but she made it very clear very quickly that I was going no place until I dealt with her. She told me that she was an Episcopalian, identified her parish and parish priest, and with much rage she quickly got to the point of our encounter.

The day before she learned that her daughter had leukemia, and with much intensity she demanded, "Why did this happen to me? Why did this happen to my daughter?" I replied meekly as I look back on the exchange, "I don't know." This made her more furious.. She went on, "What do you mean

86

you don't know? There has got to be a reason." I responded again by saying quietly, "I don't know." There is unfortunate symbolism attached to the clerical collar. Standing there numb as I was, I knew that her argument was not with me, but with her God. I knew because her questions and rage were also my own.

She held me fast, and although there was great silence, her fixed stare still asked me the same penetrating question over and over again, "Why? Why?" I couldn't find a response, and I knew that she deserved better than me giving her some pat answer that would assuage pain, something to reduce the question, something to make sense of it all.

After a period of silence she released my arm, and said that she was sorry for holding me up from completing my rounds of the rest of the Episcopal patients in the hospital.

I told her that I wasn't at Children's seeing the Episcopal patients. I looked through Joanna's door, said, "Hello," and received the gift of a mischievous smile in return. I faced the woman again and said, "That's my daughter." She burst into tears, turned, and ran up the hall. There is no easy way to learn that we are not the center of the universe. There is no easy way to accept that we aren't the only person befallen with difficulty and pain. There is no easy way to learn that we are all in this together or we will perish in loneliness.

I knew what the woman was experiencing, for some weeks before, I was standing where she was standing. The jolt that pulled me out of myself and out of self-pity happened somewhat differently. I had left the hospital for an hour after being there for a long period of time. During the time that I was away, a physician had informed Vicki about the exact nature of Joanna's illness, that it was not the common form of leukemia but a very rare form of leukemia. I received this news by phone from Vicki while I was out at Swarthmore. Getting back into the hospital through rush hour traffic seemed to take forever.

When I arrived at the ward I was in a rage, angry and frightened, by this new diagnosis for which chances of response and cure were very remote. I was angry about the bad timing of the doctor telling Vicki when I wasn't there. She could have waited. We embraced thinking, "Why me? Why Joanna?" After storming around the room, it dawned on me that sitting in a wheelchair in the middle of the room was a beautiful bright eyed thirteen year old who looked up and said, "I am Sherry!"

Vicki began to explain that Sherry was of great help to her, that she had been pacing up and down the hall waiting for me to get back when Sherry asked her to come into her room commenting, "You look as though you could use someone to talk with." Although she was young she could understand what Vicki was feeling and going through. A few hours earlier Sherry had been told that she had bone cancer and she would need to have her leg amputated later that week. I went over, kissed her on top of her head, and thanked her for her ministry to Vicki. Sometimes it is hard to realize that there is more to life than me and mine. The "Why God?" seemed unimportant and left me. What was important was that moment.

Elie Wiesel in his powerful novel, <u>Night</u>, recounts in starkly simple prose his own experience as a child during the Nazi Holocaust in Europe. Wiesel writes in his book the following exchange he had with his spiritual advisor, Moche, "Man raises himself to God by the questions that he asks

Him. That is the true dialogue, that man questions God and God answers. But we don't understand the answers. We can't understand them because they come from the depths of the soul, and they stay there until death. The true answers are only within yourself."

"And why to you pray, Moche?" I ask him.

"I pray to the God within me that he will give me the strength to ask Him the right questions. And throughout those evenings a conviction grew in me that Moche the Beadle would draw me with him into eternity, into that time where question and answer would become one." (Wiesel 2006)

The writings of Elie Wiesel seen in the light of the Holy Scripture have been very helpful to me.

There were more exchanges between the woman and me in the hall in which growth in the Spirit occurred for us both. Wearing the clerical collar that day was clearly the work of the Spirit.

But this bit of symbolism, the clerical collar, put the woman in the hall and me in touch with a penetrating question, "How could a child of God's man suffer?" she asked. All of this raises a more poignant question for all of us, "Why did the Son of God have to suffer?"

Right now I don't find pat theological answers to be of much help for they stand between me and my Lord and God. I must live the questions more fully. Why does Joanna suffer? Why does Sherry suffer? We all must live with the question of why did the Son of God suffer? You and I MUST live that question. Think. Pray on that relationship. Feel that exchange. Live in that exchange. It will change your life.

The poet, Rilke, wrote, "Be patient toward all that is unsolved in your heart. And try to love the questions themselves. Do not seek the answers that cannot be given you because you would not be able to live them. And the point is to live everything. Live the questions now. Perhaps you will then gradually, without noticing it, live along some distant day into the answer." (Rilke 1934)

Francois Mauriac, French novelist, writes in his Introduction to Wiesel's autobiography, Night, these words.

"And I, who believe that God is love, what answer could I give my young questioner, whose dark eyes still held the reflection of that angelic sadness which had appeared one day upon the face of the hanged child. What did I say to him? Did I speak of that other Israeli, his brother who may have resembled him...the crucified, whose cross has conquered the world? Did I affirm that the stumbling block to his faith was the cornerstone of mine, and what conformity between the cross and the suffering of me was in my eyes a key to that impenetrable mystery whereon the faith of his childhood had perished? We do not know the worth of one single drop of blood, one single tear, all is grace. If the eternal is the eternal, the last word for each of us belongs to Him. This is what I should have told this Jewish child. But could only embrace him, weeping." (Wiesel 2006)

I find that the Gospel of Jesus Christ sustains me as both question and answer. The cross and resurrection lead to meaningful existence. Recently I saw an inscription in a book that was given to me. I had not noticed the inscription before that time. Inside the book was written, "For someone who asks beautiful questions in the hope that we will all find beautiful answers."

Perhaps we will come to that moment where we will be drawn into eternity, into the time where question and answer become one. It may be already experienced, experienced in the present, or some day in the future.

The moment where question and answer become one. I have never heard a more poignant description of the living Lord, our Savior Jesus Christ.

Joanna's treatments continued throughout the spring. There were many hospitalizations for treatments and to manage side effects. During this time I heard from The Reverend Dr. Linwood Urban, Chair of the Religion Department, at Swarthmore College. Recall that his father taught me homiletics at Berkeley at Yale. Linwood was also a parishioner of mine at Trinity Church, Swarthmore. His son, David, was a student at the Episcopal Academy. He had received the school magazine with a job description for the new chaplain they were looking to hire.

Linwood showed me the description and said, "This is you. I think you should apply." The position described the school's desire to hire a chaplain who had significant academic credentials, advanced training in counseling, and was a great preacher and leader of worship. They wanted the new chaplain to be outgoing with good interpersonal skills and to be able to connect readily with a diverse group of people.

I was flattered that he thought of me in that way, but he knew that my focus at that time was on caring for my daughter and the people in my parish. He understood, but came back a time or two to ask me to reconsider.

I submitted an application and quickly forgot about it as each day required another important decision about Joanna's treatment. I was contacted by Jay Crawford who was Head of School at EA. He asked if he and Charles Latham, a brilliant teacher at the school who served the school in so many ways, could come to hear me preach. Charles was a modern day Erasmus who could teach any course offered at the school. Jay had a long and storied association with the school as he attended Episcopal himself and returned to teach there, eventually becoming the Head of School. They met with me afterwards and did not comment much on my sermon.

Overriding all of my professional obligations was our focus on Joanna. Her treatment was ongoing with periodic bone marrow aspirations to evaluate the efficacy of the treatment.

In late spring we learned that Joanna had achieved remission in spite of the long odds against that happening. Vicki and I were ecstatic. The doctors warned us that the remission was remarkable and would probably not last. They thought the relapse would occur quickly.

## The Call To The Episcopal Academy

During this same period of time I was called for interviews with students, faculty, board members, administrators, and parents of the Episcopal Academy. After of a period of time I received a call from Jay Crawford. He wanted me to come to the Academy to meet with him. I sat down across from him and he said, "We want you to be the next Chaplain here at our School." I was shocked. I had never entertained the possibility that I would be the candidate they chose. My whole being was at CHOP. I told him that my focus was on my daughter and this made my life very unpredictable. His response shocked me as well, "I know what you are going through with your daughter. We want you. We will help you through everything that you and your family have to deal with."

I told him I would talk to Vicki and get back to him. Then there was another crisis with Joanna and I pushed everything else to the back burner. Jay never pressured me for a decision.

Most people do not know that I had always wanted to go to the Episcopal Academy. The school's campus was about 20 minutes from my hometown. I wanted to study there for different reasons than most. I admired an Episcopal Academy student who I had met at a church camp. I have never been able to reconnect with him since he was entering ninth grade at Episcopal and then was going off to boarding school. His first name was Paul.

He talked about his love of his Classics courses at the Academy. He was influenced greatly by the religious aspects of the school. He was very polite, kind, sensitive to others, and a model of what it means to be a good person. I wanted to be like him. We raced one another. He won. He was a terrific athlete. At that age I believed that all of those great characteristics Paul demonstrated might be the result of the education he was receiving at EA.

I posed the question of going to Episcopal to my parents. They looked a bit dumbfounded as they had never heard of the school, and they indicated that our family finances would never cover such an expense. I took the attitude of nothing ventured, nothing gained, and moved on. My dream was not based in any degree of reality or possibility. It is interesting to me how deeply I was affected by experiencing the best of humanity in another student.

Vicki and I discussed the opportunity for me to become the new chaplain at Episcopal. We prayed about the decision. We concluded that, being people of faith, we should move forward and accept Jay's offer.

Jay is one of the greatest leaders I have encountered in life. I was blessed to have had the opportunity to learn from him for many years and to call him my friend. One of the secrets to his great leadership was his ability to fully focus on all personal interactions. This attribute can be taught but, like so many of the important aspects of life, it is more often caught. Jay treated everyone the same, from the most powerful to those without power. He led by example.

Jay was the embodiment of the saying made famous by Theodor Geisel, Dr. Seuss, "To the world you may be one person; but to one person you may be the world". (Geisel 10 Quotes to Live By on His 113th Birthday Website) Jay lived out our school motto, *Esse Quam Videri,* to be rather than to seem to be.

Our decision to accept the position at the Episcopal Academy was a risk for us. The parishioners of Trinity Church had been an incredible support through Joanna's treatments. It would take a leap of faith to leave that nurturing community.

During that summer we continued Joanna's treatment with the goal of sustaining her remission. We took a trip to Colorado to visit our close friends who were her godparents.

## *Many Close Calls*

One of the low points we encountered during this roller coaster ride of treatment for Joanna was when she was hospitalized with pneumonia. It was the weekend and her labored breathing concerned us. On Saturday Vicki and I looked up and standing before us was Dr. Audrey Evans, Chief of the Oncology Service at CHOP. She had been out riding her horse but she couldn't get Joanna off her mind. She came to the hospital dressed in her riding attire.

Dr. Evans took charge and moved Joanna quickly to the Intensive Care Unit. Later when she returned to Joanna's room she told us that we had to be prepared for the worst, Joanna may not to be able to live through the night. Vicki and I stood vigil through the night. Joanna turned a precarious corner and rallied. She was a fighter.

During that low point in the ICU, a tall older Episcopal priest, The Reverend Roy Hendricks came to visit us. Roy said simply that he had heard that we had a child who was very ill. To this day we have no idea how he knew this. He just appeared. He became a daily source of support and prayer for us. He and his wife, Marion, came to our home on Christmas Eve when Joanna died and prayed with us. It was only then that we learned about Roy and Marion's child, John, who had died of cancer. Our middle son is named after this remarkable person who stood with us through Joanna's treatment and death and became an important part of our life after Joanna's death. Adam Roy Squire was born 13 months after Joanna died

## *A Bone Marrow Transplant As Our Last Hope*

Before we left for our summer trip to Colorado we met with our team of doctors at CHOP and learned that our only hope for any extended time for our daughter was a bone marrow transplant. This option countered that devastating statement that there was nothing else we could do. It produced a measure of hope. At that point Joanna would be the youngest patient to be transplanted at CHOP. She was not quite four years old. A bone marrow transplant was an experimental treatment for her cancer at that time. Bone marrow transplants are devastating treatments. They were reserved as a last resort in our setting. The doctors and nurses at CHOP were excellent, caring teachers. There was so much to learn going into this complex treatment.

## Thaddeus Is The Best Match For Joanna

The first hurdle we had to make our way through was finding a compatible bone marrow donor for Joanna. The best results are achieved when a member of the immediate biological family is the donor. This is done to minimize the chance of graft versus host disease, a life threatening post procedure condition where the recipient's body attacks the donor marrow. We were all tested and our son, Thaddeus, was a match. How does one explain to a six-year-old that he may have to have surgery in an effort to save his sister's life?

Vicki and I sat down with Thaddeus and explained what a bone marrow transplant was in language that a six-year-old could understand. We told him that it would help his sister if he donated his bone marrow. We asked if he would be the donor. He quickly said, "Yes." I don't know what we would have done if he had said, "No." It was a choiceless choice. Recently he told me that he remembers everything about his role in the transplant.

Since the procedure was experimental there were many legal documents to complete. Joanna had to become a ward of the state in order to protect all involved and guard against conflict of interest and possible lawsuits. We had to go into this with eyes wide open. The decisions that had to be made were the most difficult one could imagine. This may be the unconscious motivation that drew me to pursue bioethics years later. Right and wrong decisions are easy to make. They are clear-cut. We were faced with a decision that would come under the general heading of the "lesser of two evils". Should we gamble that Joanna might stay in remission or do we put her through this life threatening experimental procedure? Do we risk the life of our one healthy child in an effort to save our daughter?

Before the hospital could schedule Joanna's transplant, our family had to be interviewed by a psychiatrist. This was to assess whether we could sustain the stress of what would be before us. We were approved to move forward with the transplant. There were only two transplant rooms available at CHOP at that time. We had to wait until one would be available. The projected date for Joanna's transplant was mid-September, just after the beginning of the school year. This timing would affect Thad since he would take part in the procedure as he was beginning first grade at Episcopal.

All of this had an emotional toll on Joanna. She was angry and confused. She would throw me out of her room. Surely her father should be able to take care of all of this and make it right. She began to resist her painful bone marrow aspirations and other aspects of her treatment, including taking medications by mouth.

By the end of the summer all requirements for the bone marrow transplant had been met and it was scheduled for some-time in September. Boxes were packed, ready for our move into the Chaplain's Residence on the Episcopal Academy Campus.

After getting settled into our home on the Episcopal Campus, fall began with a bang of activity. I had been in a high energy, busy parish, but nothing matches the pace of an independent school like Episcopal. While settling into my new position, my primary focus continued to be on Joanna, Thad, and the impending bone marrow transplant.

We continued our close relationship with and support from Trinity Church. At the same time we were welcomed warmly by the Episcopal Academy family and began new friendships. We had prayer and support from two wonderful communities.

We were contacted by CHOP with the projected admission date for Joanna's bone marrow transplant. The timing was a race against the clock. It was vital to a successful outcome to do the procedure while she was still in remission.

The day before the scheduled admission, Thad came down with a cold. We contacted the lead oncologist to report this. We needed to understand the protocol when something like this happens. The doctor did not hesitate saying, "We must postpone the transplant. We cannot risk the health of your one healthy child in the attempt to save your daughter."

## *A Nightmare: Watching Your Child Go Through A Bone Marrow Transplant*

Ten days later Joanna was admitted for the first phase of the transplant, the induction. This was a two step process, the goal being to totally destroy her bone marrow in preparation for the donor marrow. She was first given high dose chemotherapy that resulted in her experiencing all the painful and risky side effects of such therapy. Then she was taken for total body radiation to complete the process. This involved her being in a radiation treatment room by herself for about an hour.

The goal of the induction phase, destroying her bone marrow, in theory, would bring her to the brink of death. The transplanted marrow would rescue her. Witnessing the process was incredibly painful. It was awful to watch the radiation treatment, knowing the effects and watching her alone in the room for an hour with the frightening linear accelerator machine. The total body radiation would destroy her ability to have children if she survived her cancer.

During the procedure and the recovery, Joanna had to live in an isolation room for a month. All visitors had to wear gowns and masks to protect Joanna from infection. Until her recovery from the transplant was complete any infection could be life threatening. We were not allowed to be with her during the night. It was painful to leave her at night knowing she would be alone in the isolation room. The nurses on duty at night were wonderful about spending time with her and holding her.

Once Joanna had completed all the induction treatment, Thad was admitted to CHOP. He was taken to the operating room and given general anesthesia for the harvesting of his bone marrow. The night before the procedure, he slept well. I sat next to him and watched him all night.

The donor cells were harvested from Thad's pelvic bone and transplanted to his sister via an intravenous catheter. He returned from surgery with small incisions on his back and he was in moderate pain. Thad missed several days of school as he recuperated.

Many wonderful friends were with Thad through this making certain he was cared for in an extra special, loving way.

The month of October was a time of hanging on every word as the physicians would keep us updated on Joanna's progress. There were good days and bad days. The days between the transplant and Joanna's recovery were a challenging, stressful time. There was no guarantee she would recover. There were gut wrenching times watching her suffer from mouth sores, disciplining her in order to make certain she would swallow the vital medications. The medical team warned us that we had to maintain discipline but all we wanted was to love and hold her.

### Joanna Comes Home But The Cancer Returns

We took Joanna home on her fourth birthday, November 8, 1978. Thad was hailed as a hero. Hospital staff told him he had saved his sister's life. On that day we thought the procedure had been worthwhile and prayed that it would give her a few more years of good quality of life. This was not the case. The cancer returned shortly before Thanksgiving. In early December we heard the dreaded words, that nothing more could be done to extend Joanna's life. We were encouraged to take her home and plan an early Christmas while she was still able to enjoy the celebration. I took a leave of absence from the school for the month of December.

A few weeks later I was drawing and cutting out flowers with Joanna at our breakfast room table. I still could not accept the awful truth even then, but I knew I had stopped feeling that we were still in the fight. The doctors always knew that more than likely this would be her fate since we were dealing with a terrible diagnosis.

What I wanted at that point was to have her free from pain and suffering. She had been an energetic blue eyed blond haired beautiful child. She now looked like she had come from a third world country where too many children go without food. Her cheeks were sunken in. Her eyes seemed to be deeper in her sockets. The glimmer in her eyes was gone. I didn't see that mischievous fighter anymore who would not be bossed around by others. Her hair was gone. All of her strength was gone. It goes without saying that we don't always get what we pray for regardless of how fervent those prayers are.

She died a few weeks later at four o'clock in the afternoon on Christmas Eve. We were with her when she died. I remember that last breath, a guttural sound, as though it were yesterday.

She was diagnosed on Good Friday and died on Christmas Eve. Those two holy days were exactly nine months apart that year. It takes nine months to bring new life into the world and it took nine months to part with our dear daughter. The bone marrow transplant did very little to increase her quality of life. Getting through these two holidays is still difficult for Vicki and me.

Vicki and I lay in bed that night she died holding hands as the thunder roared above. We said, "She has arrived!"

I was shocked the next morning that the sun came up and that it was business as usual in the world. I thought the world would stand still after our daughter's death, for our pain was deep enough to be projected to the world. While we awoke to our first day without Joanna everyone around us was celebrating the joy of Christmas.

We had the burial office for Joanna at Christ Chapel on the EA Merion Campus. The officiant at the service was the Reverend Warren Skipp, my colleague at Trinity Church in Swarthmore.

I wrote the following reflection for the service. I was really not able to speak so I asked a good friend and one of my assistant clergy, The Rev. Richard Herschel, to read it during the service. The reflection is titled, "Wilted Flowers Bloom Forever".

> There we sat…you picking at the wilted flowers. Me…watching every motion and expression. Your question was a simple one. What happens to flowers that die? I had read to you through tear stained eyes…fed you…rocked you with starts, gulps, and stops. Why could I not say to you then what was in my heart? Why could I not make the sounds… wilted flowers bloom forever?
>
> There you were…bald without the golden hair that fell…unable to walk with legs that once would not cease to run…eyes that looked but did

not sparkle…hands and arms tinted blue from our attempts to give you life…expressions from your lips that I thought I would never hear you utter…I am afraid…Will I ever be pretty again?....Why do you hurt me?…I don't want anymore…

You are a wilted flower.

It rained the night you died. The thunder and the lightning broke the silence of that most holy night. And I told your mother in the midst of the sight and sound cascading all around…Joanna has arrived… she is home….she blossoms.

You could do nothing without spirit…without noise and disruption…that was what you had before the very last days and that is what I am certain you have this day…this hour…this moment. Those of us who knew you well thank you for your courage, your innocence, your trust, your independence, your spirit to go on that no evil could crush.

What happens to flowers that die? Some say, "nothing." But that is to live life without passion, love, and a sense of justice. That is to fail completely to risk the ultimate commitment that leads to loss, separation, and hope.

What happens to flowers that die? You know now that your courage, innocence, trust, independence and indomitable spirit are joined with Him who we call Lord who is passion, love and justice.

"Wilted flowers bloom forever" is something that you have known all along. It is the secret of your inner heart…the reason for your gift then and now of eternal life.

## Grief

There is no way to adequately describe the pain we felt in the ensuing months. Our goal was to make it to the summer. During

Joanna's final months, we didn't have an opportunity to develop close friendships within our new community.

In general, people have a difficult time supporting families who have lost a child. Our friends from Swarthmore did their best to be there for us and many in the Episcopal community reached out to us, but mostly we had to work through our grief on our own.

I did my best to take care of my family and people in need at the school. I guess the students in Middle and Upper School sensed my drive to carry on as they dedicated both of their yearbooks to me.

I was blessed that first year at Episcopal to have a great senior warden, Mark Devlin,'79 serving as the student spiritual leader of the school. The Student Vestry, which he led, was an ever present support for me in the work of creating chapel services designed to be meaningful and engaging for the students and faculty.

Joanna's death changed my life in profound ways. It broke me. It made me a more controlling person since I had lost control when I really needed it in the life and death struggle of my daughter. I now took nothing for granted. I felt that life couldn't do anything else to me that would be worse than this. That was true, but little did I know that there would be more heartache to come in my family 10 years later.

Here I should mention that I don't adhere to those definitions of the grief process that are usually put forward. Everyone's grief is different and everyone handles grief in a different way. The one constant is that grief never goes go away. You find a way to live with it. Paradoxically it causes you to live from a deeper spot.

Grief is a curious thing. What you think will upset you, doesn't, and what you don't think will upset you, does. There are two songs that even today can produce a strong emotional response in me. I simply can't listen to them. There are times when I am driving my car with the radio on and suddenly they come through the airwaves. I quickly reach across and turn the radio off. These two songs cause an immediate reaction in me of profound sadness.

The songs, both by Stevie Wonder, are "You Are The Sunshine of My Life" and "Isn't She Lovely". (Wonder 1976) Joanna would listen to these over and over in her room when she was playing. Of the two, the one that I must avoid at all costs is "Isn't She Lovely".

If you don't have faith, spend some time on the cancer ward at CHOP. It will change you in a heartbeat because faith, family, and friends will be all that you have left to cling to. The good news is that these things are sufficient for the day.

Thirteen months after Joanna died we were blessed with our second son, Adam Roy. Having this new active, happy, and loving child was a true gift for he was instrumental in bringing about the healing we so sorely needed.

## The House That Grief Built

There was important grief work to be done after the death of our daughter Joanna. Tracy Kidder wrote a book, <u>House</u>, (Kidder 1999) in which he depicted all the struggles and satisfactions of building one's own house or home. The book contains philosophical wisdom as well.

Vicki and I decided to use the building of a house as part of our grief work. We were provided housing by the school right on campus. Our goal was to establish a family homestead elsewhere.

We started with looking for land. Should it be in the mountains or by the sea? I wanted mountains and Vicki wanted the sea. We looked at many locations. The Jersey Shore was too populated. Finding something by the ocean was too expensive. We explored the Chesapeake Bay, but felt it would be too far away for weekend trips.

When we were in the search for land, the Bishop of my Diocese was Bishop Lyman Ogilby. His father had been President of Trinity College in Hartford, Connecticut. Lyman was a Connecticut Sailing Champion in his youth. He would teach all members of my family how to sail. He knew I was looking for a piece of land and asked us to come and visit him on the Upper Chesapeake Bay where he had a home on the shore overlooking the North East River.

Since we had reached a point of discouragement, we were convinced that our visit there would not yield a good prospect. We went just to spend some time with Lyman and his wife, Ruth. He was a tremendous pastor and supporter of me and I considered him a close friend.

Vicki and I walked onto his deck and said at the same time, "This is it!" Lyman knew we would fall in love with this special area on the Chesapeake. He called a real estate agent and that afternoon we signed a contract to buy land that was situated on a bluff overlooking the headwaters of the Chesapeake Bay, just three properties from the Ogilbys' home. It was a beachfront property facing west with fabulous sunsets. I read about this area of the Chesapeake in a magazine on an airplane. It was described as one of the 10 most beautiful views in our nation. Lyman and I would now be neighbors.

The home next to our property was a Lindal Cedar Home. These high quality homes are built all over the world and incorporate the best materials possible. We decided to explore this option and met a legend by the name of Chuck Goudy. He was the local representative for these homes. I could write a book of stories about Chuck and his role in the building of our home. Everybody should build their own home with their own hands ONCE for the experience.

Chuck was a very kind man who had a high regard for others. This was demonstrated by his dedication to his church community where he took a leadership role, serving on the Vestry of his Episcopal Church. When we met with Chuck to design our home, we asked for pricing for the smallest home with the least expensive options. We were disappointed when we realized we couldn't afford the materials and the labor associated with it.

Chuck was always looking for a way to help others. He volunteered, "I will teach you how to build it!" Sounds like an idle promise to get a sale. Right? Wrong. We couldn't believe it. He made good on his promise.

The building of our home was a family project. We would travel to Maryland on Saturdays to learn about construction and participate in the building process. Chuck's son framed the structure and installed the siding. We then took over doing most of the interior work and building the deck. We were required by law to sub out the plumbing and electrical work.

Chuck would appear very early in the morning as we arrived. He was a man of his word. He had been a teacher at one point in his life, and his skill came through for us. Neither Vicki nor I nor our oldest son, Thad, had any knowledge of building. Eventually I became skilled in using all the power tools Chuck would bring to the site. Thaddeus was nine years old, and our son, Adam was two. We shuffled baby sitters for Adam and took on the task as a family.

One neighbor complained to the police that she thought we were injuring someone at our house. Our son, Adam, was just as adept at imitating a skill saw as he was at speaking the English language. The neighbors soon got used to all the tools and Adam's imitation of them.

As I mentioned there are so many stories associated with the building of our home that I could write a book similar to the book Tracy Kidder wrote. I can still remember going to bed after a 12 hour day of building and feeling every part of my body aching and alive. It was wonderful! In an earlier book I wrote, <u>Watch Your Time</u>, I mentioned the need to attach feelings to moments that you want to remind yourself of later in life. This attachment to feelings was certainly true for my family and me in the process of the building of our home.

When there were extremes of weather, I left the family at home. I will never forget working against the wind blowing off the bay on the coldest days of the winter before the windows were installed.

Chuck kept his part of the bargain. I think he wanted the building project to be as successful as we wanted it to be.

I hired a member of our plant operations staff at the school to travel to Maryland to teach us how to finish the dry wall. I am convinced that one of the levels of Dante's <u>Inferno</u> should be devoted to putting dry wall up and finishing it. It is heavy, dirty work. Chuck made the comment that you only need two living beings to install dry wall. One would be a gorilla and the other would be me, and I would be the least important of the two when it came to hanging sheets of 12 foot dry wall overhead.

Brian, our dry wall expert, was in his 20s and he really loved teaching us. When we think of artists, we think of Rembrandt and Picasso, but Brian was an artist in his own right. He applied the drywall finishing mud with speed and accuracy, covering up all the mistakes we had made in the hanging of the drywall. There was no way we could come close to his skill level.

One day in the winter, when Chuck and I were working on our home, the electrician came to install the basic wiring. The electrician's name was Stormy and he had acquired this nickname because of a similar personality trait. On this particular Saturday morning he stormed into the house and asked Chuck when he was going to meet this #@#%$ owner of the home. Curse words were a regular part of his vocabulary. Chuck didn't say a word, but pointed up in the air to where I was standing on scaffolding working on the high cathedral ceiling. He pointed up and said, "That's the homeowner right there!" I don't know what Stormy expected, but it wasn't a young person covered in dirt in builder's clothing. He had an interesting response. He left the house and knocked on the door. Chuck answered. He came back in and said, "Reverend, it is so nice to finally meet you." He never missed a beat and went right to his work.

Thanks to Chuck Goudy we developed building skills but after the completion of our home I had no place to use them so I volunteered to help anyone at anytime with building issues. I have recently retired after 38 years as a school chaplain. I have the same feeling now, a desire to apply all of those years of knowledge to help others.

There are many ways that building a house is similar to the grief process. I was a novice who barely knew which end of the hammer to use. As I noted Chuck very graciously provided us with the necessary tools and instruction on how to use them. We did this as a family.

Grief begins before your loved one dies or at the moment that death takes over your life with no warning. If the death is sudden, then you just begin the crisis quickly swinging wildly against the air that you breathe. This is a world that is completely foreign to you. When your child dies of a disease over a period of time, grief begins to move around in your psyche and soul when you lose that most important word in our language. That word is "hope". Hope dies when you hear those worst words in our language that leave you helpless and still crawling forward somehow. They come as a tolling bell. "There is nothing else that can be done."

When we began the grief process we had no road map, and no way of knowing what we would encounter. We didn't know how to use the basic tools to get us through it. There is no endpoint to grief. At least with the house, we knew what it would look like in the end. In contrast, grief never ends. Could anyone build a house knowing that you would never complete it? Grief is like trying to put together one of those thousand pieces puzzles without the top of the box that pictures the final product so you must employ trial and error until something works. Trial and error is what budding novice house builders do as well. You hope that successful completion of each step in the process outweighs the mistakes.

Trial and error is key to both constructing a house and managing grief. Tasks that you feel will be difficult turn out to be easy and many you think will be easy you find overwhelming. I have anticipated days that I thought would be difficult and they were not. It was common for me to think that finding a toy or photograph would not bother me, and I was surprised when it did. The grief process unsettles your life, and as a result I sought more control.

Memory is a wonderful thing. Vicki and I can remember when each board was hammered and each piece of tile was placed. You are fine with your placement of the hardened clay as you step back to admire your work. There were times after Joanna's death that I would go alone to her room and sit and play some of her music knowing that it would upset me, but it was a way for me to process grief through memory of those last days. There were times that grew in number when I would remember the good times with her and less time was spent with memories of the wrenching final days.

I had a lot of good and bad surprises when building the house. The same was true in working through the grief process. It is filled with everything that you want to remember but also everything you wish could be erased from your memory.

There are questions in the building of a home that are identical to ones in the grief process. These questions begin with the words, "What if..." At several points in building the house we made changes in the blueprints to give us more room. What if we do it this way? These changes could be made easily because our house was post and beam construction. Posts and beams, not the internal walls support the structure. We were able to move any wall without jeopardizing the stability of the structure.

In the grief process the questions that begin with "What if...?" are like a thief in the night who steals a little part of you. What if she were alive today? What would she look like? What would hold her interest? What would her career be? Would she get married? Would her mother and I give her away at her marriage service? What would that first dance with me look like? These questions, like a thief, leave us feeling that our even keeled life would be taken from us leaving us at the mercy of questions that are painfully raised.

Grief is like making your way through an unknown room in the dark, feeling your way, but tripping over the furniture at the same time. There are many bruises that come along with that journey.

I was very slow at building. It took me much longer to accomplish a task than it would take a carpenter to do the same work. The same is true for grief. When your daughter dies, you immediately enter a club that no one wants to belong to, a club that is difficult for others to fully understand. My loss helped me to be more empathetic to the losses others sustain. Many people who have lost a child feel their pain is unique, that it is something that others who can never fully understand.

Michelangelo's *Pieta* depicts Mary holding her son, the crucified Jesus, in her lap. It conveys a message that people who have lost a child can see easier than some others can. Jesus is portrayed as a thirty-three-year-old man, while Mary is portrayed as a young woman. The message is that a parent is not supposed to outlive their child.

As I have indicated there is no way to tell others how to move through grief. Each of us can accept some guidelines and ideas, but ultimately we must choose the path ourselves.

The following statement summarizes my feelings.

> Grief never ends, but it changes
> It is a passage. Not a place to stay
> Grief is not a sign of weakness, nor
> a lack of faith.
> It is the price of love. (Parks 2010)

The house we built is still there. If its walls could talk they would tell tales of celebrations and happy moments with family and friends. Maybe we weren't trying to build a house. Maybe we were trying to build a future without the physical presence of our daughter.

Going back to Christmas Eve of 1979, the first year without Joanna was the worst. We went through the motions of life in an attempt to carry on our family life for Thaddeus who was 7 years old. He had been through quite enough in the months of Joanna's treatment, being a bone marrow donor for her, and finally living through her death and burial. As was stated earlier Adam's birth 13 months after Joanna's death helped to guide us through the grief process.

## Vicki Follows A Calling

When Adam was still a toddler, Vicki came to realize her inspiration to become a nurse. From her observations of the nursing care Joanna received while at CHOP, she finally knew what she was meant to do with her Biological Science degree from North Carolina State University. She found an evening nursing program requiring class attendance and clinical education three nights a week for over two years. Her classes from North Carolina State were accepted toward her degree, and she was awarded a full scholarship. The program was on hiatus during the summer months so she was able to spend summers with the family in our Chesapeake home.

For two and a half years, Vicki left the house at 5 p.m. and I had charge of Thad and Adam. This was good for all because it enabled me to create a special bond with the boys. Vicki excelled in her studies and clinical rotations, graduating second in her class.

Vicki found herself drawn to Labor and Delivery/Maternal and Child Health but discovered that few hospitals would hire a graduate nurse into Labor and Delivery. She settled for a position on the Gynecology Unit of a local hospital. That particular hospital had recently brought on two Gynecologic Oncologists so her unit had a majority of cancer patients in their daily census. Vicki discovered her skill at dealing with patients who were fighting a grim diagnosis. She remained in oncology for the majority of her career, earning certification in that specialty in 1996.Vicki spent most of her oncology nursing years involved in clinical research. That focus was the perfect way to combine her natural ability to connect with cancer patients and her background in biological sciences. She earned her certification as a Certified Clinical Research Professional. During the last 12 years of her career she had the opportunity to apply all previously honed skills. She was a Senior Outreach Coordinator for the Jefferson Kimmel Cancer Center Network. In that role she was a liaison between Jefferson and the members of their Cancer Network, assisting those institutions in developing their cancer programs.

Even though Vicki had found her career niche, she still wanted to add to our family. We were blessed with the birth of Spencer in 1988. This meant that Joanna would be our only daughter, a sister that two of her brothers would never know.

### *Another Challenge Of Life And Death*

Spencer was born almost eight years after the birth of Adam. Our children ranged in age from newborn to sixteen years old. It was an interesting phase of our parenting experience. We were teaching Thaddeus how to drive as we were expecting the birth of Spencer. It was a happy time with all things going our way.

Spencer was born just as the school year was starting in September of 1988. Shortly after bringing Spencer home from the hospital. Vicki developed high fevers. At first the doctors thought she was suffering from a postpartum infection.

During that time I was asked to speak at the installation of the new President of Connecticut College, Dr. Claire Gaudiani. Claire was an EA parent before being named to be President of that college. I flew up and came back the next day. Fevers still raged. It took more than six weeks to diagnose Vicki's illness, but ultimately we were guided to the team at the Hospital of the University of Pennsylvania. Ironically that institution is located next to and associated with The Children's Hospital of Philadelphia where Joanna received her care. The diagnosis turned out to be what we were dreading, cancer. Vicki had large B-cell lymphoma, an aggressive form of blood cancer. There was no established successful treatment for it at the time, but we were offered a chemotherapy regimen that had been recently identified in a clinical trial. We were told the odds of responding to the treatment were 50/50. Vicki started her treatment on what would have been Joanna's eighth birthday.

During Vicki's treatment we were blessed to have the love and support of Erma Tippett. She was a member of Trinity Church where I had served before coming to EA. She readily came to our aid and became a surrogate grandmother. She lovingly cared for the whole family as Spencer grew through his infancy and Vicki struggled through her treatment.

A thought that sticks in my mind from that time is that when a loved one is going through chemotherapy, all that you want is a normal day. All we wanted was to take a walk together with our children

One day as Vicki and I stood in our kitchen she began to cry. I embraced her and told her that everything was going to be all right. She looked at me and said, "I am not worried about me. I am worried about you having to raise our children alone while taking care of the school community." She was always thinking of others. As our marriage went from year to year, that was a common theme. She always thought of others first, herself second.

Vicki did respond to the three month chemotherapy regimen. She lost her hair and was left with some challenging, long term side effects. For a year following treatment all her joints were inflamed. She still continues treatment for the osteoporosis caused by her chemotherapy. All of this aside she recovered over time and she has been cancer free for 30 years.

### Reflections

Do you see the world as Rabbi Kushner does, that "Tragedy doesn't have a ticket into your life. It has a box seat". Do you think this statement describes the reality of life?

Have you ever experienced overwhelming tragedy in your own life? What resources did you use to cope with it? If you have not had any tragedy in your life, what resources are available to you to cope with tragedy?

Do you have friends, relatives, or others who have gone through tragedy? Are you aware of what they used to cope with their pain or sorrow? Would you turn to God for solace? Would you turn to prayer?

Does your view of the afterlife impact your life and how you live?

Can you recall examples of when the strain of life has taken a toll on someone close to you? Who was that person? What produced the strain? How do you think he or she dealt with it?

When you have encountered a personal challenge, have you ever used the building of some physical thing or another constructive task to help you move forward?

Have you ever chosen something outside of your comfort zone to help you move through a crisis?

Have you ever encountered someone like Chuck Goudy who made a big time commitment to you, promising to teach or mentor? Did they follow through to completion?

My Mother

My Father

My Brother Receiving Award for Research at the Frankford Arsenal

My Badge at the Steel Mill #368

Adam and Courtney's Wedding

Thaddeus and Meredith's Wedding

115

Joanna Lynn Squire November 8, 1974 - December 24, 1978

# FREEDOM TO

# CHAPTER 4: THE EPISCOPAL ACADEMY

## The School Experience

When I arrived at EA I felt I had come home, though it was the farthest thing from my origins in Conshohocken. Being on the Episcopal Academy campus had been my dream and dreams are the most powerful things there are if we have the courage to pursue them. Recall this dream started when, as a young boy, I met an Episcopal Academy student who awakened a yearning based in such a positive experience that it remained with me, undiminished. It was a dream about values, learning, and about being the best that you could be. Those values are like the air we breathe. They are everywhere in our school community. I had come full circle in life. I found myself wishing that everyone could have this experience.

President Theodore Roosevelt gave his famous address, "Citizen in a Republic", at the Sorbonne in Paris, France, on April 23, 1920. I have attempted to live these words out in my life.

> It is not the critic who counts; not the man who points out how the strong man stumbles, or where the doer of deed could have done better. The credit belongs to the man who is actually in the arena, whose face is marred by dust and sweat and blood; who strives valiantly; who errs, who comes up short again and again, because there is no effort without error and shortcoming; but who does actually strive to do the deeds; who knows great enthusiasms, the

great devotions; who spends himself in a worthy
cause; who at the best knows in the end the triumph
of high achievement, and who at the worst, if he
fails, at least fails while daring greatly; his place
shall never be with those cold and timid souls who
neither know victory nor defeat. (Roosevelt 2014)

When I think of this quotation, I think back to my cousin, Noble
Smith, who inspired me. I think my cousin's story is a shorter version of "be in the mix of things and never let anyone outwork you".

Truth be told, I love being in the arena. It is when I am in the
middle of things that would test others' souls that I feel most at
home and comfortable.

My arena was the arena of a very large school community. Life
can change in a heartbeat, and you never know when that change
is coming. That was part of the way I saw life then, and I continue
to see it that way today. I certainly saw this first hand in working
as Chaplain of the Episcopal Academy for 38 years. Members of
the community were dying too young or suffering from incredible
illnesses or life struggles. Granted the school was a large community where those things should be expected, but that knowledge
didn't lesson the pain for anyone.

In my role as Chaplain of the Episcopal Academy, I was spiritual leader and confidant to a community comprised of 1,250 students and their families each year, 250 faculty and staff and their
families, and a large number of alumni. All of them knew I would
be available to them at any time day or night, on any day of the
year and from any location. I recall searching for a pay phone in
Paris in 2005 so I could support a faculty member after his brother
died tragically.

Trust was the most important currency I could have in my role.
People came to realize that whatever the issue or whatever the
secret, it would be safe with me. The upside of this approach is
obvious and necessary. The downside of this is that all secrets go
with me to the grave.

### The Student Advisor Relationship

When I arrived at EA I brought with me a traditional counseling model. I had used and refined this model successfully as a founding board member of the counseling center in Chester.

I learned quickly that students don't always make appointments to seek help. For the most part that is not the way they operate. They are more than likely to just drop in. Students knew that if my door was closed I was either away from the office or seeing someone. They would always check on a good time to come back if that was indicated. Sometimes, to feel more comfortable, students would bring friends to an appointment. While this might be unorthodox in an adult counseling relationship, it could work for younger people. Friendships and peer relationship are paramount for young people, and so I felt an effective counseling program would have to leverage that dynamic.

In response to this behavior, I created the school's first student advisory system that incorporated psychological services. In this system an advisor is a faculty member, administrator, or coach who is chosen by the student (advisee) to oversee their life at the school. I am very proud of the fact that through this program I was able to give the students choice of advisor and self-determinacy.

The advisors connect into a web of psychological services established to provide mental health support for the entire community, students, faculty, parents, and administrators. This approach also included psychologists who were on campus in a part time capacity. Critical to the system is that the key interface for students seeking help is their advisor. Students were free to go to whomever they chose for they knew that some teachers may not be comfortable with certain issues that came their way. In my role as head of the program I had the privilege of acting as a resource for all members of the school community and I provided counseling as well. In most cases where the situation was particularly challenging, the faculty would check in with me immediately to get advice to guide the counseling relationship.

## *My Interactions With Students As Counselor*

Students like to communicate with others in places where they feel at home. I saw many of the students who were in need of help in hallways, classrooms, or an athletic field. I would joke with them, "Welcome to my office," and I would draw an imaginary line around us. I made it a point to be out of my office and in their space as much as I could. Because I was out there with them, it normalized my conversations with them, creating comfort, ease, and trust. Seeking help or talking about a problem can be intimidating, and some students don't want to be seen going to the "therapy office". If students saw other students talking to me in a public place, they knew it didn't necessarily have to be about a problem. It could just as well have been about how they did in an athletic contest the day before or a movie they saw. This made the space for conversation with me as confidential as it could be and provided a safe place for the students. Still the largest number of students were seen in my office.

One of my goals for our community was to have asking for psychological help seen in a positive light. I wanted that to be a goal, but society works against having counseling be seen as a source of strength. Seeking psychological guidance is still often seen as a weakness. I had as many chapel speakers as possible address this issue so students would see seeking help for emotional issues in the same way as going to a coach for help to gain physical strength.

Many of the conversations I have with people seeking help begin with the person saying, "You are the only one that I can tell." Confidentiality is always implied, and sometimes specifically requested. My standard response was, "You have come to me because you trust me. You must also trust me to handle the situation in the best way I can." I used this response because I never knew when the person may be thinking about a life threatening situation, which may require swift and decisive action that would involve bringing others into the conversation.

When working with students concerning non-life-threatening matters, I see them for a time or two without letting their parents know. In many cases, however, parents and others do need to be involved more quickly. I always let the person seeking help know the steps forward. Sharing information with others always requires thoughtful discretion.

Students empowered me. I don't know how many conversations would start with a student saying, "Could I talk with you about something. It's no big deal." They then would proceed to describe a horrific event in their lives. They taught me about courage and perseverance.

This was matched by conversations that began with, "I am not very religious but..." followed by very religious statements, if we define religion as the connections between self, others, and God.

Throughout my tenure at Episcopal I was confronted by all manner of challenging situations, such as sexual harassment, abuse of every kind, suicide, parents with weapons threatening children, and depression, to name a few. There were many times that I was asked to provide council to children caught between two parents in a nasty divorce. I encountered students, parents, and alumni suffering greatly from severe personality disorders such as borderline and narcissistic personalities as well as others who became overtly psychotic under the pressures of life. Since many people in our community had high expectations for themselves and the same coming from their families, they felt like failures and became depressed for reasons related to these pressures. Particularly heartbreaking were the several brilliant alumni who became overtly psychotic in their early twenties, a time when that descent into unreality and madness can begin to manifest. It more often occurs in men and I observed that this illness often befell the most sensitive people in our community.

I was often approached by people who felt conflicted because they were in a situation in which they had to choose between the lesser of two evils. These decisions were more difficult than decisions that were clearly right or wrong. I developed a tool kit, a set of counseling skills that fast became second nature to me, like the skills of an experienced athlete, musician, or actor. There were times when people's lives were literally in my hands, and I had to address crises when time was not on my side.

What did I learn over all these years? How did I handle these situations? First, as I have indicated, confidentiality is key. If you are going to help people, they must first trust you. Second, you must also have credibility. Whether it be a clergyman, psychiatrist, lawyer, or psychologist, people only care about one thing, that you can get the job done. An effective practitioner's reputation spreads quickly through any community, and that was certainly true of my work in our school community. You have to be able to connect quickly with all sorts and conditions of humankind.

I had had hundreds of hours of supervision of my counseling when I arrived at Episcopal. Did I handle the above situations alone? Of course not! Our faculty nurtured close relationships with students and students seeking help often reached out to a faculty member first. Most of the difficult situations were referred to me for assistance whereby I was also able to utilize the host of mental health contacts I had established in the community.

## The Importance Of Developing A Network

An important component of our counseling program was the establishment of a network of mental health professionals outside of the school to complement the work of the psychologists on campus. Someone once referred to me as the largest psychiatric broker for Philadelphia's western suburbs. We know how important it is to get the right referral for a medical condition. That is also true for mental health services. I had to know the expertise and personalities of the therapists in our network so that I could make the very best connections. To further quality improvement of our program I gathered feedback from patients to verify the efficacy of the support offered by my colleagues outside of school.

There was a particular therapist who had developed a reputation for her success in treating my most challenging referrals. We had many extensive conversations by phone. I was in Virginia to attend the marriage of one of our graduates when, during the dinner the night before the wedding, I was in conversation with the woman seated next to me. We began to talk about helping people. She looked at me and said, "Jim, you have no idea who I am, do you?" I said, "No." It turns out that she was the skilled therapist who was my top choice for referrals from the school community! All of our exchanges had been by phone. We both laughed. I had not recognized her voice given the different context. She was a family friend of the groom.

Over the years my goal has always been to quickly identify and address the issues causing pain and psychological distress in those who come to me for help. I am pragmatic. I only care about what works. I have been trained in many forms of counseling, and am a big fan of positive psychology, for example. As head of our counseling program I saw myself as a coach and the faculty as the players. A team is only as good as the players! In fact, the players are the most important people.

## Lever Therapy

Over time I developed an approach that could be used by anyone who wants to help another person. My desire was to take the mystery out the counseling process based on my experience of how effective faculty could be in helping others. I call this simple approach Lever Therapy. Recall that a lever can lift heavy weights. In counseling we can lift the heavy weight of burdens that a person has in their life. I believe it is a tool that can be used with the other modalities of counseling. In counseling we deal with the ultimate challenge facing people struggling with barriers in their lives. If the person comes to know the right thing to do, why don't they act on that insight and do it? Or in the words of Saint Paul, "The good that I want to do, I don't. That which I don't want to do, I do." (Romans 7:19) This is the important question that led me to identify Lever Therapy. There are three ingredients in Lever Therapy. One is to identify the strengths of a person, and the second is to nudge them to seek help and move in the direction they have identified as their desired goal. Between these two aspects is a consideration of how past, present and future considerations inform the development or lack thereof of the person seeking help. Issues such as self esteem, a sense of belonging, and their experience with avoiding the emotions of rejection, embarrassment, and vulnerability are also part of the mix.

When a person comes to me for help, I initially listen carefully to their concerns, but I also identify their strengths and positive personality traits. These are not always evident at first, but if you stay with the person or situation long enough, you will find something to work with. Everyone has strengths. I build on those strengths to establish a positive foundation for self-actualization and action.

Once I know what strengths and personality traits I have to work with I bring Nudge Theory into the process. Nudge Theory is a system of thought with practical implications. The theory was developed by Richard Thaler, Professor of Behavioral Economics and Finance at the University of Chicago, and Cass Sunstein, Professor at Harvard Law School and Director of the Center for Behavior Economics and Public Policy. They worked for five years on this theory and articulated it through the publication of their book simply titled <u>Nudge</u>. (Sunstein and Thaler 2008) Their theory relates to every aspect of life from getting people to slow down on a highway, to collecting taxes from people who don't want to pay them, to the latest approach to effective fundraising. On October 12, 2017 Richard Thaler won the Nobel Prize for his work on nudge theory. I think their theory can be applied to creating forward movement in the counseling process.

A typical example of Nudge Theory at work is the flashing speed signs placed along highways. When I am driving too fast and see one of these flashing signs, I am nudged to slow down to the legal speed limit. There are various ways in which counseling can nudge a person in need of help to begin to go in the positive direction that they themselves have identified. Alcoholics Anonymous employs Nudge Theory by simply having their members gather in groups to nudge each other in the right direction to attain sobriety.

As clients are responding to nudges to move toward healing, I employ the integration of how a person's past, present, and future work together as well as the issues mentioned earlier. I have used this approach with many people in crisis and feel it moves the client toward healing in less time a traditional approach does.

## *An Important Moment To Support And Uplift*

It is important to note that small nudges can also provide great support in cases that do not represent crises, but opportunities to uplift. A basketball player at our school was from an underserved part of the city. I was teaching him right after a spring break. He fell asleep in the class with his head down on the desk. I did not say anything to him during the class since I knew how challenging the combination of race and economic class could be for a student. In spite of those challenges he excelled academically.

As he was leaving, I requested him to stay. I asked him what was going on in his life that he fell asleep in class. He shared with me that he had lost track of his dates, only realizing the night before that classes would resume the next morning. He was forced to stay up late doing his laundry. His brother was the person who came to parent nights and was a tremendous support for this student. He had a terrific advocate in his brother. My understanding of his situation gave him a nudge to continue to meet his daily challenges

I taught this student again in an Ethics course in which we covered some complex ethical situations and controversial topics. He thrived in the course. He was often interviewed by the press since he had a high profile in the local sports world. He would weave into his remarks words or ideas from the Ethics course such as "teleological suspension of the ethical". The reporters couldn't get enough of him. It was great to see parts of the course appear in the sports section of the newspaper. More importantly, he had great satisfaction in sharing what he learned. He made it clear that he was so much more than a basketball player. He was a person with a fine mind and soul.

He went on to be elected captain of his division one college basketball team in his junior and senior years. He then went to Europe to play professional basketball.

I had a student who was a terrific lateral thinker, meaning that he could think outside of the box. He lived in an underserved part of the city, but he could commute by bus to our school easily when the campus was in Merion, a community that borders the city line of Philadelphia. But when we moved to Newtown Square, this student had to take several busses to get to our new campus. He would put his bike on bike racks on the front of the busses that took him close to campus. He would remove his bike from the last bus and bike up a dangerous road to our school.

When we learned about this from people who saw him doing this, we made arrangements for him to be picked up at the end of his bus ride and be driven to our campus by someone from our school. However, one morning there was a miscommunication and our student wasn't picked up. How was he going to make the rest of the journey? He went to a sandwich shop at the end of his bus route and asked the owner if he could make him a sandwich. The owner said, "Yes, of course!" Our student then asked if he made deliveries to the Episcopal Academy. Again the owner said, "Yes, of course!" Our student then asked if he could deliver him and his sandwich to the school. Suffice it to say that the owner was so impressed with his problem solving ability that he delivered our student and his sandwich to our school in time for his first period class. After graduation, that student had a very successful learning experience at a demanding college in the Midwest. He created his own nudge with the owner of the shop to solve his dilemma.

Another student in my Ethics course, Matt Sheehan, '07 was high energy and big hearted. He became the unofficial leader of school spirit. I took his Ethics class to a bioethics forum on "The Abuse of Steroids in Sports". It was going to be viewed nationally on Comcast Sports. When the forum completed, reporters from Comcast wanted to interview a student to get his view of the forum. The interview was scheduled to be broadcast on national TV. Matt was standing near me so I called him over to be interviewed and to represent the school. His response was, "I can't do that." I told him he was as good as anyone else. The interview was done and he did a great job, demonstrating that belief in a student and giving a nudge can be life changing for both teacher and student.

The next day one of our local papers used one of this student's quotes on the front page with his name attached as the source of the quote. Neither Matt nor I were aware of the quote when we entered the classroom the next day. A classmate brought in the paper to share with the class.

When Matt read the quote he jumped up with excitement. His first words to me were, "Hey Rev, can I call my mom?" This question coming from a bruising athlete delighted me. He instructed his mother to buy as many copies of the paper as she could. Nothing gives me greater pleasure than having a student succeed and grow in confidence. I saw Matt recently. He still remembers the content that was covered in the symposium. His positive spirit is still contagious.

## The Grit Of Youth

Despite their youth, all of the students I encountered exhibited grit, each in their own way. They managed through the physical injuries and pain that are part of being young. If you walked down the hall of our school, you could always find a student donning some manner of orthopedic equipment. Sports are required at our school. Sometimes the halls looked like a triage unit for an orthopedic practice.

I once scheduled a very famous professional baseball player to speak in chapel about character. The player sprained an ankle in a game the night before his scheduled chapel address. His surgeon, a friend of mine, called to inform me that the player would be unable to speak the next day but he planned to reschedule as soon as he was able.

When students asked me why our guest speaker couldn't make it, I said that he had sprained his ankle. The students looked shocked. They thought that was a poor excuse indeed! Pushing through such injuries was routine for them. Fortunately when he did come to speak, he hit a home run.

Jimmy Craig, the goalie for the American Ice Hockey Team that beat the Russians during the 1980 Winter Olympics, was scheduled to speak to our community. This particular game is referred to as the "Miracle on Ice". Some regard it as one of the highpoints in the world of sports during the last century. The topic of his address was character.

As Jimmy and I were walking down a sidewalk next to the green in front of the chapel after his address, walking toward us was a female student in an orthopedic boot. She was being treated for a torn ligament in her foot. She was loaded down with books she carried out in front of her and a book bag resting on her back. She was leaning forward with each step.

I motioned to her to come and meet Jimmy Craig. This student never complained about the multiple injuries she had sustained. She always showed up at school on time ready to learn. I told Jimmy in her presence that she was the grittiest person going right now. She beamed! I wasn't exaggerating.

I always arrived around 7A.M. at my office. One day, as I was about to enter the chapel, I saw a Lower School student walking toward me. He had a contrabass fiddle strapped to his back that was twice as big as he was. His mother was following about six feet behind. He was leaning forward as far as he could go so that the instrument did not drag on the ground. I took a picture of the student with my iPhone and sent it to our head of music with the message that this young man was learning more than just music from his experience with us. Clearly, his mother wanted him to learn a lesson about self-reliance and endurance as well!

## The Religion Department

Among the aspects that made my school life so wonderful were the four members of the Religion Department who I worked with during the latter years of my tenure as chair of the department. I called them the Dream Team. We could complete one another's sentences. I can't imagine a more talented group of religion scholars and teachers. Each had a favorite sport. I would always ask people interviewing for a position what they did to stay active. While it may seem like an unusual question, our work was as physically demanding as it was demanding of intellect and spirit.

Father Tim Gavin, Hon. is an ultra marathon runner. We began conversations about the possibility of his beginning the ordination process to be an Episcopal priest 14 years before his ordination on January 12, 2013. I was Tim's mentor and it was one of the joys of my life to go down that path with him. He was one of the first candidates for ordination to be sponsored by both a school and a parish. He served as my Lower School Chaplain for several years, and, after a national search, he was chosen to succeed me as Chaplain of the School after my retirement. He is a seeker of truth, a published poet, and a deeply spiritual person.

Tim's work in Haiti has been his signature ministry as chaplain of the school. In 2012 EA started a partnership with St. Marc's School in Haiti. Tim travels there three to four times a year. His leadership has resulted in significant improvements in the lives of students at St. Marc's School. Tim's work and fundraising have included building a new structure with solar panels for electricity, installing a water purification system, and establishing a bean farm and medical clinic. He has become fluent in Creole. The positive impact and legacy of his work there will be felt for generations to come.

The Reverend Bert Zug, '78 was born to be a chaplain, leader, and teacher. I gave thanks to God each day for having him on our team. I am a better person because I know him. Bert is a cyclist and for many years joined the Livestrong Team in support of one of our faculty members suffering from cancer. He has memorized many of Dr. King's addresses and is one of the most creative people in developing chapel services geared to Middle School. As an actor and vocalist, he is very comfortable in front of large groups of people.

There are two signature accomplishments as chaplain that characterize Bert's leadership and work. He developed a course with our Middle School Drama Department called Drama Meets Religion. This program entails a study of the Gospel of St. Mark in class, followed by a process in which the students bring the scripture alive through adapting its lessons to modern situations. These adaptations become plays, which are then performed in Middle School Chapel.

He also developed a course for eighth grade that introduces students to the study of theology. The students write a faith paper, an assignment that has become regarded by students as a hallmark moment of their education. Students then may give these papers as addresses in chapel.

Bert is also a student of poker and could be a professional player, if he chose that as a vocation. One summer he sent me emails in which he reported his successes. He described each game in great detail. The communications were filled with poker lingo like chop (split the pot), river (the final card dealt in a poker hand), flop (the first three face cards that are dealt up), and backdoor (a hand requiring two or more rounds). I had to read his emails with a book of poker terms beside me. Like a chess champion he enjoys the engagement with his fellow players who are most often colleagues and friends.

Holly Johnson is an avid soccer player and regularly played with amateur teams. She taught both history and world religions. After her undergraduate degree she received a Master's Degree in the teaching of world religions from the University of Pennsylvania. Her skills and magnetism as an educator were immediately apparent upon our first meeting. Later I learned that she had worked at our Head of School's former school and was one of the best hires he ever made. She is in constant motion and engagement in the classroom. She would use so many different teaching techniques that all students ended up riveted and committed to learning.

Holly was so demanding of excellence that I started to get calls from concerned parents who felt her course was too intense for their children. My goal was always to have a department that would to be taken seriously by all. Holly added greatly to the reputation of the Religion Department.

Dr. Christopher Row was a terrific addition to the Religion Department. Topher is one of our crew coaches. The crew team has won national recognition. The students refer to Dr. Row as the smartest person on campus. His undergraduate degree was from Trinity College in Hartford. He received a Doctorate in Art and Architectural History and a Master of Divinity from Harvard. He was also the curator of Trinity College Chapel where he did incredible work to make that place of worship come alive by his wonderful touches.

Like the other members of the Dream Team, Topher brought a commitment to excellence in teaching. He taught biblical study, ethics, the origins of genocide, and courses related to C. S. Lewis, to name a few. He also co-taught a course in sacred spaces with a member of our history faculty during our Winter Term.

One of the things that impressed me about Topher is that he used his powerful intellect to bring out the best in students while not overwhelming them. As a result, he was in high demand as a faculty advisor. Topher worked with me leading the Student Vestry in planning chapel services.

My goal was for all the members of the department to teach as though the students' lives depended on it because I believe that they do.

## Teaching Ethical Thought

I taught biblical studies in Middle and Upper School, but my signature course was a course in Ethics offered to students in Upper School. The course description was as follows: "This course in Systematic Ethics covers the thinking and perspectives on decision making of such thinkers as Epicurus, Aristippus, John Stuart Mill, Jean Paul Sartre, Friedrich Nietzsche, Thomas Hobbes, John Locke, and Jean-Jacques Rousseau as well as the ethics of religious views. The course blends the disciplines of philosophy, psychology, and theology as we explore the nature of interpersonal relationships and the dynamics inherent in the concepts of love and justice that are the pillars of ethical thought."

The students were taught to link their understanding of human nature (Doctrine of Self or What Makes Me Do What I Do) to their individual decision making processes. Lateral thinking skills were also part of the course. Students were taught to look at the many dimensions of a problem and examine how different systems of thought might be used to approach a solution to a particular social or personal dilemma. There were units on legal ethics and bio-ethics, which enhanced the interdisciplinary approach to thinking in an ethical way.

In this Ethics course, I developed a bioethics initiative dealing with current ethical dilemmas. These included such topics as "The Bioethics of NASA" and the ethical issues involved if an astronaut becomes ill on a trip to Mars. Another topic was inspired by Sheri Fink's Pulitzer Prize winning account, <u>The Deadly Choices at Memorial</u>, (Fink 2013) which chronicles the horror of New Orleans' Memorial Hospital's unusually high death rate during Hurricane Katrina. This event led the class to a discussions of critical ethical questions such as, "Which patients should get a share of limited resources, and who decides?" and "Where is the line between comfort care and mercy killing?"

## Leaders By Definition Always Work With Others

Leaders never accomplish anything on their own. There are four basic requirements necessary for any group to work effectively. I gleaned these principles from years of work with various leadership groups, most notably our Student Vestry, our elected spiritual leadership group for Upper School. This group planned our chapel services under guidance from Topher and me.

The first critical component of leadership is that everyone has to look forward to attending working meetings in the same way that a team looks forward to the big game. There has to be a positive mindset regardless of the difficult nature of the problem or endeavor to be discussed. What could be more exciting than going up against a great opponent in sports or tackling the solution to a serious problem?

Second, for a group to be successful, participants have to generally enjoy being in each other's company while working with each other. Civil discourse must be the goal. It is the leader, like a great coach, who makes sure this happens.

Third, there has to be a sense that what the group is doing is very important and will make a difference in other people's lives as well as in their own. I would always underscore for the Student Vestry the life changing potential of their work, as they shaped the moral culture of the school. I measured the success of a meeting by how much or how little I talked. The less I talked the better.

Coaches don't run out on a basketball court and get in the mix, but they enter the action when adjustments need to be made and insights shared. The important people are the students or players.

Fourth, when the meeting ends the participants, including the leader, must feel that the meeting time was used efficiently. Setting clear goals and outcomes for each meeting and reviewing those at the close of the meeting can be a good way to gauge success.

The above four principles are the basics of effective leadership. I wish that all people would commit to learning the art of leadership from leaders who have done ordinary as well as extraordinary things. This approach has the potential to guide a person to develop a leadership style most congruent with their personality. For example, my neighbor on the Chesapeake was the person who led DuPont's efforts to enter the mainstream of Chinese business. It was a huge undertaking. I asked Bob one day to share with me the most important aspect of leadership that enabled him to have the success he had in China. He indicated that great leadership frames the conversation in a way that manages people's expectations. One of the first things that he did was to introduce his people to the concept of the "dirty thirty". The dirty thirty is as follows: if 30% of your day is a difficult challenge and 70% is filled with good things, then the day has been good.

One of the most valuable lessons I have learned about leadership and human relationships is something that I also taught in my Ethics classes. Leadership can often be made strong during times of conflict and anger. Remember that anger is based in expectations. Think of the last time you were angry and seek to discover the cause of your anger in terms of a missed expectation.

I have read many books on leadership. By far the best book that spoke to leadership in an engaging, enlightened fashion that made sense to me is Doris Kearns Goodwin's <u>Leadership In Turbulent Times</u>. It is an analysis of "the transformative leadership of Abraham Lincoln, the crisis leadership of Theodore Roosevelt, the turnaround leadership of Franklin D. Roosevelt, and the visionary leadership of Lyndon B. Johnson". (Goodwin (2018)

Please know that an understanding about leadership cannot be gleaned solely from a book. It must be coupled with a deep understanding of human nature and care for others. Courage and resilience are essential.

The most important thing is to be YOU as a leader. *Esse Quam Videri,* To Be Rather Than To Seem To Be. There is a leader in all of us. We need only to discover it. The question is not "Am I a leader?" but "What kind of leader do I want to be?" You don't need a title to be a leader. You just need to see leadership as a valuable part of who you could be. No matter what your station in life, leadership awaits you.

### The Need For Listening To Others

The inability to listen is a problem that confronts all communities. Compromise has become a dirty word. Too many people are only interested in winning, not understanding different points of view. When Joe Biden came to our school to have a debate with Arlen Specter, their discourse emphasized a big problem in Washington. Nobody goes out to dinner together with members of the opposite party. The Republicans and Democrats exist in armed camps. They need to take a lesson from Tip O'Neill and Ronald Reagan, two legends of the American political landscape. They were a combative pair during the day. But after intense debate during the day, they would call each other and ask the question, "Is it five o'clock yet?", their signal for the cocktail hour even if they weren't planning to have cocktails. It was a signal to leave the business of the day aside and talk as one passionate person to another about anything in life but politics. Any community needs to develop relationships first and then let the business of the day follow.

There is a tendency today to demonize others. When will we learn that hate and love reside in all of us? I would call our drive to judge original sin. It is part of our humanity. The more you deny a feeling, the stronger it grows. I believe there is good and evil in the world. We know it when we see it. But let's not be hasty to make judgments about either side of those two moral descriptions. Randy Pausch in his Last Lecture made an interesting point that changed my thinking regarding listening to others. He states, "...that there is good in everyone. Sometimes you have to wait to discover it, but if you hang in there, you will". (Pausch 2008) It has helped me to avoid going to a negative place with others too quickly when we are working to solve a difficult issue.

### Managing Hardship

I still haven't identified the best way to describe the behind the scenes issues I encountered while serving as Chaplain at the school. Helping people manage hardships and adversity of all kinds was at the core of my role. There is no set formula or method for helping others through adversity other than knowing and employing what has worked for you in similar situations. You may not even realize the positive impact you have had on others until many years later, if at all.

### An Email Regarding An Alumnus' Flight To Islamabad: A Hero For Our Times

I received an email after my retirement was announced. A former student wrote the following.

> "To the man who saved my life...
>
> Greetings from Islamabad, Pakistan. I am currently deployed, living in a safe house in Islamabad, working out of the US Embassy. A little over a month ago, I flew in a commercial airline, alone, unarmed, in civilian clothes into the Islamabad Airport at 5:00 A.M. Of all the things that I have done, this was singularly the scariest. I was honestly unsure if I was going to make it, let alone make my connection. You gave me the tools to persevere.
>
> I remember the first time ever reaching out to you. I was a 15 years old sophomore and the first words I said in your office were "I'm scared." You

taught me to walk through fear and this lesson never left me even in my worst moments.

I have a loving wife and two beautiful daughters that will never know the childhood I knew because of you.

My mother passed just before my deployment. When she and I would talk, we would invariably ask, "What would have happened if I didn't go to Episcopal? Mom would shake her head and say, "_____, you would have died." I'm alive because of you. I got to lovingly say goodbye without regret because you taught me how to love.

Today, I have learned to give back what you so freely gave to me.

You have been in my thoughts and prayers. I am happy for you. I know that you will enjoy your retirement. EA is losing an institution.

*Esse Quam Videri*,

_____"

Fortunately when I read this email I was alone in my office. As I remembered how close this story came to not having a happy ending, I shed a tear.

What was it like for this former student who wrote me this email as he flew into the heart of enemy territory? He was terrified. He is a hero. Courage means to feel fear and move forward through it. That is what our troops do in far off lands everyday. But it is important for us all to realize that everyone is capable of heroic things when they are confronted by challenges. That includes you, the reader.

## You Never Know The Impact That You Have On Others

During our Alumni Weekends I have always made it a point to get to the 5th anniversary reunions. During the 25th reunion of one of the classes, I was standing with Vicki when one of my former students came up, greeted us, and said, "I have something I want to show you." Years ago we were required to write comments on a set of carbon copy forms for each of our students. The top page was white and the yellow copy at the bottom was sent to the student and his parents.

The student got his wallet from his back pocket and went into it. What appeared was the yellow paper that was used for student comments. He simply said, "You wrote this to my parents over 25 years ago." He handed me the paper. In the comment I described him as a person with a commitment to excellence, possessing the highest values that we cover in the Ethics course he took with me. I also indicated that I looked forward to the great things he would accomplish in the future.

He went on to say that every time someone would tell him he was not good enough, he would go to a quiet place, take out the slip, and read it, sometimes many times. Then he would put it back in his wallet. It got him through some tough times. As I held it, I asked him if he wanted to give it back to me. He held out his hand and said, "No, I'm not done with it yet." He then got a big smile on his face, and we embraced.

What is noteworthy is that I am sure every faculty member at our school could share a similar story. When I encounter our alumni, they often share remembrances of the relationships that they have had with faculty and friends. The cultivation of those special relationships is a key to the greatness of our school.

### *Treating Others With An Honest And Equal Hand:*
### *<u>Rolling Stone Magazine</u> Article*

I received a call from a writer for <u>Rolling Stone Magazine</u> who knew that Night Shyamalan, '88 was a graduate of Episcopal. I knew Night well because he was a close friend with one of the members of the Student Vestry, Graham Burnett, '88 who is now a professor of history at Princeton. At times journalists know the story they want to write and contact people who knew the subject back when hoping to get supporting anecdotes that will build interest in the story. In some cases, the story is written through the interview process.

It didn't take long for me to realize that this writer wanted to go back into Night's life and paint him as an abnormal person, based on the subject matter of his films. Each statement that the interviewer made such as, "He must have had a terrible home life.", I countered. I stated that Night had a normal upbringing with two wonderful parents. In addition to being a brilliant student, Night was a low key guy who got along well with his classmates. He was cheerful and polite. When the interview was over, the writer said in rather unfriendly terms, "Thanks, you just ruined my story." My response was, "Why don't you write a story about how normal he is. People may want to hear about that." His response was the familiar, "That doesn't sell!"

Night has the ability to cut to the essence of an idea. After Night had achieved success in the entertainment industry, I asked him to speak in chapel about what it was like growing up and to address the issues students face. I will never forget one of his lines, "You guys (referring to the students) are always trying to blend in and stand out at the same time." What a great way to describe the tension of being an adolescent.

There is a message here when you look at the life of Night. He knew in Upper School that he wanted to write, produce, and direct movies. He went to NYU to study film. After he graduated from NYU he called me on a Friday night and asked me to come the next day to see one of his first movies, which was playing in a local theater. As I recall it was a story based in India. I was one of twenty or so people in the theater. I was the only person who was not of Indian heritage.

A few weeks later he and I were talking and I asked him what he had on the horizon for his next film. He said that he couldn't tell me because it was a movie with a big surprise. I asked if he could tell me the title. He said, "Sure, it's The Sixth Sense," and the rest is history as the movie became an instant classic. Follow your dreams!

It was not uncommon for us to have children of very famous sports personalities at our school. One day I asked one of them why he chose our school and why he thought it was unique. He was quick to respond. He said that when he moves throughout Philadelphia and other places with his children, he is stopped and people ask for his autograph with little interest in his children. He understands that this is part of being a public figure.

He went on to say that Episcopal was different. Everyone is treated the same when they step onto the campus. He continued, explaining that it was a refreshing experience for his family, and it was what he wanted for his children. All people are equal in the eyes of God. This is the essence of community and family. It is sacred.

### *A Moving Gift From A Student*

A student, Julia Kathryn Adelizzi, '15, gave me a poem she wrote. She presented it to me in a frame with a beautiful picture of the Class of '44 Chapel, the sun low on the horizon behind it. She wanted to focus on the windows of the chapel that reflect the architects' vision of light, symbolizing love, as a central theme in worship.

### Windows

All can see right through
How can they, then, hold so much
Hidden to the eyes, never to be
Revealed. Thoughts,
And prayers,
Like static on mute,
Present but contained
Chilling to the touch
With an indescribable warmth. Reflective, clear
A comfortable gloss. Sun is brighter, rain
And gray defined. Like grandparents, tough
But warm, full of knowledge, many things seen and done
Yes always open. They are not opaque,

Not private. To be made they must be sturdy
As a reliant soldier.
Hopeful
If given the ability
To speak
They would tell of the hope
Within and without
As the view is equal for both
And of the mourning
But not without emphasizing
The unceasing love
They would tell the stories of those
Who've overcome great feats,
And of those
With young minds and potential
For such great wisdom.

I always felt that it was best to work behind the scenes to get the necessary help to members of our school community. The more that I did that went unrecognized, the better. I thought that I was pulling this off until I received this poem and a note from the poet that said, "Don't think that we don't know what you do here…how you help all of us in big and small ways. We do know! You are the glue that holds this school together."

I should have known that I could not get anything by our students.

## The Episcopal Church And Diversity

How can a community aligned with the heritage of the Episcopal Church include and empower students, faculty, and staff representing all religions, races, and gender expressions? As the spiritual leader of that community it was my job to make sure that everyone was included and felt cared for.

I adopted and demonstrated the view that my faith is deepened by experiencing the faith of another, and another's faith may be deepened by experiencing mine. I believe that we are on a shared spiritual and religious journey.

We had student leadership of chapel services in every division of the school. The spiritual leadership group in Lower school was the Chapel Council, the spiritual leadership group in Middle School was the Middle School Chapel Council, and the spiritual leadership group in Upper School was the Vestry. My role was that of coach and I encouraged my fellow chaplains to take the same approach. The players were the student leaders who were charged with striving to involve the other members of the community in our shared worship. This approach worked well with our school community since sports played an important role in our school.

I was crystal clear about my Christian identity and the Episcopalian heritage of the school. I feel this approach enabled me to embrace all religious traditions. It is when you are trying to be all things to all people, that you become nothing to no one. A clear identity of an institution promotes diversity.

### Diversity Or Showing Up

Showing up and being present in person is critical to bridging differences. Email, texting, or phoning just won't do. This approach was underlined for me during an encounter I had with the father of three of our Muslim students. The Toure family had spent time in refugee camps in Africa, lived in dangerous situations, and they were making a new life for themselves in our country. There were many schools in the Philadelphia area interested in having the Toure children become part of their school community, but they chose our school. One of the children, Sal Toure, '17 was elected to the Student Vestry. I wrote a recommendation for his college applications. After I retired, he called me just to make sure that I was doing well.

I asked the father of the Toure children, "How did we manage to get you to send your three children to our school? What was it about us?" He shared with me that he had received many letters from schools inviting his children who were gifted to attend programs designed to give potential students and their families a closer look at the institution. But he said that Ham Clark, who was our Head of School at the time, knocked on his front door. Ham's presence made all the difference.

College coaches know this as well. They visit the homes of their top recruits. If you want to make a difference, show up. There is a lesson in it for all of us. Take the first step. Make the walk.

## Diversity And Sexual Orientation

Several years ago I had a transgender alumnus, Clemmie Engle, '65 speak at our school. Since she would be the first transgender person to do this, I had to prepare the community so her visit would have the potential to be a positive experience for all. As a society we have come a long way with regard to embracing gender and other issues of diversity but we have a long way to go.

The proposal to have Clemmie speak came from a representative of the 50th reunion class. The 50th reunion class historically selects the chapel speaker for alumni weekend. I asked the representative why his class wanted Clemmie Engle to speak. He told me that Clemmie was a beloved member of their class, and the class felt she represented the best of an Episcopal education. I received the phone call having just finished co-teaching a course on diversity.

Fifty years ago, the school was all male. Clemmie had been an athlete and the valedictorian of their class. The class felt that she represented bravery, authenticity, character, and that she was a role model for our school motto, *Esse Quam Videri*, to be rather than to seem to be. All alumni are invited to attend this service that is held during Upper School chapel. The service kicks off Alumni Weekend.

I asked the class representative to introduce her and to share the class's relationship with Clemmie as part of the introduction. EA's alumni speak their minds. The class's attitude, however, underscored a central belief about issues of diversity. Once you get to know a person fully, all labels drop to the wayside.

I gave the school community notice the week before Clemmie spoke. Some people were direct in their criticism, but I felt strongly that we should not be so quick to cut off their voices and refuse to acknowledge that there are many opinions on any subject.

I told the critics in the parent constituency to come and hear Clemmie first hand and then make a judgment. I said that she had a high profile position in life and could handle anything they would want to say to or ask of her. Clemmie is an attorney in Denver who has been celebrated in both the straight and LGBTQ communities. Providentially an EA parent arranged for Joan Mulholland to speak in chapel about social justice a few weeks before Clemmie. Joan is an icon of the 60s Civil Rights Movement. She is seen in a famous photo from that time in which a white person is having ketchup poured over her head at a Woolworth soda fountain in the South. This may have opened some to want to hear from another pioneer of diversity.

Clemmie spoke and triumphed. She spoke about faith and social justice issues including a discussion about Stonewall and the start of the gay awareness movement. She also tied many ideas back to issues Joan Mulholland had covered. The congregation stood when Clemmie finished, and a thunderous applause followed for an extended period. That night at a dinner for the 50th reunion class, Vicki and I spent some time alone with Clemmie. She started to cry as she attempted to describe the emotions evoked by the welcome she received.

While everyone was polite to her during her time on campus, I certainly heard a great deal the following week from those who were against her speaking to the community. They had thoughtful, passionate, and angry comments expressing disagreement with my decision to honor the request of the 50th reunion class. In the end we agreed to disagree and I thanked them for their thoughts and concerns.

## Diversity And Religion

A Jewish mother and father really wanted their son to attend our school. They wanted the academic excellence, but were concerned about whether their son would feel welcomed in a Christian school. They knew that religious life is central to our school. In the end they decided to have their son apply to our first grade and he was accepted.

In their son's senior year, he gave an address in chapel, something that many seniors desire to do. His address focused on how he valued and appreciated the religious life and diversity of the community. The chapel on EA's Merion campus was contemporary with a vaulted ceiling and windows all around, symbolizing light and truth going out into the world. He used the chapel building itself as a metaphor for his point of view. He stated that the first time he entered the chapel as a first grader, he thought he was coming into a spaceship. Now that he was about to graduate, he realized that he had really been in God's living room. His parents were present and were beaming at their son's words.

Lou Fryman, an EA parent, was the first Jewish person to serve as Board Chair of our school. Lou met with his rabbi to discuss this opportunity. Before Lou would accept the chair, he also met with me in my office. He asked if I could bless this honor he had received, wanting to confirm that I supported his appointment. I enthusiastically embraced his appointment.

Lou is a deeply religious person and worships regularly at his synagogue. His Judaism is central to his life. Lou is the embodiment of what I have always held as a goal for the school, to develop great spiritual depth in all people in our community. Lou's respect for others is one of the reasons that he has received so many awards for his work on behalf of organizations too numerous to mention.

When I returned from spring break one year, Jay Crawford '57 then Headmaster of the School, asked me where we had gone. When I told him that we were on Gasparilla Island off the coast of Florida, he said, "Before you say another word, call Lou and be prepared for him to have you rolling on the floor with laughter. He has a story for you." Lou is a great storyteller. When I told him where we were for spring break, he broke out in laughter. He explained that he and his wife, Rhoda, were vacationing on Gasparilla Island when he heard the noise from several Blackhawk helicopters flying above. The island was a favorite destination for the Bush family to relax and have fun. There is only one hotel on the island so Lou and Rhoda were surrounded by the Bush family and their entourage of secret service agents. When it was time to go to dinner, Rhoda asked, "Lou, shall I lock up?" to which Lou replied, "No, we will never be this safe again for the rest of our lives." The next day Lou and Rhoda were a twosome playing golf one hole behind the President and his group. The President, George W. Bush, asked them if they would like to join him and his family. This is a great story about character and inclusion.

I was asked by Jenny Williams, one of my students from the class of 96', to bless her marriage. Jenny was raised with religious choice so that she could be open to all faiths. Her family is half Jewish and her parents let their children decide on their own religious heritage. Her mother, The Honorable Constance Williams, has played a key role in the political life of our state and nation. Jenny's father, Dr. Sankey Williams, has made important contributions in the medical field. Both Connie and Sankey have been enormously supportive of our school in general as well as me in particular. Jenny was marrying someone whose family had a long history in the Quaker tradition. Jenny worshipped for years at our school in the Episcopal tradition. I met with the young couple, and we crafted a service that included all of those religious perspectives. Since it was a service that included several different religious traditions, we wanted everyone to feel included. To that end we developed a unique liturgy. The newspaper reporter who came to write about the wedding indicated that he might write about the service as well.

The service was held on Mount Desert Island in Maine down by the water. After the service everyone headed up the hill to a tent where the reception was to be held. As I was making my way to the reception, I was intercepted by a man who simply said, "Thank you for a ceremony where all of us felt included." What a great revelation, beyond the magic of the wedding ceremony!

Following are the words I spoke at the service, reprinted here in full. Please take note of the quotations of Elie Wiesel and Rainer Maria Rilke. These two quotations are an important part that point to an essence of life, so I use them frequently in addresses at weddings hoping that the bride and groom will find them to be helpful too. For me Jesus becomes the answer to the questions that are raised. I referred to these questions when Jay Crawford and Charles Latham came to evaluate my preaching when I was a candidate to become Chaplain.

On the Occasion of the Blessing of the Marriage of Jennifer Lee Williams and Thomas Sanford Weymouth

July 1, 2006

Jenny and Sandy at this time you are beginning a new stage in your lifetogether. This celebration of the blessing of your marriage is symbolized for us in the questions that have been asked and the answers that you have given to each other.

"Will you love and honor each other as husband and wife for the rest of your lives? Do you promise to be true to the other in good times and in bad, in sickness and in health, to love the other and honor the other all the days of your life?" and you answered with an emphatic, "I will!"

Questions and answers are the rhythm of life. Each of you are question and answer for one another. Two important authors, one a poet, one a writer, focus this symbolic ebb and flow of question and answer for us.

Rainer Maria Rilke wrote, "Be patient toward all that is unsolved in your heart and try to love the questions themselves. Do not seek the answers that cannot be given you because you would not be able to live them. And the point is to live everything. Live the questions now. Perhaps you will then gradually, without noticing it, live along some distant day into the answer." (Rilke 1934)

You will spend a lifetime living the questions asked and the answers given during this marriage ceremony.

And Elie Wiesel, author of Holocaust literature, wrote about questions and answers in his book,

Night, which recounts in starkly simple prose his own experience as a child during the Nazi holocaust in Europe. The following is an exchange between Elie and his religious teacher, Moche the Beadle.

Wiesel wrote:

"Man raises himself toward God by the questions he asks Him. That is the true dialogue. Man questions God and God answers. But we don't understand the answers. We can't understand them. Because they come from the depths of the soul, and they stay there until death. You will find the true answers, Elie, only within yourself.

And why do you pray, Moche? I asked him. I pray to the god within me that he will give me the strength to ask Him the right questions. And throughout those evenings a conviction grew in me that Moche the Beadle would draw me with him into eternity, into that time where question and answer would become one." (Wiesel 2006)

When the questions asked tonight and your answers become one in your life you will know the Eternal One who we call Lord.

On December 13, 1895 in the Berlin Concert Hall the world heard for the first time words that I will leave you with this evening, "Der Grosse Apelle", the Great Calling, the Finale of Gustav Mahler's Symphony Number 2 "The Resurrection".

The text translates from the German as follows:

"With wings that I seized for myself in the ardent struggle of love, I will soar away to the light to which no eye has penetrated. I will die so as to live. You will rise again my heart in an instant! Your victory will carry you to God." (Mahler 1895)

That is my prayer for both of you as you begin this new adventure in living.

Amen.

Embracing diversity of religion is predicated on embracing shared experience. I had a student whose sister was undergoing a significant health issue. I was ministering to him and his family. The Reverend John "Jack" McNamee, a Roman Catholic priest who had been assigned to St. Malachy Parish in the heart of North Philadelphia, was ministering to the family as well. He always had a calling to serve the poor. St. Malachy was a struggling parish that Jack transformed into a place for everyone. It was a beacon of hope in a place where hope was not present. Jack pondered, "What are the consequences for faith and belief in a landscape where there is so little to believe in?" Jack wrote a book, The Diary of a City Priest (McNamee 1995) that answered that question. The book was turned into a movie.

Jack and I were in regular communication about my student's sister. I had also asked him to speak in chapel. He was taking great risks to help those who were so underserved in his part of the world, a story and ministry worth sharing.

My student's sister died in her mid twenties. The service was set in a nearby parish. In the Archdiocese of Philadelphia, it is up to the parish priest to determine whether clergy who are not Roman Catholic can participate in a service. Jack was to be the designated officiant for the Mass of Christian Burial.

I attended the service with some other administrators, students, and teachers from EA. The church building was a small place so there was standing room only in the aisles and at the rear of the church where I was standing.

I noticed Jack came into the sanctuary looking around trying to find someone. He walked down the center aisle. He saw me in the back behind other people and immediately came forward to greet me. He asked, "What are you doing back here? We are going to do this together in the same way that we ministered to the family together." One can have different views within any one faith. The shared experience is what becomes the most important ingredient.

## *Diversity And Welcoming the Neighbor*

Since the Merion Station campus was along a city bus route we had interesting people attend chapel or wander onto our campus from time to time. Diversity can take many forms, including people who have mental health issues and are separated from society on account of their illness. It was not uncommon for me to have visitors who needed money or who just needed to come in and talk about challenges they were having in life.

Our stated policy was that the Head of Plant Operations and I would handle people who had challenges of mental illness or financial need who came onto our Merion Campus. It is important to note that this was during the time before Columbine and our current era of much greater safety awareness.

Once a woman who was psychotic made her way onto our campus. The Plant Operations staff took her to my office even though I was off campus at the time. When I returned and approached my office several people said that they were sorry for what had happened to my office. I couldn't imagine what they were talking about! The police had put her in my office and seated her in my office chair. An additional larger policeman arrived and stood in the doorway. The woman was frightened by his size. This induced a psychotic episode and she destroyed my office, even knocking a cup of coffee onto my computer.

The outcome from this situation was favorable. I asked the police to take her to the nearest hospital with a psychiatric unit and she received the help she needed.

## *An All Ivy Half Back Who Defined Back Up*

Another similar event occurred during a Middle School Chapel service conducted by an assistant chaplain. The Assistant Head of Middle School came into my office about halfway through the service and told me that someone was lying on a back pew and refused to leave. He was uncooperative and somewhat threatening.

I told the administrator to get everyone out of the chapel and then call the police. In the meantime I would see what I could do.

I went to the rear pew and asked the visitor to sit up, which he did. He was confused and angry, apparently about our plan to move to a new campus in Newtown Square. Everything was low key until he stood up. I am tall, but he was taller. The more we talked the angrier he got. I had run out of every strategy I knew. This is where real back up came into play. I thought the visitor and I were the only people in the chapel. Then I felt a tapping on my shoulder and turned around. There standing behind me was a muscular member of the Religion Department, Chris Ryan, who was an all Ivy running back at Penn. He said simply, "Rev, I got your back!"

The police came and escorted the man off campus. As I understand it, they didn't take him for evaluation at a local hospital which I thought was a missed opportunity. I learned later that he had attended our school in the lower grades, which is why he was confused about our move.

## A New Campus For The Episcopal Academy At Newtown Square

We moved the campus from Merion Station to its current location in Newtown Square, PA in 2008. The new location is a 20 minute drive west of the old campus. The Newtown Square campus is some 90 acres bigger than the Merion campus. The much larger site allowed us to build everything we thought was necessary to enhance the education of our students. We were hemmed in on all sides at the Merion campus and repeatedly failed to get zoning approval to build even a simple structure there.

Despite the strong alignment of our school community behind the move, it quickly became obvious that there was real resistance to leaving behind the Merion campus chapel since many important events and special moments occurred in that place. At the same time the community was behind having the new chapel be the signature structure on our Newtown Square campus.

### *Key Leadership In Building The New Campus*

Building the new campus entailed splitting our focus and it felt much like working two full time jobs. We had to keep the quality of education at our old campus at a high level while planning the new. We were blessed during this challenging time to have had a dynamic Head of School, Hamilton Clark, who guided the planning, building, and transitioning to the new compus. Ham possessed the kind of energy that was needed to get things done. I asked him to give a chapel address describing his style of leadership. He expressed his belief that the key to leadership is to be everywhere. He would be in classrooms, sports events, corridors, and any place else that defined the school, listening and learning. He believed that leaders had to be visible in the community. Our board chair at the time, Ed Vick, once said, "leadership is either given or taken." He went on to add that Ham was someone who took the reins of leadership at our school.

During this period we also had terrific board members and board chairs, including Rush Haines, '61, a great friend and real estate lawyer. He was one of the key leaders during the planning and building of the new campus. Rush was followed by our first female Board Chair, Gretchen Burke, an EA parent. Gretchen brings great leadership to any project in which she is involved and building the new campus was no exception.

Gretchen Burke was the Chair of our Board of Trustees during one of our most significant periods in the history of the school. It was quite an ambitious undertaking to go from a 32 acre campus to creating a new campus on 125 acres of undeveloped land. Our goal was to improve our physical plant in order to transform our school into one of the best schools in the nation. Fundraising was no small part of the project.

Following are excerpts from a letter Gretchen wrote when she became the new Chairman of the Board of Trustees.

"It is with a sense of both pride and humility that
I assume the chairmanship of the board of trustees
at the Episcopal Academy. I'm honored to become a

part of the school's esteemed tradition of leadership during this momentous time. Particularly, I would like to acknowledge the strong advocate and tireless leader that Rush Haines, '61 has been over the past six years. His guidance and foresight have provided us with a very solid foundation for the future.

My focus over the next three years will be on finalizing our move to Newtown Square and managing the construction process, securing the necessary funds to build our incredible new campus, and strengthening our endowment to ensure a vibrant institution over the long term." (Burke 2005)

It was a daunting task but I think of the success of Gretchen's leadership and respond with the words of the hymn, <u>Come Labor On</u>, "Servant well done!"

Gary Madeira, '72 who is a wealth manager brought significant expertise to the board chair position. Schools have always been thought of as places where "readin', ritin', and 'rithmatic" are at the heart of the learning process. My experience with Gary focused my awareness on an additional three "r(s)" of learning, respect, response, and responsibility. His leadership demonstrated humility and a love of school. For me those are the ingredients of a great leader.

I think we all learned something very important from Ed Vick,'62 who was board chair when I retired. We all learn our leadership skills from important people and events that shape us into who we are today. Much of this book is my examination of how I made my way through life carrying with me the seeds of leadership skills learned first in working class culture. For Ed the seeds of his leadership skills were discovered and nourished in the Vietnam War where he led over 100 combat missions throughout Vietnam's Delta and the Cambodian border.

Ed was Co-chair of our Strategic Planning Committee, an entity that oversees other committees charged with examining every part of school life. I was on the Religious Identity Committee serving with a diverse group of people. I wish everyone could have heard the exchanges in those meetings that reaffirmed the school's Christian identity and Episcopalian heritage as our foundation. Ed played no small role in making sure that supporting the religious life of the school was goal one of the Strategic Plan.

Members of our Board of Trustees were talented and committed to being supportive of our faculty, staff, and students in all aspects of our school life during this challenging planning, building and transitioning process.

I overlapped a few years with our present Head of School, Dr. T. J. Locke. T. J. has brought a passion for the use of technology to enhance learning. Opportunities to integrate technology on a new campus are endless and with T.J.'s leadership we continue to keep pace with the most advanced use of technology. He also is balancing the long history and tradition of the school with innovations in learning. One of T.J.'s key characteristics is that he never settles. He is always looking to improve the life of students through faculty training and any new approaches or programs to make the student's life rich and fulfilling. A few paragraphs from a recent letter will indicate in specific terms how he accomplishes this. The complete letter referenced is in the references and endnotes section of this book.

> "Beginning in the 2018 academic year, the Computer and Engineering Department will equip our students with more than technological skills -- It will prepare students for tomorrow's careers by providing a foundation in concepts like computation thinking, the engineering design process, and digital citizenship. These lessons transcend technology, and provide a basis for designing innovative solutions that can be applied across disciplines.
>
> Creating this department was a true community effort. In May of 2017, a small multi-disciplinary group of 23 staff and faculty created the Computer Science Study Group to examine our current computer science and technology offerings and assess how to strengthen our programs. Over the

next seven months the group conducted site visits to cutting-edge peer schools, universities; and technology firms; spoke with leading thinkers in computer science; shared articles and studies; and surveyed EA parents, students, faculty, and alumni." (Locke 2018)

Teamwork and vision are evident in his leadership for our school.

## World Class Architects Robert Venturi, '44 And Denise Scott Brown Design The Class of 1944 Chapel

It was thrilling for me to be part of the planning and building of the Class of 1944 Chapel on our new campus in Newtown Square, working with renowned architect Robert Venturi, who was a member of the Class of 1944. The class donated the money and Denise Scott Brown, Bob's spouse, was his partner in the project. They are two of the best architects in the world. They were selected to design the extension to the National Gallery in London, considered the most prestigious new building project in Britain. Vicki and I had the opportunity to see their work in London first hand and to read accolades authored by Prince Charles praising their creation.

A group of representatives from various stakeholders in our school served on the Chapel Committee, providing feedback to Bob and Denise along the way. Meg Hollinger, Hon, Head of our Development Office, worked closely with the class of 1944 to secure the funding. She did it with such style, grace, and energy that the class made her an honorary member of the Class of 1944.

I know everyone in the class is grateful for their classmate, Bruce Mainwaring, for taking such a leadership role in the building of the new chapel. It is important to keep in mind that all of the members of the class of 1944 made a significant investment in having this chapel be the school's new place of worship. Both architects knew that leaving Christ Chapel on the old campus was an emotional pain point for the school community, being aware of the many significant events of joy and sadness that occurred in that place.

Before I met with Bob and Denise, I was given several books authored by them on the theory of architecture so that our conversation about the design could be an informed one. I came into my first meeting with Bob and Denise knowing that we needed to capture the essence of Christ Chapel at the Merion Campus and translate that essence to the Class of 1944 Chapel in Newtown Square but in a different way. Bob and Denise asked a very direct question, "What do you want to see when the new chapel is completed?" I simply replied, "I want something that communicates awe and intimacy. I want a chapel that is one of a kind, an original."

There are so many stories that could be told about the building the chapel. When you have so many stakeholders involved, there are clashing points of view. This was tempered by the fact that everyone wanted the best structure possible, as the chapel would sit at the head of our campus and would be the signature building for our school. It would be the first structure that people would see as they enter the main drive onto the new campus. The placement of the chapel was to be a statement of the central role of worship in the life of the school.

Every possible detail was discussed in an effort to get things right. An interesting fact is that architects work out seating in structures by assuming that everyone has an 18-inch-wide buttock. This assumption is used to calculate the actual seating capacity. The organ was moved from the Merion Campus and was expanded to meet the sound requirements for The Class of 1944 Chapel. This expansion was supervised by one of our chapel organists, John Powell, '75. The cross that hung in Christ Chapel on the old campus was transported to the new campus to be hung in a similar way in the new chapel.

The cross hangs high above the sanctuary in the new chapel. It seemed to me to be just the size for the space. I was present when it was taken down at Merion and made ready for shipment. Viewing it at close quarters lying on the ground, its presence was enormous. Perhaps there is a symbolic lesson here. When your faith becomes part of who you are, Christ and the cross can loom much larger in your life.

## *The Topping Of The Steel And A Misunderstanding*

There was a moment during the building of the chapel that required important dialogue and conflict management. We had a topping of the steel ceremony, an event that celebrates the final work of the ironworkers in the building of any structure. At this ceremony there is an evergreen placed on one end of a beam and the banner of the Iron Workers' Union is placed on the other end. The beam is hung about 30 feet up in the air by a crane.

It was pouring rain during the ceremony. Four hundred and fifty ironworkers were present, proud of their accomplishment. Through the driving rain I could see there was a stick on one end of the beam near the evergreen and the banner of the Iron Workers' Union on the other end. I didn't know anything about the symbolism of what appeared to be a stick.

Once the ceremony was over, we all sat together and had a celebratory lunch. The rain continued. During the next few days I received calls from passersby saying that they thought it sacrilegious to have an American flag at the top of the chapel where a cross should be. The stick turned out to be the furled American flag that I was unable to see in the driving rain during the ceremony. We are on a busy thoroughfare so there were many who made their concerns known.

The on site supervisor, Charles Boschen, and I talked since he had been getting calls as well. I suggested that we install the cross on top of the chapel and lower the flag down the vaulted roof about 6 feet. It seemed like the perfect solution.

When I arrived in my office the next morning, Charles Boschen was the first call of the day. He said, "There are 450 iron workers packing up their trucks with their tools, and they have called Action News to let them know how unpatriotic we are as a school for moving the flag down below the cross." This was very ironic as I can think of no school that is more patriotic than we are. We have services to remember those who lost their lives on 9/11. We have special chapel services for Veterans Day and Memorial Day. We send many students to the service academies. To be fair to the workers, they had not built a church before and were not aware of the protocol for a chapel.

My first response to Charles was to suggest that I come out to speak to the ironworkers. The head of the union was in Charles's office, so he put him on the phone with me. My only question was, "What is needed to make this situation right?" I had to clarify for him the protocol concerning churches. I also related to him how patriotism was valued by our school.

He suggested that an apology was needed. I apologized for failing to go over protocol issues with the workers prior to the ceremony. I also indicated that it is difficult to apologize for something that I could not see. If it had not been raining so hard, the flag would have been unfurled, and I could have addressed the issue then. This was not a disagreement that I was interested in winning. I just wanted to get the men back on the job.

The head of the union said that he understood what occurred and went back to address his men. Charles and I agreed that it was a beautiful sight to see the men getting the tools out of the back of their trucks and returning to work.

### How Did We Do? Will We All Fit?

The Chapel was completed in July of 2008 before the start of school in September. I met with Bob and Denise in the chapel. They referred to our first meeting regarding what I wanted to see in the new chapel, a sense of awe, intimacy, and a unique structure. They couldn't wait to ask the question, "How did we do?" I quickly and enthusiastically responded with, "You met and exceeded our expectations!" They had accomplished all the goals and then some. They had created a spectacular worship site. Others referred to the Class of '44 Chapel as possessing a wow factor.

Ham and I stood in the middle of the chapel surveying the finished product one August day before the start of school that first year on the new campus. The first chapel service was to include the Middle and Upper School, their faculty, and anyone else who wanted to attend. We reviewed the seating chart for the service. We both had the same concern, "Can we fit everybody in?" The seating chart indicated that we could. The chapel is designed with a bleacher arrangement of seats in the back sections without compromising a sense of intimacy. However, we both had the same thought. What if we can't get everyone in the chapel? What an embarrassing moment that would be. The first service occurred with more than 950 people in attendance. We had room to spare!

We were unaware that <u>The New York Times</u> was looking for school buildings across the nation to recognize with a "Too Cool For School Award". The chapel was one of eight to win the award. Students of architecture from all over the world have come to the chapel to behold the work of Venturi and Scott Brown. Some have even done an academic treatise on the unique and awe inspiring design of the chapel.

### Architecture: An Old Boys Network

One of the things I came to realize about the field of architecture is that it is an old boys network. Historically it has been difficult for women, specifically Denise Scott Brown, to have their work recognized. Bob was very sensitive to this and always made it clear to all that they were equal partners in design. We had a special evening to pay tribute to Bob and Denise. The tribute included a video in celebration of their work in creating our school chapel. For the video those involved in the project were interviewed. My interview included a statement about Denise's special talents and her contributions to the design. She sat in front of me in the theater as the video was shown. Afterward she turned and with a tear running down her cheek she mouthed the words, "Thank you."

After she was overlooked for a particular award, students at Harvard started a petition on her behalf to receive an award but she was overlooked once again. I thought it would be a great thing for our students to petition on her behalf as well, and they agreed.

A reporter from our school newspaper who was doing an article on Denise came to interview me. I told the student reporter that I could do her one better. I asked if she would she like to talk directly with Denise herself. I knew the student reporter had her questions ready. After she gathered her composure, I put her on the speakerphone with Denise and listened to a fabulous interview between the two. When they were finished, the student thanked her and left while I continued the conversation with Denise. She let me know that her book on photography of architecture was coming out soon. She also informed me that a show of her photographs of architecture was to be held in Venice and she said, "I don't mean Venice, California." She has a wonderful sense of humor. She finally had her due recognition.

## *Reflections*

Do you like things calm or chaotic or in between these two extreme states of being?

Do you have someone who you can call at any time for help?

Has anyone ever broken your trust? Were you able to repair the relationship?

When, where and how did you develop important character traits such as courage and integrity?

Do you have a momento from another person that helps you to remember your goodness?

What have you lost to gain something more important to you?

Would you define yourself as a religious person?

How do you relate to people who have a different sexual orientation than you?

When do you feel out of place? What do you do in those situations?

What nudges you to act in ways that help you and others?

Is there a label you feel has been placed on you? If so, have you thought of ways to alter that perception?

Can you think of someone in you life who has made you a better person simply by knowing him or her?

Who is a leader that you admire? What leadership traits does that person have?

How do you regard people with a different sexual orientation than yours?

# CHAPTER 5: REMEMBRANCES OF PEOPLE AND PLACE

In the course of my daily life at Episcopal I encountered a staggering diversity of experiences, from events that were light and humorous, to people and happenings of great import and life long significance. Here I would like to share a mere sampling of these with you so that you can walk in my shoes as chaplain.

### Frequently On The Insider Track

Given the diversity of movers and shakers that made up our school community, I often found myself with knowledge of events shaping our local and national landscape, some minor and some major, all shared in the context of the relationship of trust and confidence that I cultivated with deliberate practice. Here is just one of those.

John McCain is one of my personal heroes. We differ on certain political issues, but he is a model of character and courage. In his last book, <u>The Restless Wave</u>, McCain discusses his campaign for president and shared the fact that he wanted to have Joe Lieberman, a close friend and democrat, as his vice president. He also talks about his choice of Sarah Palin instead as his running mate. This announcement was to be made at 12:00 P.M. on a Thursday. Everyone, democrats and republicans alike, was eager to find out who the vice presidential candidate would be.

At 9:00 A.M. the morning of the announcement I was meeting with an alumnus of the school who was a Washington insider and a member of George Bush's administration. I had asked him to speak in a lecture series about a very timely but somewhat controversial topic. We were discussing what he should say. In the midst of our conversation, his cell phone signaled an alert to indicate receipt of a message. He looked down at the phone and then up at me and said, "Do you want to know McCain's choice for Vice President?" I said, "Sure!" He said, "I know that I can trust you to keep it quiet until the announcement at noon. It's Sarah Palin!" I was listening to NPR later in the afternoon and learned that even Sarah Palin's parents were not informed until noon.

## The Joys Of Celebrating Students' And Coaches' Accomplishments

Episcopal has produced many renowned athletes over the years. Two in particular come to mind from my time at the school. Wayne Ellington, '06 went on to UNC and Gerald Henderson, '06 went on to Duke University. They graduated from Episcopal the same year and our community was privileged to witness exceptional basketball as they played together. They performed at the highest level at our school, at college, and in the ranks of professional basketball. Wayne received the MVP award when UNC won the National Collegiate Basketball Championship. Both Wayne and Gerald were high picks in the National Basketball Professional draft. They were students, gentlemen, and athletes.

Both Gerald and Wayne were blessed to be coached by the legendary Dan Dougherty, Hon. or "Coach Doc", as he was affectionately called. I remember vividly the first time I met Wayne. He had just entered our school in ninth grade and Coach Doc and I were having lunch together in the cafeteria. Dan said, "Jim, I want you to meet someone." He called Wayne over and introduced him to me. When Wayne left the table Dan indicated, "He is the real deal!" That turned out to be a prophetic statement. Coach Doc never gave idle praise.

Wayne's father was tragically shot and killed in the city. The memorial service for him was at a church on North Broad Street in Philadelphia. It was a cold day. Wayne's father meant the world to him, and, in his time of grief, Wayne received great support from our school and from the basketball community.

Our community was blessed to know another outstanding coach, Jay Wright, Head Coach of the Villanova University basketball team, who was also a parent at our school. He epitomizes everything that is transformative about college athletics. I have my Villanova Final Four hat on top of my bureau. Jay came from a solid blue collar background. Neither of his parents had the opportunity to go to college. His coaching mantra is, "Attitude is everything!!!" He treats his players with great respect. He has a basketball court in his backyard so that his children and his players can have pick up games.

Jay's wife, Patti, keeps everyone moving in the right direction. Her empathy and warmth is palpable. She commands respect and keeps everybody in line. On top of that she knows a lot about basketball. Jay and Patti were present in chapel when their son, Collin,'12 was inducted into the Student Vestry to lead the group as Senior Warden. Jay saw me after the service and said that Patti had given him an elbow during the service because she thought he was texting. He said, "Rev, I was getting down everything you said. Look!" Jay was taking down a piece of the net after winning the NCAA National Championship and was overheard saying, "I don't deserve this!", which speaks to his humility, an attribute that shapes players and coaches into champions.

Bruiser Flint '83 who coached at Drexel was a graduate of our school and Fran Dunphy who coached the Temple University basketball team was an Episcopal parent. Jerome Allen came from an underserved area in the city and overcame many hurdles to graduate from EA and from the University of Pennsylvania. He returned to Penn to become the coach of the men's basketball team. He has moved on to become assistant coach of the Boston Celtics.

## The Enduring Value Of Relationships

Several years ago I was hospitalized at Philadelphia's Jefferson University Hospital for a heart issue. Jefferson is a teaching hospital. Dr. Pavri, my cardiologist, who heads the Heart Institute there, entered my room with his entourage of residents and interns.

He discussed my case with them and then said, " I have appointed a special resident to watch over you. His name is Dr. Jon Finkel."

I paused for a moment and asked, "Are you the same Jon Finkel who went to the Episcopal Academy?" The chosen resident moved from the back of the entourage to the front so I could see him and responded, "Yes, it is sir!" Jon was a member of the Class of 1999.

I always tell people to treat others as though your life may depend on them some day. My life literally depended on this former student. I noticed that Jon was a frequent visitor to my room and I suggested that he look after the folks who were more critical than I was. Residents have a large number of people to take care of. He looked at me and said, "If you die on my watch, I am a dead man. Look at all the people you have taken care of."

In a recent conversation with Jon I learned that he is now a cardiologist at Crozier Chester Medical Center. He has a busy life and is married with two children. To this day I am grateful to him for his terrific medical care. He was still interested in how I was doing. He remembered all the medical moments when I was his patient among the many patients he has seen since then.

## Sacred Presence

During that stay in the hospital I had a visit from Drew Mason,'86 also a former student. We have maintained a close friendship since his graduation. I co-officiated at his wedding. He and his wife Mary have nurtured a wonderful family; they have transferred their goodness to their children. Drew asked if he could pray the rosary with me that night in the hospital and I said, "yes." The students refer to this as "a lap around the beads". Drew knelt by the bed on the hard linoleum floor and prayed the rosary. At one point a nurse entered and offered a blanket, placing it under Drew's knees. I am sure the doctors and nurses who were waiting to come into the room were wondering who this guy was. It was a special spiritual experience for me.

When Drew was a senior at EA, I received a call late one night from an admissions office of an Ivy League School. They apologized for the late call, but they were anxious to ask me about Drew and they knew that I would give them honest answers to their questions. Drew was a great student athlete who was a quarterback on our football team.

They asked me to verify his athletic prowess, and I indicated that their facts were true. Then came the long pause. They continued to get to the real reason for the call. They had tried to schedule a meeting with Drew, but they learned that he was planning an overseas trip to see the Virgin Mary where she was appearing in Medjugorje. I indicated that was true as well.

I didn't tell them as a tenth grade student he had smuggled bibles into a communist country, an illegal action. The punishment for doing this was severe. All of his life he has been a risk taker and has taken the road less traveled.

One day after a meeting in my office, he indicated that he would take me home in his baby blue VW, a dilapidated model with some of the floor missing. Instead of going the right way he took a shorter route that was against school rules and we got stuck at the top of a sidewalk on a hill next to our tennis courts. If that wasn't bad enough, it was the day of our Board of Trustees meeting so we were stuck there as a parade of trustees passed by. Each said, "hello," with smiles on their faces. Drew didn't know what to do.

After Drew graduated from Wharton at Penn, he kept in close touch. When the school receptionist would not put his calls through, his way of dealing with that was to tell her that she should leave a message for me indicating that my psychiatrist had called.

After various medical challenges, my brother died suddenly in 2008. I was with his wife, June, and my niece, Teddy, when he was taken off of life support. I co-officiated at his funeral service in Alexandria, Virginia. We had his body brought from Alexandria to West Conshohocken for his burial.

There was a graveside service at his burial with only members of the immediate family present. As I began the committal service I looked to my left and there standing at the end of the drive was Drew. He had a ministry of presence. He never said a word. He stood there to offer quiet support. He is one of a kind. We need more like him.

## **Passion, Commitment And Levity In Balance**

The Chambers and Shanahan brothers provided a lot of support and comedic relief. In these families, the good stuff from their fathers and mothers was ingrained in their boys.

Pat Chambers,'89 was my advisee. He coached basketball at our school, at Villanova, and at Boston University before becoming the head coach at Penn State. He is working hard to coach his team to the next level. Pat did not find his passion in academics although he was a solid student. He did, however, channel his passion into everything related to basketball. It has been a thrill for me to watch his career, but more important to me was a photo of him with his children in the local press as he was taking them to their first day of school in the fall.

There was a humorous moment at one of Pat's games when he was coaching for us. I was sitting with a scout for a college team who leaned over and said, "I think it is great that you have a priest for a coach." I had no idea what he was talking about. I looked at our bench. Pat was wearing a black sweater over a white turtleneck, and could readily be mistaken for a priest. We had a great laugh when I let Pat and his coaching staff know of the scout's observation.

Pat Chambers' brother, Paul, '88 excelled at sports at Penn as did one of the best athletes to graduate from our school, Chris Flynn, '84. Chris played both football and lacrosse at Penn. Chris has told me that he can still remember his first class with me. He reminds me that he wasn't prepared for how difficult the course would be. He excelled in the course and provided levity with his imitations of me.

Paul understands expectations and priorities. That is what made him such a great student athlete. Paul was a member of the Student Vestry. We had a meeting scheduled for the Saturday that Paul had been given tickets to a Penn State game. It was to be the game of the season. He came to the vestry meeting forgoing the hyped football game. I found out about all of this after the fact and not from Paul. To this day he may not know that I knew of his choice.

Tim Chambers, brother of Pat and Paul, an EA parent and All Ivy Defensive Back at Penn, wrote and directed a movie titled, The Mighty Macs. It is the story of Cathy Rush as coach of the Immaculata College National Championship Women's Basketball Team. Tim wanted it rated G so that all family members could attend. Vicki and I attended the premier in the city.

I had Tim address chapel about the value of perspective, and he told this story about himself. He was coaching a football team of young boys, giving them an impassioned speech about hard work and dedication with a "win one for the gipper" tone. When he finished his impassioned address, giving it everything he had, he asked if there were any questions about their road to success. A player in the back of the room raised his hand and asked, "Coach, do we have practice on Halloween?" Even Tim had to laugh. Perspective in all things is key.

The Shanahan brothers were gifted athletes with a great devotion to family. One of the brothers, Brian, served as Senior Warden of the Student Vestry. He also has had an outstanding tenure as a basketball coach at another independent school and recently became head basketball coach at EA. The Shanahan brothers arrived in my office one day and were talking about the upcoming marriage of their sister. I told them I could only imagine the hard time the future groom would get from this feisty bunch. All at once they chimed in stating, "She is the toughest one of the family. You should feel sorry for us." They always managed to make my day!

The father of the Shanahan brothers, Jim, died just a few years ago. He would occasionally stop by my office when he was on his way to one of his sons' games on campus. He was someone who was a terrific support, along with the boys mother, Jeannie, of their talented sons. One day he stopped by my office, and sat down with a big smile on his face.

As a graduate of Villanova University, Jim had attended a fund raising event where the university was seeking financial support from the gathered assembly. He said that he and his friends looked around the room and noticed something. There were no A students in the room. The successful people were all C students. He had a successful trucking company, The Shanahan Express. Still with a smile on his face, he asked, "What do you think of that?" He already knew the answer because he lived it! You need grit and social/emotional intelligence, as well as the ability to read people and to get along well with others with integrity. They are just as important as anything that is learned in a classroom. His children learned that lesson. He and I left together to see one of his children play their sport. The smile never left him! I mention this incident for another reason. We have all heard the expression that "character is what you do when no one is looking". I was aware that he did a lot behind the scenes that no one knew about to help others and he probably did it with that big smile.

## Opportunities For Character Development Can Appear When You Least Expect Them

Vicki and I were going to Larry's Steak Shop on the campus of St. Joseph's University to have dinner on a Saturday night when an event occurred that demonstrates the power of perfect timing. At least it was perfect timing for me.

As we were entering the restaurant three of my students were leaving the beer distributor located right next door. They were carrying their six packs, arms wrapped around their valued possessions, as though they were football players heading for the goal line. They took one look at me, turned on their heels as one and headed back into the beer distributor. I waited for them to come back out empty handed.

They raised the question, "I guess you want to talk to us next week?" I told them to think about what they wanted to say to me. Their school day started at 8 in the morning so I indicated that we should meet at 7 on Monday in my office just to make it inconvenient for them. They were all there on time. Their words to me were exactly what I would have said to them.

I needed these students to own their actions. Parents can be quick to let their children off the hook. The students will tell you that the greatest words in the English language are peer pressure. If a student is caught drinking, some parents will say, "It was peer pressure." Any unhelpful behavior can be justified by those two words. The students know this so some will play their parents like a well tuned fiddle.

## *There Is No Great Success Without Sorrow And Struggle*

One of my students, Leonard,'96 seemed to have it all. He was handsome enough to be recruited for modeling, was a terrific academician, a fine lacrosse player, and one of the most mature and moral individuals one could find. When Leonard was in 8th grade his father died tragically. The word crisis in Greek describes something that can be a positive or negative influence on your life. Leonard always chose the positive way. He went on from an undergraduate degree earned at New York University and University of Pennsylvania to Harvard University to earn his Ph.D. in Islamic Studies. He earned a Harvard law degree as well.

When Leonard was a senior at Episcopal, I blessed the marriage of his mother to a graduate of our school. It was a joy to see her experience happiness in a new relationship.

In 2016 Leonard asked me to bless his marriage. He was marrying an amazing political writer, Kristin, who appears on network news shows. The wedding weekend in New Hampshire was idyllic. Leonard made sure that Vicki and I were very comfortable and enjoying the weekend. The occasion was further blessed by coinciding with the release of books authored by both the bride and groom. Leonard's book was about Sharia Law in the Middle East and Kristin's book focused on problems with the politics of Washington from the perspective of a millennial.

The backdrop for the wedding was Mount Washington, and the ceremony was held at one of the grandest hotels in the world. The couple had reached a summit in their lives and they were enjoying it to the fullest. They also knew their life together would hold challenges as they juggled careers. The groom and I had gone down many roads together. It was clear that his bride shared his passion for life and learning. I was filled with so much pride during the service as I was reminded that there are no overnight successes. There is always a backstory of grit giving birth to resilience during the quest for excellence. It was a thrill for me to join them on this summit as they looked into their future.

There was a humorous moment when I asked the groom the next morning at breakfast how he thought the evening went. I was talking about the ceremony and dinner reception. I should have been clearer about my question for he thought I was talking about their time together after everyone retired for the evening. He was quite funny when he reflected, "Now let me see. Our room was next to my parents and across the hall from my spiritual mentor and advisor. I should have planned that better." We can still laugh about it.

## The Challenges Of Straddling Two Cultures

There are times when it is difficult for a student from an under-served community to navigate the seas of an independent school. I was asked to be the advisor of one such student. He had a difficult time transitioning to the demands of our school, acting out in various ways. I wasn't making much of an impression on him so I told him that I would be checking in with his mother. It was important to let a student know when I planned to check in with a parent because of trust issues. I called his mother. His dad had worked for the electric company and was killed in an accident on the job. I communicated the long list of infractions that her son had been involved in and asked if she could support me on her end. There was absolute silence. His mother had a one sentence response, "You will not have any more problems with my son." And I didn't. A picture may be worth a thousand words but so are the simple words spoken by a parent that draw a line in the sand.

This student went to college in western Pennsylvania where he got into a fight and was suspended for a term. When it was time to go back to college, he called me just to talk. I asked him how his mother was and suggested that he call me once he got settled in back at college.

When I received his call I asked, "So how was the trip? Did your mother give you some last minute advice?" His response was, "Yes!" When mother and son got on the elevator of his highrise dorm he thought he was home free until she pushed the emergency button and stopped them between floors. When I first met his mother I thought that she would be 6 foot 6 and look like the incredible hulk for she communicated great power. Instead she was a petite lady. Suffice it to say that between the floors of his dorm his mother communicated a clear message of her expectations. He has the greatest love and respect for his mother and she for him.

Today this fellow has a wonderful wife and children and is a school principal. No one will ever be able to get anything by him. He knows all the tricks. I still receive information from him about his running competitions and his race and workout times. I am very proud of him.

### *Overcoming Labels And Respect through Discretion*

I had a wedding to co-officiate at the New Jersey shore. As Vicki and I were driving there, the thought crossed my mind that the groom and his groomsmen were all athletes of note, terrific lacrosse players. When I arrived, the other clergyman was quite out of sorts and feeling hassled. I asked what was wrong. He indicated that he couldn't get control over the group. They were all over the place and he could not get them to focus. I asked him politely if I could run the rehearsal and he readily agreed. I gathered the wedding party together for the rehearsal and things went smoothly. When we finished, my co-officiant asked the secret to getting the group going in the right direction. I indicated that they were high-spirited but well meaning. All I had to do was have a private word with a few of them to bring things in line. Offering words of criticism, especially in groups, requires discretion; you always want to leave everyone's dignity intact. Public criticism is never the way to go in handling a negative group dynamic.

One member of this group had served on the Student Vestry. All Upper School students and faculty can vote for the slate of candidates running to serve on the Student Vestry. It is not unusual for us to have 24 students run for 4 positions. When this groomsman was elected, I received a number of emails expressing the opinion that his election was a joke. They claimed he wouldn't take it seriously.

He went on to be a key leader in the group with total commitment to the group. He grew so much from his role and the expectations that were placed on him. He later would tell me that it was the most important aspect of his high school experience. The lesson is, once again, drop a label and you will give a person an opportunity to succeed.

## Relationships For A Lifetime

Lawyers tend to get a bad rap, but the following three attorneys get the highest praise from me: Tom Bergstrom, Rush Haines, and George Noel. Question: Who would you call if you needed legal help at three in the morning? For me it would be one of these three. Beyond being tops in their profession, they are good friends, and I can always count on them. I would hope that they felt they similarly could call me at three in the morning.

Tom is one of the highest profile litigators in the country. His cases tend to receive a lot of press.

He was one of the first people to locate the land for the new campus. All three of these gentlemen lawyers give new meaning to the word loyalty. Tom is also a great husband and father. His son, also named Tom, was a member of the Student Vestry. Tom's wife, Dee, had surgery to treat throat cancer and needed to use an assistance device for speaking. We had the good fortune to have Dee speak in chapel while her son was a member of the Student Vestry. I will never forget her chapel address. She spoke about grit by describing the challenges she faced in confronting her cancer. Sadly Dee lost her battle with cancer the year after her son graduated from Episcopal. Both Tom and Dee were marines, so her funeral was held at Quantico. It was a beautiful tribute. Her son, Tom, sang one of her favorite songs, "The Impossible Dream."

Rush is totally dedicated to his family, the Episcopal Academy, and his college alma mater, Princeton. There is a New Yorker cartoon of someone in a Princeton sweatshirt ascending through the clouds to meet with St. Peter. The caption is, "To enter heaven you must give up all earthly connections." The look on the man's face indicates that he may not want to give up his affiliation with

Princeton for heaven. That is Rush! When he is committed to a cause or a person, he is committed for good. When Rush's wife, Susie, was receiving treatment for cancer, Rush shaved his head as a gesture of solidarity. One of my great memories is blessing the marriage of their daughter, Jen, to Chris Butler. Jen was one of my advisees. The wedding was on Nantucket. Rush and Susie made the event a very special time for their daughter and the assembled guests. It was a magical five days.

Rush and I could always talk freely about problems and challenges. One of the things I admire about Rush is that he always speaks his mind and he communicates in a direct fashion.

George Noel is a Notre Dame guy who believes that sports build and transform character. As a result, his children didn't have a chance to be anything but great athletes. George's passion was to support and encourage his children. He is measured and reasonable. George's wife, Mary Ellen, also strongly supported and encouraged their children in athletic pursuits, but she had a more direct approach. Their son, Matt, was scheduled to compete in the Penn Relays which are held off campus. Before boarding the bus to travel to the competition, Matt indicated to his mom that he wasn't feeling well. He thought he should pass on the competition. His mom quickly decided otherwise. She instructed him to lie down in the back seat of their car and she drove him to Penn. She figured that way he could run the race and then she would drive him back home. I laughed when Mary Ellen shared this with me as we watched the races. Today Matt is a successful lawyer, husband, and father on the West Coast.

George and Mary Ellen's other son, Jon, was a member of the Student Vestry and a terrific punter on the football team. He graduated from Penn, has established a successful business, and is a dedicated husband and father.

I had the privilege of watching George's daughter, Mary Beth, inducted into the Sports Hall of Fame at another independent school in our area. She continues in athletics and coaching, while enjoying her roles as mother and wife.

George's, wife, Mary Ellen, died a few years ago. Needless to say, George was the model of how a caregiver should care for a loved one. She was an integral member of her garden club so we had a lovely period of reflection for her at one of the historic homes in the city of Philadelphia where she had provided flower arrangements.

All three of these parents and I share a common experience. We can pick up the phone and begin a conversation with one another as though no time has passed by. Pay attention to those times of shared experiences. They could turn into three o'clock in the morning phone calls.

## The Wonder Of Self-actualization

Always be ready to look for advice, support, and solutions from others, even if you might not think of someone as a resource. One student played on the Middle School football team while I was coaching. He was always self confident. One day during a game, I called in the play from the sideline. He barked the commands with hands under center, and then there was silence followed by a long pause. He looked over at me and asked, "What was that play again coach? I forgot." I told him and he went right under the center to receive the snap as though no interruption had occurred even though people were laughing on the sidelines. He went on to become an All World Goalie in lacrosse. Yes, he was the best in the world at that position.

I asked this student for his advice on how I should guide student athletes who want to play at the Division One college level. His response was, "Tell them, depending on their choice of school, they will be required to do the sport eight hours a day and school on the side." For some dedicated athletes that is the name of the game. Others require more balance in life.

One of our graduates who had a learning disability went on to a very competitive college and played a sport at a Division One level. He became captain of his college team. He came back to see me during his senior year when he was on Christmas break. He and I had many conversations when he was a student at our school so it was appropriate for me to ask the $64,000 question. How did you achieve your success in college? I told him that I wanted to share his story anonymously with other struggling students.

He paused for a moment and then said, "It is really kind of simple. My roommate was an outstanding student, and we were taking the same courses. Pretty soon I realized that what took him two hours to do would take me twice that amount of time. I asked myself if I could do that for four years. It was gut check time. I said to myself, 'I can and I will.'" And he did!

He went on to say, "That's what people like me need to be told. It isn't right. It isn't just. But it is the way it is." This student probably was told this insight a number of times. The difference this time was that he embraced this truth because it came from within him.

## *Reflections*

Have you had the experience of being in a place that was new and different where you had to figure out the rules of that group or culture?

What role does humility play in your life?

Do you know people who always seem to be there when you need them?

Think about people who make you laugh and who inspire you?

Character is seen in what we do when no one is looking? Can you remember an experience where you have exhibited character in this way?

Can you recall a time in your life when a difficult situation did not deter you from continuing to move forward with your goals?

Who would you call at three o'clock in the morning if you needed help?

Can you recall an experience that caused you to face your limitations and accept those limitations as part of who you are?

# CHAPTER 6: LIFE AND LEGACY

## Life And Legacy, Loss And Legacy, And Promoting Diversity

Our lives are a constant thread of loss and legacy. What do those who have departed this life leave as their legacy to make our lives better? I have already indicated that the loss of my daughter shaped my life and who I became. Throughout life we encounter individuals who are examples of life and legacy. I have many examples of each but will share a few with you. Everyone mentioned here has given me permission to share their names and stories. Everything I relate about them is in the public domain. There are no secrets. Their stories reveal deep understandings of how we are touched by the loss of life and the gift of life of those still among us. Their stories inspire us and make us better people.

A book title, Necessary Losses, (Viorst 1986), describes life in a precise manner. Life is a series of necessary losses but I would add that each life gives us a necessary legacy as well.

## Givers and Takers

Adam Grant adds another dimension to the spiritual experience in his book, Give And Take (Grant 2013). One may wonder what a professor at the Wharton School of the University of Pennsylvania could tell us about spirituality in action? As it turns out, he can tell us a great deal.

He divides the world into givers and takers. One of the characteristics of givers is that they do things for others while not seeking public praise. The givers' efforts are other-directed. Their motivation is not to gain recognition. Takers want others to focus on what they have done. Takers are motivated by reward and recognition. It is hard to believe this in our culture, but givers do better in the long run as everyone recognizes their selfless nature. Grant goes on to prove this with research data.

The actions of the giver have no strings attached with no *quid pro quo* relationships. There are always strings attached to the taker's actions.

EA is a community of givers with some giving large gifts and others giving small gifts based on their ability to contribute. I have often summarized Grant's research by the spiritual koan, "We only get to keep what we are willing to give away". The givers have had a wide range of impact on our community. They are responsible for endowing buildings or places within buildings and establishing scholarships and educational programs. Givers in our community also act with the ordinary gestures, putting others before themselves. They receive joy through this perspective.

## Gratitude Is Where Psychology, Theology, And Ethics Meet

Gratitude is the hallmark and characteristic of people who live to benefit others. Their attitude and actions create true happiness. Gratitude is where theology and psychology meet.

Since the chapel services and lectures are the centerpiece of the spiritual experience at The Episcopal Academy, this communicates a distinct sense of gratitude for God's gifts and grace to each and every one of us. A grateful heart is the beginning of a true religious experience. In my career I have experienced this phenomenon over and over in connecting to others, young and old alike. The chapel experience at EA is a place where the community is reminded of this important aspect of creating meaning, happiness, and purpose in our lives. You will see this as a theme in a sampling of chapel addresses included in this book. Gratitude is the source of giving. It is important to recognize this aspect of theology.

Gratitude plays a large role in psychology. Students at Penn, who take the Positive Psychology course, do at least two assignments

179

focusing on gratitude as the central tenet of being happy and creating a sense of purpose and a commitment to something important beyond one's self.

The first assignment is the gratitude letter. Students write a letter to someone who they are grateful for in their life and describe what has created this gratitude. The student must hand deliver the letter to the person and wait as the person reads it. It is an emotional experience for both the giver and the person who is receiving the letter. This is a perfect example of "you only get to keep what you are willing to give away." I always tell people to keep these letters and reread them when they are having a bad day to be reminded of their goodness.

Although it did not take the form of a gratitude letter, I saw this over and over again in the Ethics course I taught. At the beginning of the course, the students go through an exercise to identify the core personal value that guides their decisions. They also have an assignment to identify the core interpersonal value that reflects what is most important in their relationships with others. Where the personal core value and the interpersonal core value intersect is a powerful force in how they make decisions.

In my Ethics course I indicated that I did not want them to reveal their core personal value. It was just for their eyes. I also indicated that I would be the only one to read their essay on their core interpersonal value. When I graded their essays and returned the papers to them, I made a point to encourage them to guard the privacy of these very personal papers. There were certain essays that were a powerful statement about the students' parents as a guiding factor. At times I would include in my comments that they should consider showing the essay to the person who has affected them the most. It was always a suggestion not a requirement.

### An Early Morning Visit

This activity became as moving an experience as the gratitude letter was in the course at Penn. One example will demonstrate this. I arrived at my office one morning and was in the process of unlocking the door when I heard, "Good morning, Reverend

Squire," coming from someone in the conference room across from my office. I must have jumped a foot off the ground as I wasn't expecting anyone to be there. The woman was crying. Tears streaked her face. I was contemplating what problem could have put this parent in such a state of despair. I was wrong. She had tears of joy. She was a parent of one of my Ethics students. The student had written her essay on how her mother was the greatest influence in her life and how grateful she was for all her mother did for her. She showed me the essay that she had clutched in her hand and proceded to say, "I felt like dirt under her feet. I never knew how deeply she appreciated me." I learned that daughter and mother embraced and cried together. The mother left saying, "Now I feel as though we have a much better relationship. It is the nicest thing that ever happened to me."

I have literally taught thousands of students and I always asked a question of them in Ethics class, requesting they raise hands to answer in the affirmative. I asked them, "How many of you feel that the greatest influence on shaping your values has been your parents or a parenting figure such as a grandfather?" All hands went up affirming that parents are, for better or worse, the value makers of their children.

I asked another question resulting in all hands raised, "How many of you spend too much time avoiding the emotions of guilt, vulnerability, and rejection?" All hands went up. Does that surprise you? All adolescents feel they are under constant evaluation and scrutiny, real or imagined.

The second gratitude exercise practiced in the Penn Positive Psychology course has been documented with scientific research to support its efficacy. The exercise entails writing on paper what you are grateful for that occurred that day and focusing on those things or events before bed. This is seen as an exercise that promotes sleep better than other approaches including medications. I would add that offering a prayer of thanksgiving for those positive occurrences enhances the exercise.

## **Service To Others Counts**

While being at The Episcopal Academy had been a long time dream during of my youth, my early days at EA found me coming to terms with the contradiction of my past of no back up and the affluence of a good many of the EA community. I recalled the story of John Kennedy speaking in Boston, when a person shouted, "Kennedy, you were born with a silver spoon in your mouth." And that key response from a blue collar worker which is what I also would say, "Yea, John, and you didn't miss a thing." This became an iconic insight that was forged in the smithy of my soul. That attitude on my part became liberating.

As already noted I often told my students and my children that money will never guarantee happiness, but it will give you choices. The more choices you sense you have the freer you will feel to determine your own destiny.

This theme arose throughout our school community as students returned from community service projects. We had one initiative in particular, founded and shaped by one of my colleagues, The Reverend Tim Gavin, 'Hon. that took our students to Haiti to assist in building a school. Tim was fully informed of the culture of Haiti and he made an effort to learn the language of the people. The conditions and the faces of poverty startled our students, but they were also startled by the high levels of meaning and happiness they observed in the children they were there to serve. How could these children who had so little be so happy? The answer is that it's not all about money or material wealth.

Closer to home, I remember one day a student who had very little in terms of material things confronted another student who was from an affluent family. He accused the student from an affluent family of having it easy. The affluent student responded by saying, "My mother got on a plane at 5 A.M. this morning and she will be out of town all week working every hour until she returns home for the weekend. If you call that easy, you need to think again." All of us are paying a price. What is it? Is it worth it? That is the reality I wanted our school community to continuously examine and keep at the forefront of its conscience.

Whether we come from terrific wealth and privilege, or from meager means, we all have challenges to face, and can all know joy and happiness in different ways. We are all made from the same clay.

## Life And Legacy

The following two sections highlight people who leave a legacy by their life lived. The first is titled <u>Life and Legacy</u>. The second section is <u>Loss and Legacy</u>. It highlights the impact of some members of our school community who have died. Their lives became a compass pointing us in the direction of a true north of ethical behavior and lives richly lived.

These two sections are the tip of the iceberg of stories that I could tell to highlight people who have inspired our community. The stories communicate the importance of legacy. The stories I could tell are too numerous so many of them will just remain close in my heart.

## The Recovery Of Candace Gantt

Encountering a real life miracle makes an impact on any community. Candace Gantt, a parent of two Episcopal Academy students, is a real life miracle. She was an elite athlete at the time she was hit by a truck on a busy road while training. She was thrown from her bike into a telephone pole and fence. She was airlifted to The Hospital of the University of Pennsylvania (HUP) where her surgeon, Dr. M. Sean Grady, performed an emergency craniotomy, removing the left side of her skull to relieve the pressure from her life threatening head injury. This occurred in July of 2005.

Some time later with the support of her husband, daughters, family, Penn doctors, and members of our school community, she returned to HUP to thank all of the medical people who had been so helpful to her. She now chairs "The Mind Your Brain Conference" at that institution.

She was in a coma for two weeks after her three neurosurgeries. The outlook for her recovery was unknown because of the severe nature of her injury. A book was written about her that sits on the coffee table in my office. It is there to always remind me about what can be achieved against all odds.

When I visited her while she was at HUP, I wondered about what medical miracle could return her to some sense of normalcy. Eventually she left HUP and was transferred to a rehabilitation facility. I will never forget visiting her there one afternoon while she was in the occupational therapy room. When I located the room, I saw her across the large space and started to make my way toward her. She held up her hand as a policeman does to stop traffic. It stopped me in my tracks.

Candace, wearing a helmet on her head, crossed the room with a slow deliberate pace until she reached me and we embraced. She advanced to walking more, then running short distances, then longer distances, and on eventually to compete in ironman races and marathons once again. In fact, I wrote her a congratulatory email upon her successful completion of the 2018 Boston Marathon, competing in some difficult weather of cold and rain.

If you go online you will discover a great deal about Candace's accomplishments in her recovery from a traumatic brain injury, but there is more to the story than what she achieved by making her own way back to being an elite athlete once again.

I am afraid that too many of us would be stopped after such a horrific experience at the question of "Why me?" I know Candace well and have never heard that question raised to me or to others. She has chosen to raise another question, "Why not me?", and to live to help others. Candace became a leader of the Altar Guild in the Class of 1944 Chapel so I saw her on a daily basis. The Altar Guild takes care of all arrangements, floral and otherwise, involved to make the chapel a special place. The members of the Altar Guild work tirelessly at their tasks.

Candace is a leader who is soft spoken but you can trust that she will take your ideas to a place where they will be valued and acted on. She is much more than the poster child for recovery from brain injuries. She is the model for how we should lead our lives and treat one another. She is a spiritual person who is family centered and is always willing to help others. You don't get medals for those attributes, but you do get a reminder of what it means to be a good person and how your life can be a legacy for those around you.

Candace took this horrible accident and turned it into an important piece of wisdom for our students in a chapel address.

"Looking Back To Go Forward"

Good morning.

I'd like to speak to you this morning about experiences that tend to mold people's lives, and sometimes provide profound wisdom.

On a bright Wednesday morning in July 2005 I was cycling with my triathlon training partner on Goshen Road in Chester County... not too far at all from the location of our new campus.

It was one week after my birthday and two weeks after completing a pretty grueling half ironman competition in Lake Placid, New York.

Evidently I was hit by a truck that morning while the driver was passing me while going over a hill. I suffered a number of injuries including a traumatic brain injury.

I say evidently because I have no idea what happened for the next three weeks or so other than what people have told me transpired.

Looking back, I know I experienced a number of blessings on that day and during my recovery and I'd like to share my story.

During the accident my momentum from my own bike speed and that of the truck bounced me off Goshen Road and into a nearby telephone pole at about 20 miles per hour.

I suffered a broken clavicle (collar bone), several broken facial bones, and a severe concussion.

Evidently my training partner was just a little behind me and arrived in time to see me conscious but squirming around and trying to rip off my helmet.

Blessing number one...I was wearing a helmet and I can _assure_ you that without it I would not be here today. She called 911.

The Willistown police arrived very quickly as did emergency medical staff who immediately characterized my flailing behavior and speech as that of someone with a possible severe concussion.

They immediately decided (and here's blessing # two) to get me to a trauma center capable of handling these potential life threatening injuries, not to send me to a more local hospital for stabilization. They immediately called to have me medivacked to The University of Pennsylvania for care.

In the meantime, the medics gave me injections to paralyze me so that I would stop flailing around and so that they could insert a breathing tube down my throat to assist in my breathing.

The helicopter arrived in short order but unfortunately for me as they were inserting a required needle into one of my veins in my chest, they inadvertently pierced my lung on my left side and thereby collapsed my lung and it started to fill with blood.

I arrived at Penn and immediately was moved to the emergency room where I was stabilized and sedated. Apparently that's standard procedure for this sort of thing.

My husband had been called out of a meeting at work and joined me at Penn where he was introduced to two neurosurgeons who to this day he claims looked like they were no more than twenty years old...the surgeons advised that a cannula or straw be put into my head to measure the intracranial pressure to make sure my brain was not swelling from the concussion.

My husband (before giving permission to drill a hole in my head and insert a straw) insisted on seeing the "senior neurosurgeon" on duty.

The two surgeons relented after a short debate and finally brought back what my husband describes as "an adult".

(Blessing three) As it turns out the man they brought back to see my husband was Dr. Sean Grady the Chief of Neurosurgery at HUP who had finished with his surgery of the day and was on the verge of going home…and who by the way has a particular interest in traumatic brain injury.

My husband tells me it didn't sink in with him about what he was being asked to consent to until the surgeon had to get two surgeons on the line to hear my husband's confirmation.

The surgery was otherwise uneventful and I was rolled back to my room in the emergency trauma ward about 11 p.m. that evening still with an ICP "bolt", as they call it, in my head.

My husband tells me he and all the visitors watched that ICP reading for two days as a barometer of my recovery.

In the ensuing weeks while I remained in a drug induced coma a tube was inserted into my collapsed lung to drain the blood, a tracheotomy was performed to insert a breathing tube directly into my trachea to reduce the potential for pneumonia, and innumerable MRI and CAT scans were performed.

While life was OK for me… what did I know? I was in a coma?… life was very stressful for my family and friends.

During this period there was absolutely no way to tell what the outcome or prognosis would be for me.

At one point in the second week at Penn one of the neurosurgeons told my husband that through my injuries I had suffered serious damage to the temporal lobe of my brain and that I would likely not be able to understand what people say to me and that I would not likely be able to speak again.

My husband tells me that was his lowest moment.

Throughout it all, I had my family and closest friends around me with much love and support including Reverend Squire and the whole EA community who stayed close to my husband providing much needed prayer and support.

My friends tell me I was prayed for in prayer groups all over the country.

Eventually the prayers were answered. As the doctors weaned me off the drugs that were sedating me I showed subtle signs of recovery. First some voluntary body movements demonstrating I could move my own muscles to my own commands and then some response to light and verbal requests that I started to show.

The physicians told my husband that if I said anything it may be profanities at first as I came out of the coma or if I was to gather my senses I may be completely without any sense of vanity... fortunately neither happened although I'm sure most of you know that hospitals are no place for anyone with a sense of vanity...

Eventually I was moved to another part of Penn where I didn't need the care of the trauma surgery staff and eventually moved to Bryn Mawr Rehab Center to regain my motor skills, memory, and speech skills.

My neurosurgeon tells me that I was as close to death as one can be and not die...

I know that many of you haven't had the opportunity to be close with God...and really haven't had to lean on Him for help…but I can tell you all that one day you will need to…and He will be there for you…

It may not be in the way you want or the way you expect but He will be there for you…

So I would like to leave you with a verse that was conveyed to my husband and meant a great deal to him during my recovery and on many instances ever sense…

And it comes from Jeremiah 33:3…Call unto me and I will show you great and mighty things thou knowest not…

Thank you

## The Snyders, Bioethics, And Richardson Merriman

Greg Snyder, '05 and I communicated after he graduated from our school while he was a student at Princeton. We had many discussions centering on bioethics as he was a student leader in that area at Princeton. Greg knew I had a great interest in that field and had been involved in bioethics programs at our school for the better part of a decade.

The bioethics initiative was just one of the programs I was able to develop at EA because of a very generous gift from Richardson Merriman, an EA parent. Rich's gift supported other programs as well including the National Conference On Understanding Islam.

After my retirement Rich and I were able to meet, usually after reading a particular theology or science book, to discuss theological questions that others seem to avoid, topics ranging from issues of diversity to an understanding of how God operates in our daily life. Rich is a lay theologian who sees the world through the lens of faith. He is also Founder and Chairman of the Pennsylvania Trust, a financial services group.

The bioethics initiative was a high powered program in our school run by student leaders in Ethics and AP Biology. My partner in the initiative was Crawford Hill, '70 teacher of AP Biology and Chair of Science. So that the program would be across all departments, we took twenty four faculty members to the Penn Center for Bioethics for two weeks during a summer to be trained in bioethical issues and decision making. Later Cheryl Mitchell, teacher in AP Biology, took over for Crawford after his retirement from the school. Presenters to our group at Penn included Art Caplan, now head of Bioethics at NYU, Paul Wolpe, bioethicist for NASA and now Head of Bioethics at Emory University, and scientists who discovered stem cells. Topics that represented the most difficult medical decisions that were occurring in society were discussed in detail and shared with the entire Upper School.

## A Moment Can Change Your Life

Greg Snyder is smart and committed to all that is good in the world. After he graduated from Princeton, he took some time to do some important work in Guatemala before he entered medical school at Thomas Jefferson University to fulfill his dream to become a doctor. In Guatemala he was a Princeton Public Health Fellow and also taught English and Biology in a small Catholic school. He is always driven to make a difference for the better in the lives of other people.

Upon completing his junior year at Jefferson, during the month of June, Greg set out to do some bouldering with his dog. Bouldering involves low level climbing on some difficult rock formations.

During this athletic endeavor Greg fell 30 feet as he was completing his last climb. He suffered a devastating injury that severed his spine. He became a paraplegic and was treated by his teachers and peers at Jefferson. One of his peers was his fiancée, Christina. They had been at Princeton together, but did not happen to meet each other there even though their eating clubs were located next to each other.

Once Greg had dealt with all of the immediate medical issues that encompassed him, he moved on to a rehab facility. I visited him as often as I could. I knew him as an athlete so it was painful for me to watch what he was going through. After many months of grueling physical therapy he was able to go home. It was fortuitous that his mother is a physical therapist.

With sheer guts and grit, Greg returned to medical school in a wheelchair to complete his senior year. He only missed one year.

After his recovery and return to medical school, I asked Greg and Christina to speak at our bioethics symposium. They chose to speak about access or absence thereof in the drug industry to clinical trials for spinal injuries. They were in search of a clinical trial to help with nerve regeneration. Christina is a poised woman who stood next to Greg in his wheelchair as they shared the stage. They were terrific, demonstrating great courage, as they communicated this very personal issue to the gathered community.

Once this amazing couple had chosen their wedding date, Greg asked me to bless their marriage in the Princeton Chapel in the coming fall.

When we were closer to the event itself, Greg told me that he was going to recite his vows to Christina by looking her directly in her eyes. Until the day of the service I had no idea how this could be done.

All of us were in for a surprise. He arrived in a special wheelchair, strapped in tightly. The wheelchair could be raised so that he could assume a standing position. It was motorized so he could also move it forward and backward.

Following is the homily I delivered at their wedding service in an effort to capture the essence of two physicians being united in marriage. There is great similarity in the characteristics that are needed to be a caring physician and a supportive spouse.

> Christina and Greg, I am going to focus on two words that will enrich your married and your professional lives as physicians and as husband and wife. These words will also connect you to the religious life when they become habits of the heart.
>
> The words are practice and presence. You have already made friends with these two words but let's underscore them as you build your professional lives and your married life and look at how one life can inform the other.

Both of you have been athletes. You, Cos, were a Division One soccer player at Princeton and you, Greg, have been an accomplished ice hockey and soccer player so you know that hard practice creates winning moves that become second nature.

Philadelphia sports fans are among the most, shall I say, expressive in all the land. Anything can set them off. Allen Iverson, talented basketball player for the 76ers, found that out the hard way. In an interview after he missed a practice, a reporter asked him how he could justify that level of irresponsibility.

Regarding the missed commitment, he replied, "We are talking practice not a game. We are not talking about a game where it really matters. How can I make my teammates better by practicing." After that comment it was all down hill for him in the eyes of the fans.

Clearly Iverson did not understand practice as Dr. Atul Gawande does. He was a surgeon at Brigham and Women's Hospital where you, Greg, are doing your residency. Dr. Gawande is also a prolific writer who wrote describing how he was able to successfully insert a central line while others failed that procedure. He reflected, "I still have no idea what I did differently that day. But from then on, my lines went in. Practice is funny that way. For days and days you make out only in the fragments of what to do. And then one day you've got the whole thing. Conscious learning becomes unconscious." (Gawande 2007)

Practice is important in your married life when you repeat behavior that reflects the highest religious values such as compassion and concern for each other. In the Christian life in the Book of James we hear the bold articulation "faith without works is dead." (James 2:14) Those sentiments are also expressed in the Hippocratic Oath that you both recited as you entered and completed medical school.

Your vows and the questions raised and answered in today's marriage ceremony reflect the habits of the heart, the things that you need to work at day in and day out as husband and wife. You will need to practice them, if you will, so that they become second nature for your hearts. It is interesting how your vocation is referred to. You are entering the "practice" of medicine.

Practice takes on a whole new meaning in your professional life and practicing the habits of the heart will take on a whole new meaning in your married life. One will inform the other.

Presence…being fully present for one another and for your patients, living as much as you can in the holy now is important for us all. Do you remember when I asked you both to do a bioethics seminar for me at the Episcopal Academy on stem cells and access to clinical trials? When I asked you for a couple of dates Greg said that there was only one week when you would be together in February, and you could schedule the presentation one day that week. The life of a resident is a busy one. That means that you have to savor the moments when you are together.

After you gave a marvelous symposium where you were present for one another in your professional life, the three of us went back to my office. I forget what it was, but it was something that you needed Cos to do, Greg. You looked at one another, kissed, and kept your gaze fixed on the other. Time stopped and your love for one another was seen in the snapshot of that moment. It was natural. It was just you two. I was not even noticed. With the busy professional lives that you will have, carve out as many moments like these as possible. Don't let those moments go by unnoticed. You both are compassionate and engaging people so I know that your complete presence with your patients will be important to them as well.

Finally, I spent a day every other week for two years meeting with Dr. Ernest Rosato, a legendary surgeon at Penn and one of our past parents. Those meetings began after he was diagnosed with pancreatic cancer. Ernie was one of the premier surgeons in the nation and taught many surgeons in the Philadelphia area and beyond. He was also a great friend. We talked about life and death. After he died, we had the service for him at the Class of 1944 Chapel at EA. The week after the service, Dr. John Morris, Chief of Surgery at Penn, sent me a photograph of himself on the left and Ernie on the right with a resident in between. The inscription below the photograph reads, "Ernie's last surgery October 3, 2011." The photograph catches them being fully present to the patient, and I can hear Ernie saying his most famous line to a resident who failed to follow acceptable practice, "Now why did you do it that way?"

He was all about practicing the procedure that was proven best for the patient.

The photograph hangs in my office in such a way that I can view it frequently during the day. I will now think as well of you two in the middle of the experts, learning from and practicing surgery and internal medicine. I trust that you will do that with the habits of the heart, with love and compassion, as you are present for one another as man and wife and present as physicians for your patients.

God bless you both!

Christina and Greg looked each other in the eyes for the whole service. Vows were exchanged. When the final blessing was given, they kissed and Greg motored down the aisle upright with his new wife, Christina, at his side. I don't think there was a dry eye in the house, myself included.

The Snyders are now residents at hospitals in Boston. Greg earned an MBA from Harvard and continues as a resident at Brigham and Williams Hospital. Christina is a resident at Massachusetts General Hospital. They would agree that the most important moments of their married life so far were the births of Adaline Marie, who is now two, and Caden, Adaline's new baby brother.

I don't know how they are managing their busy lives in Boston. Their professional obligations are challenging enough, then add a new child. I was in a wheelchair before one of my spine surgeries, and I thought of Greg. That thought inspired me. Everyone should move through a day in a wheelchair and confront the challenges that go with that.

## The Importance Of A Second Chance

One of our students who tested the boundaries of school life was expelled from our school for several major infractions. I knew this student very well. We talked frequently. Because of the nature of his infractions only one independent school would consider his application for admission

The student called me, and promised he would get help to turn his life around. He asked if I would recommend him to the one school that was open to admitting him. We had an in depth discussion. At the end of the conversation, I was convinced that he had learned many lessons and that the ongoing help he promised to seek would be key to his moving forward in life in a positive fashion. I recommended him to the one school.

During the summer months before the student was to enroll in his new school, Vicki and I visited friends whose home was on the border of Bowdoin College in Maine. Our host, Henry, was a publisher and a real character and his wife Jody was just as engaging.

The phone rang and Henry answered it. I could catch bits and pieces of the conversation. He was telling the person on the other end of the line that I deserved a vacation and to contact me at another time. Finally I realized that Henry was speaking to the head of the school that I had petitioned on behalf of the expelled student. I raced across the room, took the phone from Henry, and quickly apologized to the caller.

The Head of School indicated to me that he would accept the boy if I was still good with my recommendation for him. I told him that I was. He then stated that if the boy becomes a trouble maker, he will come right back to me and let everyone know that I made the recommendation. After that threat, he again asked if I still wanted to stand by the recommendation. I affirmed that I did. All the while my internal voice was saying, "I got a lot riding on you, kid. Don't let me or yourself down."

The student made it through high school, went on to college and I didn't hear much from him during those years. About six years later I had a phone call from him during our Christmas break. He asked to meet with me. In our time together I learned that he had become successful in the world of finance in New York, but he was more interested in showing me pictures of his wife and children. He felt his family was the greatest blessing in his life. At one point in our meeting there was silence. He finally said, "Thank you," and he couldn't get anything else out as he became overwhelmed with emotion. We embraced. He left with a smile on his face.

## *David Cornell: Ethics In Practice*

I received a call from David Cornell, '82 the week before alumni weekend in May of 2012. David had taken an Ethics course with me. He was a center on our '82 football team that was undefeated, the first time this had occurred in 53 years. David's jersey number was 53, assigned to him at the beginning of the fall season. What a coincidence. In a recent phone call, I pointed out to him that the center touches the ball on every play but doesn't receive the fame that is garnered on other team members. We should change that.

David came to alumni weekend and provided my students with a class they will never forget. It was the last period on a sunny Friday afternoon. The students were thinking, I am sure, about the weekend as they entered the classroom. David arrived and sat down in our semi circle. The Ethics classes are usually large. I introduced him. At one point during the class I called on a student who was seated off center and I asked him a question. The student responded by saying, "Rev, you put me on the spot."

The next thing I knew my guest was almost out of his chair responding in an intense fashion with, "You want to achieve success in life. You're going to spend your life being put on the spot. Get used to it!" That was just the beginning. David went on to talk about practicing ethical behavior in the real world. The students were completely engaged and entered into active conversation with him.

One of the beautiful things about teaching is that it is an art form full of surprises. I was proud of my students because they did not back down from this important exchange. They were practicing civil discourse. When I said goodbye to David, he thanked me for permitting him to come to class. I want anyone who is as moral and engaging as David to have the opportunity to address the student body in chapel so I requested that he do so. Below are experts from his address delivered on October 26, 2012.

> A 58 year old man sits alone at a desk in a one bedroom apartment. His childhood kitchen table serves as his desk. To his name he has a closet full of suits, white shirts & ties, and scant else in the way of amenities. He is armed with a phone, an idea, and an unstinting core ethical belief that integrity (defined as doing the right thing regardless of the cost) is more important than success at any cost. He dials the phone trying to line up his fledgling company's first deal. The man had left two "C" level executive positions when asked to do things that went against his code of ethics.

Forty years earlier he left home with nothing but one pair of blue jeans and five white shirts. He rose through the ranks of corporate power. He knows he can do it again. Eight years later his company is listed on the NYSE, and his one bedroom apartment has been traded for a 22 acre estate in Aspen. Even though the road may be bumpy and indirect at times, the good guys do win.

That man was my father and namesake, David M. Cornell. He had the foresight to send me to Episcopal Academy in 1978. I am forever grateful to him for the environment he placed me in and the lessons I learned here and at home. What has been most interesting to me, however, is that the single most influential class I took here was taught by a young teacher who, you all know now, as I did then, as Reverend Squire. The course was Ethics. If you have the opportunity to take the course, PAY ATTENTION, the lessons taught in it will come up again, and again, and again.

I distinctly remember walking down the lane of the old Merion campus as a graduating senior and musing that at that point in time I knew more about Biology, Physics, Chemistry, Calculus, English Literature, and Art than most of the inhabitants of the world then and certainly more than any prior generation. Attending an elite educational institution such as Episcopal arms you with all of the answers to all of the questions presented to you.

The larger un-insulated world outside of Episcopal Academy's hallowed halls and your parent's seemingly restrictive oversight, however, presents you with very complex questions that don't follow simple formulas. Ethical quandaries actually creep up on you. If you place a frog into boiling water it will immediately jump out, if you raise the temperature slowly in an incremental fashion, you can boil it alive. "Don't get boiled alive" could be the title of my talk today.

I never in my wildest dreams would have thought I would have a front row seat to some of the greatest and most sensational ethical lapses in America over the past decade or so. Once great proud companies and institutions violated ethical codes and are no longer in existence. Their leaders went from the "smartest guys in the room" to "just another couple of guys in a cell". There is NOTHING wrong with being smart and highly educated, there is plenty wrong with being unethical.

Let's take a look at a few examples of some of the companies I have worked for directly as a consultant or as a service provider before they disintegrated years later under a cloud of disgrace.

(David went on to describe the ethical failings of Enron, Lay, Fastow, Bernie Madoff, and John B. Goodman.)

My father died of cancer on November 29, 2008. He was buried the following week in Aspen.

In attendance at his funeral were his friends of some 15 years from the community. Only a week after dad's service the Bernie Madoff's $64.8 billion Ponzi Scheme finally came crashing down with his arrest on Dec. 11, 2008. He pleaded guilty three months later and was sentenced to 150 years in prison. Many of the people in attendance at Dad's funeral had their personal fortunes wiped out by a man more focused on "appearing" than "being".

There is nothing more important that you can take from Episcopal than understanding the essence of its motto. **Esse Quam Videri: To be rather than to seem to be.**

If you live your life with integrity and are genuine in your presentation of your skills, you will do well. That is not to say that you might get away with something sinister for a loooooooong long time, but you will ultimately have to pay the piper.

Don't get too caught up in other people's success or appearance thereof. I once looked at the top of a hill and admired a house sitting on top of it. A girl I was dating at the time said, "that house is a sad house." I said, "how can that be, it's gorgeous." She then laid out the backstory. The father was a highly successful Hollywood producer. He had great financial riches. The costs for those riches, however, were the lives of his children. In their early twenties, one had committed suicide, one had overdosed, and one was in rehab. Gorgeous home, but unattractive lives once the façade of houses, cars, and clothes were pulled back.

My mom has always struggled to understand what her entrepreneurial son does for a living. When I left the Academy and completed all my pre-med courses and took the MCAT she knew I was going to be a doctor and save lives. At a minimum, I would heal people and make them feel better. Instead of becoming a doctor, I followed my father's footsteps into business. My decision to not go to medical school can be summed up with: I don't like to be around sick people. I had to be honest with myself, I do not possess the healing gift that in my mind a doctor should have. So I chose a different path. Much to my mother's chagrin at the time I might add.

At EPM Associates, my new consulting company, simply put, we save lives. We help companies prosper by implementing better processes and controls. In the exciting world of accounting and operations management there are two guiding principles we adhere to:

1. It is not **would** someone commit theft or fraud, but **could** someone commit it.
2. It is not impropriety, but the mere appearance of impropriety that undermines confidence.

If all those involved in the financial scandals of the past had gone to Reverend Squire's Ethics class, and PAID ATTENTION, their lives, those of their families, and tens of thousands of lives of employees, investors, and charities might have been saved from ruin and despair. These men deviated from the path of truth and righteousness. They were caught and punished, but they destroyed the peace and happiness of so many. That said, had proper controls been in place, their frauds would likely not have occurred in the first place.

When my dad was dying we had multiple conversations on God, death, and what lies beyond. He asked did I believe in God. I said yes, but I also recognized that my understanding was limited by my and humanity's current capacity to understand. I told him to take solace in the fact that no matter what either of us or any human being alive today thought, we were most likely wrong.

Our collective comprehension of God on our insignificant planet – the 3$^{rd}$ rock from the sun called Earth (ironically for a planet actually 2/3 covered in water) is limited by our experiences and perspective. Seeing as we have such a small glimpse into the actual universe, how can any perspective be definitively "correct"? Certainly people shouldn't be killing each other over their disparate views as they have for thousands of years.

With our cosmically short scientific track record, do you honestly think we've got God "figured out"? I do not. That said, I believe in God. I was raised a Catholic, went to an Episcopal high school and currently attend a Methodist Church.

I don't have "the answer", but neither does anyone else. What I have is knowing that our current representations and explanations are the best we can do with the evidence we have and they provide a solid framework for peaceful living and coexistence as long as we take a contextual and not literal approach to the ancient teachings.

The gift of attending Episcopal Academy is that it teaches you to think and not merely recite. Free thought though comes with responsibility. Once you graduate and start to enter the world, rely on the foundations of faith and knowledge you gained here. Know that you are not alone. You have hundreds of years of tradition to reflect upon. Episcopal may not live forever, and your teachers certainly won't be around to give you demerits for misbehaving (assuming they even still do that) but God will always be watching, so behave. I say behave because 10, 20, 30 years on you want to proudly be able to come back and say to your colleagues, the world is a better place because I am in it. Not that you made the most money, but you have enriched the lives of others, raised good kids, and helped those in need.

On my wall in my office I have the 5 quotes that form a simple ethic to follow in life and business.

1. **"Esse Quam Videri"** - To Be Rather Than to Seem to Be
   a.  So simple – never forget it. Live your life proudly and with integrity in whatever endeavor you choose. Be real, have substance, don't sell others a bill of goods

2. **"Fix, Close, Sell"** – Jack Welch
   a.     Simple enough to say, tougher to implement. Don't have a Messiah complex. You can't fix everything or everyone. You have to know when to move on.
3. **"No battle plan survives first contact with the memory"** – Helmut von Molkte the Elder
   a.     Understand this axiom. It doesn't mean that you shouldn't "plan", it means that whatever you plan is likely going to need to change when implemented.
4. **"Never be afraid to reinvent yourself"** – George Foreman
   a.     See quote three. People of my generation per the Bureau of Labor Statistics will have on average 11.3 jobs. Each job is an opportunity to reinvent yourself. My former administrative assistant is now a Vice President at a large energy company. A former busboy I know now runs one of the largest restaurant operations in the USA.
5. **"Wishing is not a corporate strategy"** – David M. Cornell
   a.     My dad had this quote posted around his office as a reminder to himself and his employees that wishing alone won't get you anything in life.

Remember, life is not about CAN you do something, but SHOULD you do something. Can you steal? Yes. Should you steal? No. Can you drive while texting? Yes. Should you drive while texting? No.

I had the privilege of attending a speech by Dan Ariely an Israeli American professor of psychology and behavioral economics. He teaches at Duke University and is the founder of The Center for Advanced Hindsight. Dr. Ariely studied and observed:

"While ethics lectures and training seem to have little to no effect on people, reminders of morality — **right at the point where people are making a decision**—appear to have an outsize effect on behavior."

According to Ariely's experiments, his observations arise from hard data that supports a contention that having regular, recurring reminders of what "to do" are far more effective than being told what NOT to do.

In closing, I am not going to tell you what to do or not to do. I simply recommend that you find your own quotes and sayings and put them on your wall to remind you daily of the right course. After you leave Episcopal, you will no longer see outsized *Esse Quam Videri* appropriately etched into the wall of the Chapel. But, never forget the words or their meaning or the lessons learned in Chapel. Take Episcopal's spirit with you wherever you go. Lastly, if you get a chance, take Reverend Squire's Ethics class – it will serve you well. Thanks for your time.

David continues his business consulting work of assisting organizations to implement accounting systems and process controls to better manage day to day operations and protect against fraud. A current program management client of his is a federally charted credit union that refreshingly provides comprehensive training in the Hall-Tonna values framework for all of its employees in order to help them implement the organizational mission of assisting people of modest means achieve and maintain financial slack (e.g. savings relative to debt and income relative to spending). This organization is also taking a leading position relative to environmental sustainability in the building of their new corporate headquarters as part of its desire to be a community and global leader in ethical business operations. David feels blessed to be able to work with companies that are putting the systems and processes in place to ensure their employees are fully supported in doing the right things every day.

It is possible to do good and do well at the same time!

## Bernadette Tankle: EA Grit

I recently had a conversation with Bernadette Tankle,'14. Bernadette was an elite swimmer both at EA and at Colgate University. She was on track to try out for the US Olympic Team. A conversation with Bernadette can lift anyone's spirit. Her strength of character is present in everything she does. She was in Florida during the winter hiatus from Colgate practicing with her swim team when she began to experience changes in her body that frightened her, numbness was taking over. She spoke to her coaches and then gave her parents, Joe and Karen, a call to let them know what was happening.

They brought her home immediately. As she was getting off the plane, she fell due to the weakness in her legs. The diagnosis was Guillain-Barre Syndrome that left her paralyzed from the neck down. She went from being an elite Division One athlete to being unable to move or feel her body from the neck down almost overnight.

A statement that is challenging for anyone to hear, "We don't know how much of your previous health and strength you will be able to recover," was what Bernadette lived with throughout her recovery.

When I entered her room at the Bryn Mawr Rehab Center, I was greeted by her million dollar smile, a hello, and a request, "I want to speak in chapel about this experience." I responded, "You got it!"

I exchanged texts with her and later learned that she was hitting the keys with her nose to compose those texts. She worked hard in rehab and was able to return to Colgate in a wheelchair several months later. The school was amazing in their support of her. She didn't miss a beat. She became familiar with and conquered all the challenges of living life as a paraplegic. Her family and friends were reluctant to have her leave the safety of home for college, but Bernadette found that being with her friends and her swim team members was what she needed. When she was finally able to return to her swim team, she had to confront another hurdle. She had to accept that she had gone from being an elite swimmer who finished first in most races to a swimmer who then finished last.

She is now taking her experience not to the Olympics but to law school where she would like to be an advocate for those who live with disabilities. She is passionate about that goal. Being an advocate for others now runs through her veins.

When I asked if she was 100% back, there was a pause as Bernadette considered the question. She knows that she has come a long way, but she also knows that she is not the same person she was before her illness. As far as she is concerned she is back 100% since she is still giving her all to everything she does with what she has left, and she has a lot left.

I went on to ask the question that was the elephant in the room. "How did you do what you did, coming back in record fashion?" She shared with me that there were low periods, and when she was experiencing them she simply said to herself, "Don't focus on what you can't do. Focus on how far you have come. Don't quit." As a result of everything she has been through, she saw an upside to the experience. "I feel that I can do anything now!" What powerful words resulting from one of life's greatest challenges.

What follows is her chapel address.

Thank you Coach Kline for your warm introduction. Thank you Reverend Squire and the vestry for allowing me to speak today. Thank you to all the students who have welcomed me back to my alma mater today. It is truly an honor to have the opportunity to address the student body. Before I begin I would like to take a moment and dedicate this speech to my mom, who has been my fearless guide throughout this unexpected journey.

Like you, for four years, I sat in chapel and listened to many inspirational and informational chapel speeches. And for four years, I hoped that before I graduated, I would deliver a chapel speech. However, my hopes were barred by my own inhibitions- believing that I had nothing either inspirational or informational to say. Little did I know that my life's journey, shortly after leaving Episcopal, would bring me to this moment to deliver the message that, I believe, God intended me to give.

Graduating from Episcopal - as you all know, is a significant accomplishment- And I can tell you that when you leave EA and move onto college- you are better for having been here. You have this "edge". It is not palpable. You can't touch it or see it and you may not even realize you have it, but it is there. You've all heard of the people who find themselves faced with a physical challenge - like the person whose loved one is trapped under a car and with Herculean strength, they lift the car never thinking about whether they had the strength or not to do so. The EA "edge" is like that, only it's mental, emotional and it's the essence of our stripes- courage, gratitude, faith. It is what I have come to learn is known as EA grit.

In November of my senior year, I was fortunate enough to sign with Colgate University to be a member of their division one swim team. Colgate was a perfect fit for me and I quickly set about defining both my academic and athletic goals. Following in true EA fashion, I enrolled in a heavy academic load first semester and embraced a very challenging athletic season. By the time December had rolled around I had a very particular goal set in my mind. I wanted to set the freshmen 200 butterfly record, and I was going to do it. Everyday I ate, trained, and slept with this goal in my mind. During sets I would go to the side of the pool where the record board was located and would focus my gaze onto those numbers that read 2:02.36. I could picture my name up there ….My goals were set and my mind was clear and I was ready to take on anything.

So what brought me here today? Well, I'm going to tell you that I never reached those goals that I set last December. Instead I had circumstances forced upon me that have changed my life forever.

After struggling with numbness in my legs and body fatigue for a few days on our winter training trip in Florida, I made the decision to fly home and see a doctor. Within hours they had diagnosed me with Guillain-Barre Syndrome, or GBS, a post viral infection that ferociously attacks the body and leaves the patient paralyzed. The doctors were very swift with their actions and guidance. "Your paralysis will get worse before it is better; your internal organs will struggle. You may need a tracheostomy and breathing tube and a feeding tube. You will be in the hospital for at least 2 weeks and rehabilitation for at least 3 months. You will need to relearn how to walk, talk, eat, drink, everything." There it was….All before me. No time to think, prepare, or decide if I had the strength...I had to lift the car...Within minutes my goals had drastically shifted from breaking a school record, to just keep breathing. In my swimming career I've always strived to take faster, more efficient breaths, now I just hoped I would be able to breathe.

### First goal - I will not get a tracheostomy.

I asked the respiratory team – what I had to do to NOT get one. The answer- breathe- strong.

Got it- swimming has given me lungs of steel. The respiratory team checked my deep breathing every 2-4 hours. It was hard, but I managed to keep my lungs working strong. Goal one- check!

**Next:**

Tolerate and respond to treatment. There are only 3 known treatments for GBS. My treatment involved five hours of lying still while being infused with medicine that felt like fire pumping through my veins at a painfully slow rate. After five days of this schedule and much to the doctor's surprise -I responded so well to the treatment, that I was released to the nearby rehabilitation hospital a week sooner than anyone anticipated.

When I arrived at the rehab, the treatment team of 10 clinicians gave me a grim glimpse of the journey ahead—it was the standard prognosis and plan for a GBS patient- three-four months of intense physical therapy, speech therapy, AND a recommended medical leave from Colgate.

In my room at Bryn Mawr Rehab they had a whiteboard on my wall and on the first day they ask you, "what is the end goal you wish to achieve upon leaving here?" There was that word again: "goal". It seemed to be following me around more and more. Now looking back I realize that most people in my situation probably would have said something along the lines of " walking or talking" but me.... No.... I said with mumbled words and struggled breath ... I need to be able to stand well enough to cheer my team on at their championship meet. My comment was followed by an eerie silence and the next thing I knew, I looked at my physical therapist and she's crying. "Never have I seen anyone think of others while in such a terrible situation as yours," she said. That's when I realized I was fighting for a bigger goal. My team was my goal. The team was my motivation.

They were the reasons I got out of that hospital bed every single day. It was then that I understood the importance of setting goals in your life. Whether they are motivated by self or by others, they have the power to change everything.

So that was the turning point for me. I wasn't going to feel sorry for myself. I wasn't going to take the easy road. And I wasn't going to let my illness win.

I woke up everyday with a "can do and will do" attitude. I enrolled in a full course schedule at Colgate and did my work in between physical and occupational therapy sessions. At night I did reading assignments and dictated my papers onto my computer through a voice app, or with the help from my mom. I listened to podcasts, read lecture notes, and stayed in constant email or phone contact with my professors. They were on board and wanted to help me to achieve my goals. That's another thing that I learned throughout this process. It's okay to ask for help in route to reaching a goal and it's rarely done as a solo act.

So now that I had my life in rehab pretty much down to a science, the next goal was to get out of rehab and back to my life. I needed to relearn how to walk, how to talk, and how to use my hands. Given my age and physical strength, I asked if we could progress more quickly through the rehab and, while they were hesitant, they ultimately honored my request. Most importantly, I found a physical therapist who was willing to challenge the status quo and allowed me to get in the pool. It's as if the pool had healing properties because once I got in the water, I recognized that by questioning the standard plan, you can achieve a superior, unexpected, and even unimaginable outcome. With that in mind, I had to persuade the treatment team that I could return to school in half the amount of time required for a typical GBS patient.

On February 19th my mom drove me to Bucknell University where I slowly inched my way onto the pool deck with my walker as my guide. And for the first time in three months I was able to STAND with my teammates once again. I watched each one of their races and cheered them on so loudly that sometimes I would throw off my center of gravity and have to grab my walker for support. Then came the 200 butterfly. I had to sit idly by as I watched the women move effortlessly across the water, I heard the announcer say my name, and I watched as my heat went off and my lane remained empty. When the girls finished, all I could do was smile and think ...new goal... beat them next year. On February 21st I returned to a very snowy Colgate with the support of my wheelchair and walker. Over the next few months I focused on learning to walk and completing my coursework.

When I arrived home to West Chester for Easter break, it was my EA grit that carried me across the threshold of our front door with my leg braces in tow and my walker and wheelchair folded up tightly.

**So here I am today -- Achieving one goal in place of another:**

It doesn't matter that it didn't happen according to the standard plan. It matters only that I am able to stand here today to share how my EA experience made the difference.

Through it all the EA grit was there in full force.... The faculty who sat by my side and offered strong words of encouragement; the EA athletic teams who came in numbers and in force with the strong "fight" message; Reverend Squire, who remained in constant contact with my parents and myself and Coach Kline who drew on the strength of his own difficult journey and delivered it to me with EA strength. It is those moments in life, when you are faced with adversity, that make you grateful for what you have been given: Every family member, every friend, every teacher, every step, every breath.

Sometimes experiences like mine suggest that people slow it down a bit, smell the roses.... My experience set me on a different course....a positive, forward moving and intense course that is driven by steel determination and laser focus. To tackle my goals, adjust when needed. To portray grit, not fall prey to my circumstance and to take charge whenever and wherever possible. It's all the grit that makes up "me". It's God given grit and family driven grit and... and forever and always... EA grit. You have it. It's all around you. Recognize it, appreciate it, embrace it ... and never let it go.

### Christy DiSilvestro Rivard: Grit, A Spiritual Leader, And Spiritual Growth

Christy Rivard,'10 is an outstanding EA graduate. She served on the Student Vestry as Senior Warden, the chief student spiritual leader of our school, and was well connected with her peers and faculty. She was a key member of our water polo team. Harvard was thrilled to welcome her into their student body.

What follows is Christy's final chapel address to the school community as Senior Warden. I include it because it states so well a student's journey of faith and a reflection on her years at EA.

Seven years ago, I stood at the pulpit in Christ Chapel and delivered my first speech. It is hard for me to believe that an entire seven years has passed because I vividly remember the speech. It was Thanksgiving chapel, and I spoke alongside my brother and sister. Now I stand before you, delivering my last speech and, let me tell you now, it is not going to be easy for me. I guess you could say this is my goodbye to Episcopal and represents my appreciation for everything the school has given me.

I have been in upper school for four years, surrounded by students and teachers who enlighten me every day. After all this time spent together and moments shared with one another, what will I take away with me when I leave? The most important thing I will remember about Episcopal is the love. It's not the facts, the figures, or the grades that will stay with me. It's the love that surrounds me here every day. That is the legacy that Episcopal will leave in my heart as I move on to college and further into my life.

This love is always here on the Episcopal campus. We may not realize it, but we are surrounded by love in this community because we are surrounded by people who genuinely care about us. Sometimes this love and caring is most evident when we are struggling. In every memory of a time that I have struggled at Episcopal, there have been people I have always been able to fall back on. These people are not always the same, and I have learned that sometimes the people that can help us the most are the ones we least expect. They are also there to celebrate with me and to share in my moments of joy. Episcopal has taught me to keep my eyes open for love and support everywhere I turn. I might find it in a smile, in a teacher's comment, or the advice of a friend. Episcopal has also taught me to share this love with others. The more we spread the love, the more we will receive in return.

Throughout my time at Episcopal, I have learned many important lessons that I remember and record, our teachers put together a play that incorporated everyone's stories. We practiced and performed the play as a class. This experience was very meaningful for me. We took the love and lessons that others had enjoyed and acted them out ourselves, sharing this love with those around us.

In lower school, I was taught to love without restraint or judgment. This is when my strong support at EA started to take form, and from then on I have always had the comfort of feeling a natural connection with those in my class and knowing that they will always care for me. This continued to develop as I moved through middle school, joining with the Devon campus, and building a stronger group of supporting friends. The beginning of sixth grade was frightening for all of us.

Not only would we have a completely new system of scheduling, but we would be mixed with "Devonites." The lower schoolers who attended class on the faraway Devon campus were frightening, and many times we felt that they were extremely different from those at Merion. After a short period of adjusting, however, we learned that the "Merionites" and the "Devonites" were backed with the same education and community, and could surprisingly live together in harmony. I have learned from this experience and similar experiences not to hold on to a first impression, but to be open to meeting and befriending new people.

Middle school was not only a time for making new friends. It was the first time that I was pushed to evaluate and develop my personal faith. I ran for the chapel council in sixth grade after enjoying my experiences in lower school and middle school chapel. Time spent with Reverend Zug deciding on speakers to schedule for services connected me with the chapel, the faith based center of the school.

In seventh grade, for the "Drama Meets Religion" class, groups of students wrote skits to perform in chapel that focused on the values laid down in the Bible. In eighth grade, the development of faith was more personal to each student. Anyone who was here in eighth grade knows that each eighth grader must write a paper about the fabric that composes his or her faith. This was the first time I really thought about the substance of my beliefs and how they apply to my life. I read my paper during middle school chapel in eighth grade. Since that middle school speech, my faith has been molded and strengthened, with the same core beliefs driving my thoughts and actions.

My time in upper school has only continued to teach me important lessons. Upper school is often oriented around setting goals and trying to reach them. We set goals for classes, for sports, and for colleges. There is no limit to how high we set these goals, and they are often for the distant future. With hard work and dedication, we might reach these goals we set, but we might not reach them. We often do not celebrate until we come upon this final result. We are fearful of raising our hopes up, only to bring them down. While this concern is valid, I think there are many situations when we follow this standard thought process too strictly. I believe that we should celebrate each moment instead of waiting for the final product. I have found tremendous happiness in high school by finding joy in each and every step of the way. We should celebrate each win instead of waiting to see the final season record. We should celebrate each college we are accepted to instead of waiting to hear from our first choice.

By embodying this mindset, I have maximized the joy I find in each moment of my life.

I cannot count how many things there are at Episcopal that I will miss when I am gone. There are 10 years of memories that I will carry forward with me. First, I will miss the people here. I will miss my friends, the students, and the faculty. It is said that friends come into our lives for a reason, a season, or a lifetime. Each of you is significant in shaping my character and affecting the way that I think and act. Those who come for a reason may not spend a long period of time with us, but they are extremely important. We often do not realize how valuable these people are until they are already gone. These are the ones who take hold of our lives, and they pick us up when we fall; they capture our attention and cause us to change. They force us to move on from tough situations. Those who come for a season are no less important. These are the ones who might teach us for a school year, or play on the same team as us. We work together with them and learn from them. Although they may not have such an explicit effect on us, they help us grow and develop our character. They are there for us in times of need and times of celebration, and we remember them forever as we move forward. They are the ones who help us evolve into a better person. Then there are the friends whom we keep for a lifetime. I believe that I have many of these at Episcopal, both students and teachers. They are the ones who give me love and support without fail. I care about them completely, and cannot imagine my life without them.

As I move on, I will miss the comfort of familiar faces and sites at this school. I will miss the Newtown Square campus, the big green leading up to the chapel. I will miss walking around and knowing almost everyone I see. I will miss all the teachers. While I have not had all of them in class, I have learned something from almost every teacher here. I will miss the vestry. Three lunches spent together a week have made the members of the vestry some of my closest friends.

Mostly, out of everything at Episcopal, I will miss the chapel. Out of all the places here, the chapel is where I feel the most comfortable, the most complete, and most connected with God. It is where my life is put into perspective as part of God's plan. It is where I remind myself to carry out God's will. It is where I ask forgiveness. It is where I can pray in silence, or express myself out loud. It was in the chapel that my parents decided to send me to Episcopal when they visited the school and sat in on a service many years ago. In the chapel, I take a break from the rest of my life to piece together the people and events that have affected me, further developing my faith.

My faith is constantly growing and strengthening due to the chapel, my participation on the vestry, and my reflection on my life. There are certain beliefs I hold to be true that stand at the foundation of my faith, influencing everything I do. I believe that I am always safe in the hands of God, and this gives me reassurance through any time of trouble. I believe everything happens for a reason, and that God can provide light in any time of darkness. I believe God has a plan for me. He will guide me as I move forward, looking over me every step of the way. I have looked up at the same cross for ten years, and it reminds me of these strong beliefs that build the basis of my faith. I will miss this cross, these pews, and this altar, and I will miss speaking to all of you.

I will miss Reverend Squire. While the chapel is the heart of Episcopal, Reverend Squire is the heart of the chapel. He has taught me much more than he realizes. He has taught me how to trust in God, and how to listen to God's word and apply it to my own life. He has taught me how to be a leader. He has shown me how to work together with everyone, how to listen to their perspectives and learn from their thoughts. He has taught me that there will always be people who disagree with you, and it is important as a leader to make consistent, thoughtful decisions. Most of all, the Rev has shown me how to be resilient, because he is the most resilient person I know.

The chapel is the place where one can see and feel the respect of the Episcopal community. Last fall, I organized a chapel service to commemorate those who died or lost loved ones on September 11th. To intensify the power of the service, I asked the student body to enter and exit the chapel in complete silence, something we had not done before. On the morning of the 11th, I was one of the first students to enter the chapel. I looked at the cross and goose bumps swallowed my arms as I thought about the tumultuous events that transpired eight years ago. I walked to the vestry room and rehearsed my speech, unable to see those entering the chapel. A few minutes later, I looked back into the pews in astonishment as I saw that they were almost filled with students. Every member of the Episcopal community had entered with such silence that I did not even hear them come into the chapel. My eyes welled in appreciation for the reverence our community expressed.

The chapel is a place of worship and a place of learning. I learn a new lesson every time I come to the chapel. From Reverend Zug, I learned that everyone in a community fits together like a puzzle, each piece being just as important as the next. From Gigi Constable, I learned that caring for others should have no boundaries. From Victoria Kielty, I learned that each person defines "home" independently, and it is more important to value the significance of the word and what it represents, then to only associate it with the material structure that makes up a house. From Julia Fabiani, I learned to appreciate every day I have with my family. From Randy Teti, I learned the importance of the constant comfort of the cross, which I mentioned earlier. From my brother, Kevin DiSilvestro, I learned to embrace the true meaning of the Lord's Prayer, and to forgive those who have trespassed against me. Today I am learning how hard it is to move on, even when I am excited for the future.

I am sad that this is the last time I will stand here in front of you. Each time I stand here, I am astounded at the view I see. From this pulpit, looking out at everyone in front of me, we are one body. People are distinguishable from one another, but everyone blends together as one group. Never have I seen the upper school so united as I do from the front of the chapel. I am sad that I will not be here next year, sad that I won't be able to enjoy the coming school year with the same students and teachers. After all the love that I have been given at Episcopal, how do I now pay it back? I will carry forward this feeling of love and support with me as I leave upper school. I will share it with others, so they may further share it, and the spirit of Episcopal can grow outside of the campus.

It has been a privilege to be a student here. It has been a privilege to be a member of the class of 2010. It has been a privilege to share my faith and experiences with all of you. And it has been a privilege to serve you as senior warden.

One April night when Christy was at Harvard, she went to bed feeling fine. The next morning when she awakened she couldn't walk. She had a medical condition that caused her groin muscles to become inflamed and very painful. Her condition was difficult to diagnose and it took multiple surgeries to address the issue. There were times when she would have flare ups of the inflammation to the point where she was unable to get on top of the pain. She had to take certain examinations standing up as it was too painful to be seated.

The truly remarkable issue is that Christy did not miss a beat during this painful condition and the treatment needed to relieve it. She continued her education at Harvard, addressing the academic rigors at the same time she was addressing the rigors of her medical situation. Simple acts that most would take for granted were major challenges for her. Just getting around campus was a major challenge that took much effort and planning.

We would talk by phone. She was undaunted. There was not a moment of complaint about having to endure the horrific experience. She moved forward through prayer and sheer grit, courage and perseverance.

At one point I asked Christy how she was getting around campus when classes could be far from one another and far from her residential house. She casually said that there was a particular guy who, at times, would carry her from one place to another. This guy was part of other conversations that we had.

She graduated from Harvard on time with her classmates and was chosen as the Class Day speaker at graduation, quite an honor.

About a year after her graduation, Christy called to ask me to bless her marriage. I immediately said, "Yes!" and then asked, "Who is the lucky guy?" She said that it was the guy who carried her around campus when she was unable to walk. His name is Laurent Rivard and he was one of the greatest basketball players in the history of Harvard.

The wedding was magical. Following are the words I spoke to capture the essence of their relationship. I have come to realize that addresses I give at weddings express the core elements of my faith, elements that are important to share with others. There are five file boxes of sermons in storage at my home containing sermons I have given over the past 45 years. Sharing some of these sermons seems to me to be the best way to express the essence of my Christian faith.

November 19, 2016

What do basketball, faith, school mascots, porcupines, and rings and hands have to do with what I think that you, Laurent and Christy, and all of us should strive for in our relationships and in our marriages?

Christy is an incredible person, kind, respectful, a person of faith, full of grit and determination. She is a superstar, a model of the best of humankind.

As you know she had an injury that was painful and highly problematic. She navigated her time through Harvard with a limited ability to walk to many areas of the campus.

Whenever I would talk with her by phone she was upbeat, a person of prayer, and committed to finishing her Harvard degree on time. Each time I got off the phone I reflected, "How is she doing this?"

During one phone call she shared with me that there was guy who carried her from place to place on campus. I thought, interesting!

When Christy asked me to bless her marriage, I simply asked, "Who is the lucky guy? She responded by saying, "Remember that guy I was telling you about who assisted me across campus, it is him...Laurent."

And then I met him... in premarital counseling. When I asked him if he played a sport at Harvard, he simply said that he played basketball. That was it! Christy quickly leaned forward and told me he was one of the best basketball players in all of Harvard history. This was followed by a litany of his achievements, three point scoring record, NCAA tournament appearances, and many more accolades. Laurent was humble. Christy was effusive with pride. I searched his basketball career online. His coach at Northfield Mount Hermon School wrote that he was tough and hard working. Tommy Amaker, his coach at Harvard, may have summed it up best. He said, "I am always surprised when he missed a shot."...a superstar.

Our premarital sessions together continued and I came to realize that these two superstar athletes were also superstars as human beings and shared the same personal attributes. Since you both have made significant achievement in sports, Christy in water polo, you know that even in the pool, positioning and stance are what make for greatness.

In sports we think of stance as physical posture. But when we think of Christianity, it is moral imperative and stance. We think of stance as spiritual and moral posture. A central belief in Christianity is all in the stance...Christianity has reciprocity at the heart of ethical behavior. We know it as the Golden Rule. Do unto others as you would have them do unto you.

This day with the merging of these two wonderful families, we find our common ground to be that you, Christy and Laurent, should always treat each other the way that you would want to be treated. It is the hope of all of those gathered here today that your lives would be a reflection of that truth. That is the starting stance for marriage, but there are at least two more stances for you to inculcate into your married life together to take you to a higher form of love and the first involves school mascots.

Laurent's school mascot at Northfield Mount Hermon was the hogger. Christy attended EA where the mascot is a church mouse. Now we also have a student running around dressed as Bishop White, our founder. These two school mascots remind us that choices of mascots can be interesting, like the Oregon ducks.

But if I were to select a school of marriage mascot for you it would be a porcupine. The philosopher, Schopenhauer, offered the image of the porcupine as metaphor for a successful marriage. Porcupines must huddle together to find warmth during cold days that the philosopher likened to the absolute need that we have to be with one another to gain spiritual warmth. Yet if the porcupines stay there together too long they prick one another and they must move apart, symbolic of our need to be independent of one another. The ebb and flow of this image leads to interdependence where you both have your individual gifts that are made even more complete when you provide the warmth of relationship with one another.

The final level that will lead you to oneness of Spirit in the Christian tradition is the act of considering the other more important than your own self. Harry Stack Sullivan, founder of interpersonal psychiatry, was asked the simple but profound question, "What makes someone mature?" He didn't hesitate for a millisecond when he responded by saying, "It is the ability to put another person first."

Finally, it is only the wise ones in Christendom who know about the miracle of empty hands. We do a lot with hands in this service. We hold hands. Give and take the hand of another. Put rings on fingers of hands. Extend your hands out to one another and turn them over. In just a few moments each of you will place a ring on the hand of the other. When you feel and see that ring in your married life for years to come, I want you to remember that a secret to a happy life together are these empty hands. The miracle of empty hands is that you only get to keep what you are willing to give away. St. Francis said it thus, "Lord, make us instruments of your peace. Grant that we may not so much seek to be consoled as to console; to be understood as to understand; to be loved as to love. For it is in giving that we receive."

It is the physical stance of the empty hands captured by St. Francis and the Golden rule that will empower you to live your lives together with the fullest form of spiritual love.

In basketball, water polo, and many sports, success may be in the stance of feet firmly planted or proper position achieved! But in marriage, success is in the spiritual stance of equal and shared care for one another firmly planted. That is the hope and prayer for you, Christy and Laurent, today and in your years to come. Amen

## A Pair Of Docs: Paradox

Kevin DiSilvestro, '08, Christy's brother, also served on the Student Vestry at EA. Kevin and his wife, Jessie, are both residents training at hospitals at Brown University. They were apart for all four years during medical school. That was a challenge for them since one was in Maryland and the other in New York, but they found ways to keep the fire of their love burning.

Following is the homily I gave at the wedding of Drs. Jessie and Kevin.

What do we call two doctors such as you two who will be joined as one during this Blessing of Your Marriage? We call them a pair of docs or today a word that sounds the same. You and your life as well as the lives of all gathered here today are a paradox....a contradiction of terms. Paradox is cognitive dissonance where two things seem impossible to exist together.

Paradox defines the heart of the Gospel and the heart of your life which you will be reminded of each day of your life for you will always know that you are a pair of docs... a pair of physicians. You are two who will become one! How can this be?

As doctors and husband and wife you will know that paradoxically you will only be able to keep what you are willing to give away. As you will give your hearts and souls to your patients and to each other as husband and wife, you will receive that joy that passes all understanding.

You will discover, as the Bible tells us, that the "last shall be first" for the sign of real maturity is the ability to put the other first whether it be patient or spouse. You will discover that, indeed, it is better to give than to receive for it is in giving to your patients and to each other that you will be empowered with feelings of pure joy in your married life and in your chosen profession.

Bringing joy to each other and to others is the fastest way to experience joy yourself.

You will need to get into the shoes of one another and your patients. This will require practicing empathy. I love the Dalai Lama's description of the paradox of empathy. If we see a person crushed by a rock, the goal is not to get under the rock and feel what they are feeling; it is to help to remove the rock. Empathy is not passive. It is active. It strives to make a situation better.

In your marriage and profession you will have opportunities to identify problems and come up with a solutions all at the same time.

As you studied in your physics courses (or maybe you would rather repress those memories) you looked at Planck's Constant that describes all matter as both a wave and a particle at the same time...impossible to comprehend but a fact in science...a paradox.

But let's look at the paradox that will be at the center of your life...Jesus is both human and divine at the same time.

He died but rose again. How can that be? These are facts that are at the heart of the Gospel and need to be nourished by your faith.

You both know that I like to give homework. You completed all assignments responsibly during our premarital counseling and you shared the results with one another and with me.

I have one last assignment, because I can think of no better statement about the paradoxical nature of faith, life, and work as a physician or spouse than the prayer of St. Francis. Google it, print it out, and put it in your wallet or appointment book. Read it whenever you need to be reminded of what it means to live the good life...the good moral life... as husband, wife, and physician.

Lord, make us instruments of your peace. Where there is hatred, let us sow love; where there is injury, pardon; where there is discord, union; where there is doubt, faith; where there is despair, hope; where there is darkness, light; where there is sadness, joy. Grant that we may not so much seek to be consoled as to console; to be understood as to understand; to be loved as to love. For it is in giving, that we receive; it is in pardoning that we are pardoned; and it is in dying that we are born to eternal life. Amen

Now here is the head fake...remember those head fakes from the <u>Last Lecture</u> by Randy Pausch that you viewed and discussed as part of your homework. Here is my head fake for today!

The attributes you need to be successful as husband and wife are the same attributes you need to be successful physicians. Your marriage and chosen profession will feed and strengthen each other since they require the same attributes.

You will remember to pray the prayer of St. Francis periodically (I know this) because you will always be a pair of docs.

## Ordinations At Christ Chapel On The Merion Campus

Special moments took place in the EA chapel as seminary students were ordained there. In fact my ordination occurred in the chapel on the Merion campus in 1970, eight years prior to beginning my tenure as head chaplain of the school. I was asked by one of my students if he and his sister could be ordained in our chapel to an independent Christian Church. They requested that the service begin at 6. I assumed that it would begin at 6 in the evening. Wouldn't you? When I asked for clarification, I was told that the service would begin at 6 in the morning. A band would be arriving at 4 A.M. to practice.

The service lasted over 6 hours and was an amazing experience. It was a religious event of pure joy and a thrill for me to watch and be part of as, not one but two, of my former students were ordained into an independent Christian Church. To use the students' words, "The place rocked."

## Chapel Speakers of Note

Uplifting and inspirational moments occurred in both EA chapels as we were privileged to have a long list of internationally famous people share their lives, legacies, character, and faith. The list includes college presidents, political figures such as Joe Biden and Arlen Specter, actors, the Archbishop of Canterbury and great sports figures and coaches including Jay Wright, coach of the NCAA Championship Villanova basketball team, and Jimmy Craig, goalie for the Olympic Ice Hockey Team that beat the Russians. They all had an important message to share with students and faculty centered around our chapel theme for the year. Each year our students and faculty select a theme for chapel. Then chapel addresses are focused on the exploration of the theme to make it come alive with meaning and give guidance for the lives of all.

A person who generated a great deal of conversation for unexpected reasons was Morgan Freeman. I had a connection to him through a student. He spoke from the heart about faith and social justice, focusing on racial issues in America.

The students' reaction was disappointment. When I asked why, they responded by saying, "He is just like us." We reflected that actors are reading lines written by others. Mr. Freeman was speaking directly from his heart so he connected directly with the students about issues of race and character. They wanted an actor. He gave them a human being. I am glad they got the latter. It was an important lesson learned.

During a meeting of our Student Vestry, one of the members of the group, Nicole Spagnola,'07 asked, "How would you like to have John Bogle speak in chapel?" Her family knew him well socially so Nicole could tell the students in the group a bit about him. John is the founder of the Vanguard Financial Group, one of the most successful financial groups worldwide, managing many trillions of dollars. I knew John was in demand by various groups, colleges, and universities. The Vestry and I were excited by the possibility of hearing from him. I knew Nicole would have some difficulty getting John Bogle to speak since he was in such demand, but I didn't want to rain on her parade. Never underestimate a student. At our next meeting, she said in a matter of fact fashion, "He can come to speak in two weeks! What date would be best?"

A good number of people are unaware that John Bogle has his moral compass set on true north for the highest level of morality. When he came to speak to our school community, his address was not about money but about success in life and living a life with purpose.

Nicole did a wonderful job of introducing him. You can learn more about Bogle's philosophy of life by reading one of his books, <u>Enough: True Measures of Money, Business, and Life</u>. Bill Clinton wrote the forward to the book, but John introduced where he was heading in the book by beginning with a story to set the tone. He wrote, "At a party given by a billionaire on Shelter Island, Kurt Vonnegut informs his pal, Joseph Heller, that their host, a hedge fund manager, had made more money in a single day than Heller had earned from his widely popular novel, <u>Catcher-22</u>, over its whole storied history. Heller responds, "Yes, but I have something that he will never have. I have enough." (Bogle 2008)

John gave a terrific address to our community. He was a down to earth person of significant wealth but he only flew first class on an airplane once. He took only half of his earned salary, donating the other half to charities. In his presentation John focused on what it means to have enough in a world that is focused on status. He also made the point that we need to focus on supporting our families, communities, and nation. In essence he is a person who believes in and practices the highest moral principles.

There is more to the story. Somehow the word spread that John had spoken at our school. Various groups, schools, etc. were calling to ask me the secret to getting him to speak at our school as he was normally booked way in advance. He was in very high demand.

I simply told those who asked, "I didn't get him. A student did. You have to know a kid who is a good friend with him." Most famous people will never turn down a young person who they know well. I have learned over the years to never underestimate the ability of a student to accomplish a task.

### Chapel As A Family Photo Album

There wasn't an ethical subject or issue related to character that we didn't cover in chapel during our worship services. We tried to establish a balance of conservative and liberal views as well.

I think the best metaphor for our chapel services that occurred every day is the family photo album. You cannot just pick out one picture from a photo album and say it is who we are or that it represents what occurs in chapel. You have to take in the whole to have the right perspective.

## *Reflections*

When have you been a giver? When have you been a taker?

Write your own gratitude letter to someone and give it to that individual. Who would you choose?

Do you put yourself in situations to avoid guilt, vulnerability, and rejection?

What role does service to others play in your life?

What do you want your legacy to be?

Have you had a traumatic experience that you had to overcome? What or who did you draw on to for support as you moved toward recovery?

Do you have a slogan or quotation that directs you to do the right thing?

# CHAPTER 7: LOSS AND LEGACY

## Pull For Paul

Paul Pratt, '14 lived out loud. He was a force of nature, cherished by all who surrounded him. He was prone to accidents so his parents decided to surround him with one of the safest vehicles on the road, a huge Suburban. The night before the Stotesbury Regatta, crew's biggest and most prestigious competition, Paul stopped at Five Guys Burgers on his way home from practice to get something to eat before his dinner. Crew practice was very demanding, and I am sure he was very hungry. Paul turned his Suburban over as he rounded a curve near his home. The speculation is that he was reaching down to get a burger out of the bag and took his eyes off the road for an instant, causing the accident.

An EA alumnus, John McMeekin, '86, saw the accident and stopped to render aid. First responders were called, but nothing could be done. Paul died in the accident.

John noticed that Paul was wearing our school colors. Neither the police nor any of the first responders could find identification on him. John called to inform me of the accident since he knew that I probably would be able to identify the student. The police requested that I come to the accident scene to help with the identification. I am very proud of John. He attempted to revive Paul using CPR and he kept his cool in a very tragic situation.

When I arrived I parked in front of the suburban, got out, and made my way back to the rear to identify the student. It was a series of difficult steps to take as I moved toward the body for I had no idea who would be lying behind the end of this over sized car. The distance I covered was short but every step seemed to take forever.

When I reached the rear part of the car where Paul was laid, the police asked if I knew him. I answered, "Yes." I then accompanied the police to the Pratt home to have one of those encounters that you wish you never had to have. Joe Pratt, Paul's dad, came to the front door and we informed him of what had occurred. As you can imagine, Paul's dad was inconsolable. We waited for Paul's mom to arrive home as she was traveling home from upstate New York after having picked up her other son, Doug, from college.

The family felt as if they were living a nightmare from which they would soon wake up but there was no waking up from the reality of this tragedy. The school community was stunned and in shock. We had the Memorial Service for Paul in the chapel on our new campus. There was standing room only since many from the Philadelphia rowing community attended along with our entire school community. I received many emails expressing the following, "We never got the true nature of the Episcopal community. Now after that service for Paul, we get it!"

Paul was one of the best rowers in the nation and was destined for Harvard where he would have played an important role in their crew program.

I got to know Paul in depth when he took Ethics with me. He came to me with various labels such as "difficult", "challenging", and "hard to handle". He lived up to those labels in our first few classes. He saw me after the first class and said, "I apologize for stepping over the line today." My response was, "You were fine. I'll let you know when you do!"

I had a question about Paul that I needed to answer, "If he is perceived as so difficult by others, why is he so highly regarded by his peers since he had no need to impress others?" My Ethics class was right up Paul's alley since it contains complex theory but also controversial topics that, if not handled well by the students, could become a real problem.

I began to see Paul apart from his labels. He was a seeker after truth. This is what his peers saw as well and his parents confirmed his questioning spirit. He had question after question but was also sensitive to the fact that his peers needed to be as involved as he was. I allowed him to deep dive into the issues. He would still come up after class to make sure that he had not stepped out of line. I finally said to Paul, because he really wanted to be seen in a positive light, that I would let him know if he crossed the line. I encouraged him to keep questioning. I also told him that I would never correct him in front of his peers. I would only do that privately.

Something magical occurred in Ethics class when I was teaching Paul. He became a class leader who empowered others in the course. When I thought about the transformation Paul made in this class, I also discovered why years after his death he is still mentioned in chapel addresses by students who didn't know him but knew of him. He was about as real as a human being could be. Our school motto is *Esse Quam Videri* that translates to "to be rather than to seem to be". That is a powerful characteristic to model for others and Paul did just that.

Paul's labels dropped off in the class and once others could see who he was deep inside, they wanted to be like him.

Paul's father, Joe, raised an important question when he gave the eulogy for Paul at Bryn Mawr Presbyterian Church. The anecdote that describes the question Paul's dad raised is as follows.

> At the first race of the 2013 Stotesbury Regatta, a time trial on May 17 at about 1pm, four oarsmen, Nick Mead, James Konopka, Guillaume Furey, and Jack Alden, rowed the Episcopal Academy shell. Paul would have been there, rowing bow seat, had he not died 17 hours earlier. At the five hundred meter mark, which is about where the St. Joe's boathouse is located, the four oarsmen were met by an eruption of cheering, yelling, and screaming from the crew community from all the participating schools lining the banks of the Schuylkill River. These passionate rowing fans were not yelling the names of schools. As one, the community chanted one name, and one phrase, "pull for Paul; pull for Paul; pull for Paul; pull for Paul." The Stotesbury Regatta is the largest and oldest high school regatta in North America. Long time observers of

crew racing have said they cannot recall such an outpouring. In the days that followed, I pondered the question, "Why did Paul's death cause such a reaction?" As time passed, I also could not help but wonder why Paul's death grew in the minds of our greater community, not only among rowers, but among those who publish national blogs.

The answer to these questions came in the form of letters and notes sent to his father and mother expressing what Paul meant to so many and the grief that reached into the hearts of family, friends, faculty, and the rowing community. I have read some of these. They are poignant and moving in their expression of love for Paul and his amazing gift of filling each minute with life and love. His legacy continues to this day. Many who Paul touched questioned whether they were filling their time in a way that honored the time that we have on this earth.

Paul's mother, Kimberly, as well as his father played a large role in shaping who Paul became. When Kimberly and I would meet after Paul's death to talk about the most sacred of things, she would always bring a gift…apples…flowers…candles. These small tokens placed on the table between us made the time sacred as she was filled with gratitude for the life of Paul. Could this be how Paul learned to do the same in his life, to fill every minute with meaning? Kim who is a deeply spiritual person found solace that Paul became a person of faith. She played no small role in that journey.

Paul's life is a powerful legacy!

I gave the following eulogy at the memorial service for Paul.

For those of you who knew Paul well, you know he never met an argument that he didn't like. He could make an issue or argument out of anything even if there wasn't an argument anywhere in sight. He could wear you out as only his family and friends know. If I were asked to summarize Paul's life, it would be three words… question and answer.

Can you imagine what it was like to have this engaging spirit in an Ethics class where virtually everything that was covered could be debated and argued about with great passion. He would sit to my right in our semi-circle leaning forward, head slightly bowed, with that little grin that said, "just you wait," written across his face, and he didn't disappoint. Some of you from that class of 17 students are here tonight. Boyle, Fox, Jacoby, Keffer, Langfitt, Marino, Regillo, Robinson, and Zahan.

Nothing went unchallenged by Paul. Following one class that was very engaging he came forward and said, "I think I crossed a line today. I apologize." I will never forget that moment for at that point in the course he had written two incredible essays on his core values and what made him do what he did. His questioning was real and important so I said simply, "Paul as long as I know that your questions come from your questioning heart and not for the sake of drama, everything will be alright. When I don't think that is occurring, we will have a different conversation." It is a tribute to Paul that we never had to have that different conversation.

What Paul didn't know is that "why I do what I do" is based, in part, in the words of the poet Rainer Maria Rilke who wrote, "Be patient toward all that is unsolved in your heart. And try to love the questions themselves. Do not seek the answers that cannot be given you because you would not be able to live them. And the point is to live everything. Live the questions now. Perhaps you will then gradually, without noticing it, live along some distant day into the answer." (Rilke 1934)

Paul's life was a series of questions and answers. In talking with his mother, I learned that as recent as this Mother's Day he came to a new understanding of how God was both a question and an answer for him. He came to believe!

Elie Wiesel, author of Holocaust literature, states that his spiritual advisor, Moche the Beadle, voiced the following wisdom, "Man raises himself toward God by the questions he asks Him, he was fond of repeating. That is the true dialogue. Man questions God and God answers. But we don't understand the answers. We can't understand them. Because they come from the depths of the soul, and they stay there until death. You will find the true answers, Elie, only within yourself.

And why do you pray? I asked. I pray to the God within me that he will give me the strength to ask Him the right questions." (Wiesel 2006)

Paul asked the right questions. He had lots of practice driven by his desire to know. I believe that where question and answer become one, we find the eternal one who we call Lord and God! That's what Paul knows now. I know that he may have his head slightly down and that grin on his face that says "just you wait" but that has changed to his bright smile that we all know so well for he now rests with his Answer.

In honor of my retirement the crew team, coaches, and parents named a shell after me. Paul was honored by the same action. Recently both those boats won in national competition. There is a picture of both boats being carried upside down. Seeing that photograph, Joe Pratt was inspired to write the following message on Facebook. It captures some of the essential nature of Paul.

Dear Everybody, it is a quiet hot Sunday and our compressor broke last night so no A/C yesterday. I went down to the boathouse, The Fairmont Rowing Association. Molly Konopka mentioned that the shell named for Paul had won a few days earlier at the nationals. And then this morning I got an email with the picture (people carrying both boats named after Paul and Jim Squire). Jim Squire and Paul Pratt were upside down. Whoa, let's think about that.

From almost being thrown out of EA in 8th grade for some relatively benign insults. (The faculty vote might have been 50/50). Paul molted into something very big in this community; loved, admired, and respected in his sophomore and junior years. Even Harry Parker invited Paul to spend an afternoon in Cambridge in his launch as he coached an eight. On 5/16/13 and thereafter, there was much weeping and gnashing of teeth.

One of the major forces that molded Paul was the very right Reverend Jim Squire. Jim stood tall many times in Paul's life when in class, in chapel, and on the river at practice or in a race. Paul looked for guidance as to values, morals, and behavior. Jim, to Paul, was like the general who needs to only look at his lieutenants prior to battle, and they know without him saying a word, what is expected of them. Few young men have been fortunate and privileged to have such an imposing and wise leader as Jim Squire. Paul's story was very intertwined with Jim's story. Just listen to Jim's eulogy for Paul. Paul had immense respect for "Reverend Squire" as Paul referred to him at home.

At about 10 PM on 5/16/13 on Eagle Road, near CabriniCollege, Jim's prayers to God elevated Paul's spirit to Heaven as Bear and I stood shoulder to shoulder with Jim, a few feet away from the very spot where Paul died two hours earlier.

(General image found in Pecock's words in an interview: Pecock, https://www.youtube.com/watch?v=oYaveihFlXk)

## *Alex Bilotti: Live From A Deeper Spot*

Alex Bilotti, '12 gave an important chapel address when she was a senior. She won the Class of 1890 Prize for the Best Essay in Religion when she submitted this address to the Religion Department. I had the honor of giving her this prize at her graduation. I treasure a photograph of her receiving the award that sits on a shelf directly across from my desk in my office.

I first got to know Alex when I taught her in an Ethics class. She asked me to be her faculty advisor. Alex is a one out of a million kind of person. She will tell you of her medical troubles in an address that follows. She had the support of the entire school community. She worked very hard having to make up lost time at school because of chemotherapy. She missed the junior class ring ceremony. When I asked her how she wanted to handle that she simply said, "Why don't you just give it to me in your office." She was someone who didn't want to call attention to herself or her struggle, and life for Alex was a struggle. There were occasions when she willed herself to make it through a difficult hospitalization. Alex never let her illness interfere with her quest and passion for living.

I will never forget the day she was accepted at Penn. It was one of the happiest moments for Alex and her family. It also was an occasion that communicated subtly that she had a long future ahead of her.

When someone has a serious cancer such as Alex had, her treatment becomes a family matter. It is rare to see such courage, faith, and perseverance as I saw in the support and care that her family gave to Alex. Her mother, Sandy, is in a caring league of her own. She was a constant presence in Alex's life when care was needed. Alex's life was like a roller coaster ride with the best of times and the worst of times. One summer she was very ill in the hospital due to a disease that had taken advantage of her compromised immune system. The medical team was not sure that she would make it through the ordeal.

On one of my visits, as I entered Alex's hospital room, Sandy was there as always, small but mighty, cuddled up in a chair. She was as exhausted as a human being could be. I asked her to share the most recent information regarding Alex's progress. She said that she had asked the doctor to leave the room as she thought that he had a negative vibe. I will never forget her words. "He doesn't know Alex! He doesn't know what she has come back from. I told him I didn't want any negative stuff in the room." She was so tired she could hardly speak. That pretty much summarizes the relationship between this mother and her daughter. It was powerful!

Alex died when she was a student at Penn. It was crushing for us all!

Following is Alex's inspirational chapel address.

Thank you, Kathryn, '12. (Kathryn Burke, a very close friend introduced Alex) Please be seated. In ancient Rome, for a period of about 500 years, there lived a group of people more powerful than anyone has ever been. They were the emperors and they had absolute control over perhaps the greatest dynasty in history. They could do whatever they wanted. They could enslave people, create laws, declare war on entire countries, or, if they really wanted, nothing at all.

And yet, the Romans didn't stick around for 500 years by letting whoever happened to hold power really do whatever they wanted. Further, it would seem, that without laws, there was no way for the emperor to be controlled. But there was. For though the emperors were powerful, the greatest among men, what they were also was mortal. And in this they were like every man or woman who ever lived before them, and every man, woman, or child who has lived since.

And so, to be sure that their emperors behaved and remembered what mattered, two servants were always placed behind the emperor, they were his constant companions. And if ever the emperor was full of himself or too angry or wanting to do something for personal reasons that would potentially damage Rome, the servants would always whisper, *Memento mori*, which means "Remember Your Mortality." For although at his peak today, tomorrow the emperor could fall. And thus, although *Memento mori* means remember you will die, what it produced in the emperors was a consciousness of the moment, of the fleetingness of life and of time. And thus, for them, to remember death was really to know what matters and remember how to live.

All of you here probably know my story, or at least the one that has attempted to define me. And part of the reason I am here is to tell it, and of course, to tell what I have learned from it. But much more than that, I would like to speak about the universal things – the things far, far bigger than myself – that my small, personal journey has brought me into contact with. Though they start with three big words: life, cancer, and death, they end at a very different place. Although they are big words, what I don't have are big, easy answers. I don't have any answers about life or how to live it. In fact what I've gone through has only taught me that any easy answer to such a wonderfully complex thing is foolish. But what I do know is that though we think of life and death as two totally separate things, opposites in fact, without one, the other does not exist. And for me (and maybe long ago some Roman emperors), the start of living a life as opposed to just being alive, began not with life and adventure and happiness, but frankly with becoming aware of death.

I know how that sounds. We as a culture, as a society, as a school, as individuals, are terrified of that word. But like a lot of the things that we're scared of, we're not necessarily scared of them, more we're scared because we don't know how to integrate them into the rest of our lives. We have trouble admitting we were wrong as if it would negate our future abilities to be right. We don't know how to admit that we've been a bad friend, because we think it would mean that we were never a good one. And we couldn't possibly confront something like death because, from our perspective, we view it as an indefinite end. However, from another perspective, I feel as though it can make you view life differently.

As we have seen in this community through the loss of Mr. Mandeville, its permanence is tragic and assured. But I am not talking about dying. I am talking about confronting death, which even though it may use the same words, I promise is a radically different thing.

On June 21, 2004 I was diagnosed with Ewing's Sarcoma, a rare childhood cancer. I was eleven. I know being so young for such a serious thing as cancer sounds scary, but, in truth, I think I was more terrified by what I couldn't comprehend than what I could. See, no one in my life had ever died, at least no one I was close to. I had never even been to a hospital before, not for me or for anyone else. The first time we went there, my mom and I didn't even know what the word 'Oncology' meant. It had started with a pain in my side that just wouldn't go away. Or, to see it another way, "it", being my life with cancer, began a few weeks later, when I was called back into the hospital after receiving scans to check up on the pain on my side that everyone originally had thought was pneumonia. But then they saw on the scan that the "pneumonia" was growing larger.

The scene at my house upon hearing this news was just as frantic as you would imagine. I vividly remember hearing my dad whisper to my mom,

"She might not make it." Everyone was crying all around me. Up until this chaotic point in my life—chaotic, I promise you, being an understatement—I had never contemplated not living or even that dying was a possibility. I didn't completely understand what was going on. As we arrived at the hospital and entered the lobby where the elevators were, we didn't have the slightest clue as to where we should go. All we had was that awful word repeating in our heads and a fear for the worst. Our fragility, our absolute inability to fit into the scene was so apparent that an elderly woman who worked at the hospital appeared out of nowhere with a wheelchair to take me to where I needed to be. After that, for a year, I underwent treatment.

First, I was given another scan to find out exactly what the mass in my side was. Then, I underwent biopsies, which showed that the cancer was not only in my side but had also spread to my head and a few other places in my body. Starting immediately I received six rounds of chemotherapy; each lasted around a week and would give me fevers between cycles that would put me in the hospital for a few days in addition to the treatments. So, you can imagine, I was miserable. After all the chemo, I had surgery in which they removed the large tumor on my side along with some of the ribs themselves. Finally, I underwent two bone marrow transplants and localized radiation. All of this, as I said, lasted a year. And I don't know if you can recall when you were eleven, but, back then, a year was a very, very long time.

Cancer is a peculiar thing. During what can only be described as a pivotal moment, life, as I remember it, was a somber blur of treatments and sickness. However, I seem to have retained a small collection of distinct moments of clarity. It's these moments, characterized by their melancholic nature, which pushed me to stop dwelling on death and to work for a life I didn't have.

I got sick right before sixth grade. Having gone to parochial school, where you stay in the same classroom for every subject and have to bring your lunch to school every day, I was so scared I would miss out on all the new experiences I'd been yearning for at the new middle school that I was going to attend. I wouldn't be able to experience having a locker (I really wanted a locker), experience the unexpectedness and fun of switching classrooms in between periods, of waiting in the lunch line with my tray to buy food from the cafeteria. I can remember sitting in my living room, watching a Cinderella Story, with no hair on my head, wondering if I'd ever have friends again or be able to go to a party. Because all that had been taken away from me, I began to find how much I appreciated the littlest things.

I remember, commonalities such as food and school became twisted and unfamiliar. Chemotherapy altered my taste buds so badly that everything seemed to have an almost poisonous taste. I wasn't worried about how good the food was but whether eating it was even bearable. That same year, while going through treatment, I was only able to attend five or six days of school. I was repeatedly absent throughout my first year of Middle School and so I decided to repeat the sixth grade in order to experience what I had missed.

And yet, as terrible as going through a year of treatment was—and it was terrible—life after that torturous year was completely the opposite; it was great. There's magic to pain. It hurts so much when it's there, but, unlike a failed test or a broken relationship, it disappears as quickly as it came.

And because all of my senses had been dulled and affected by my treatments, when they returned, I became just that much more aware and appreciative of my surroundings. I tried to attend every social event possible, couldn't get enough of my friends, (a lot of the time staying with them for almost the entire weekend). And, frankly, it was amazing just not to feel sick. But then, here's the funny thing. At some point, somewhere, I began to forget. I guess that's the thing about pleasure, about good things, too; too much of them can dull our senses just like the worst chemotherapy.

See the trouble with our society—or at least the trouble for me—is that it all feels so great. Our phones—or, should I say Siri—can provide restaurant suggestions, text all your friends where and when to meet, and supply driving directions. Our Rom-Coms depict perfectly constructed and easily predictable fairytale lives. And, we have, at max, one month to wear our newest clothes before we spot our own picture in the, "What Not to Wear," section of Us Weekly.

But see, as great as all this stuff is, collectively and repetitively, in dosage after dulling dosage, it leads to one thing and that thing is forgetting. See, when we forget that we are going to die, then we forget everything else too. Wrapped up in materialism, we don't pay attention to the richness of life that can at any moment be taken away from us. We forget that if we don't stop this minute and fix our relationship, apologize, move on, whatever it may be, that we won't, that we never will. We forget that simply saying "hi" to someone might completely turn that person's day around and that if we don't, one day when we can't, we will yearn for the opportunity to do so. We forget. And instead, we go for the next meal, the next nap, the next run, without even thinking about it.

But here's the thing. I know it sounds, right now, like I, the girl who had cancer, am telling you what you don't know about life. That because I was so close to death once, I would appreciate life so much; that I would never forget. And sure, when I was really sick and had no hair all I thought about was how nice I would look when it grew back. But when it grew back, sometimes I complained about my hair. It was wavy when I wanted it to be straight, straight when I wanted it to be wavy, and was never thick or shiny enough. See that's the thing. The stuff that matters in life never comes easy, not to anyone, no matter what good or bad you've been through.

Although my cancer resurfaced sophomore year, and I was treated for another two more years, finishing in November, I am currently in remission and loving every second of it. As far as cancer is concerned, it is not who I am but rather a situation that, whether I like it or not, is a part of my life. It will never take away from my personality but rather allow me to view the world in a different way than I would have. As far as I am concerned, I now know that I can deal with the good and the bad and that every day I am still learning to handle situations as they occur.

I don't come here today claiming to know the answers and I hope that's not what you will come away with. If I were asked, "Do you wish you never had cancer?" I would hesitate before responding. Of course I didn't enjoy going through all of the horrible things, but if I knew that I would be okay in the end, would I have gained from my experience? It was my wake up call to appreciate life's beauty, to think about what I was doing on a much deeper level and savor the experiences that pass us by.

But I do know this. Because cancer chose me and because of what I've gone through I've been given a rare glimpse of death. If I would like to leave you with anything, it would be to think of one of those servants whispering to the emperor *Memento mori*, remember death. Don't dwell on it, don't get lost in it, just remember it and live your life accordingly. And though I think each person is entitled to figuring out what that means for themselves, for me at least, it has meant to live from a deeper spot. Not to do more, but to appreciate more. Not to always be happy but to figure out why I'm sad. To carve into this stuff called life because I know that at some point, I and those around me will no longer be here to do so. Thank you.

## The Lantern Of Love And Suffering

Following is the address I gave at Alex's Mass of Christian Burial at her parish church in the city.

In the Gospel of Matthew 5:14-16, we hear these words, "You are the light of the world. A city on a hill cannot be hid. No one after lighting a lamp puts it under a bushel basket but on the lampstand, and gives light to all in the house. In the same way, let your light shine before others, so that they may see your good works and give glory to your Father in heaven."

(Holding the lantern up for all to see) This ceramic lantern is constructed with a lattice pattern so that an image is projected from the light behind. Alex did this in a ceramics class at the Episcopal Academy. Small in stature but big on courage she was called "Big Al" for her toughness. She presented this lantern to me in my office, with a message attached and said, "I have a surprise for you." The message attached read, "Rev, when you light this, think of me. Love Alex." This lantern and her note sit in a prominent place in the Squire home.

The lantern and the note go to the heart of who Alex is and the essence of our faith.

Light shines forth from it in a distinctive pattern that Alex has engaged and crafted. To me this pattern takes up a lot of space and symbolizes for me the many things that attempted to block out the light of love she had for all of us here this day and our love that we have for her. The ceramic pattern is formed by the rigors of her disease, Ewing's Sarcoma, a particularly insidious form of cancer. This was a pattern in her life that attempted to block out the light. The pattern contained weavings of pain, nausea, surgery, and a delay of her dreams, among others.

We can't ignore the pattern because it is part of who Alex is. It was half of her life. The pattern of pain and suffering gave another gift to us as people of faith as she stated in her chapel address at Episcopal. She indicated that her illness had caused her "to live from a deeper spot". There was no place for the superficial in Alex's life.

Her words, "Think of me when you light this", are closely tied to the words of Jesus at the last supper said in the midst of his own suffering, "Eat this bread...drink this wine...do this in remembrance of me."

Alex has given each of us our own lantern with our own memories of her, created by her hands and heart and engaging creative spirit...helping us all to live from a deeper spot. Our lanterns will cause us to see her light of love. I know that her family wants us to celebrate her life. In fact Alex required us to live with more joy and courage as a result of her being with us.

Our dilemma is that we are flooded with many lanterns today. It is hard to focus on one at a time.

But we know that when we need a bit more love in our life…more hope...more joy…more courage… more inspiration, those lanterns that Alex gave us will appear again and again. They will shine forever as Alex does now in the arms of her Lord.

When your lantern lights up with a pattern of hardship woven into your life, think of Alex and her deep desire and passion to live. Now she lives in a place where pain, suffering, and sorrow are no more.

What I want you to do now is close your eyes and think of a lantern that Alex has given you. You have to keep the pattern in mind. It can be a moment when you were just having fun with Alex, when you were inspired by her courage, faith, passion for life and joy. Before you open your eyes, say the following to yourself, "When you light this, think of me. Love Alex"

Alex's family told me that many people purchased lanterns after the service to remember Alex. The service for Alex occurred in a church in Philadelphia. As we planned to honor her, I asked her father, Peter, to give me an estimate of the seating capacity of the church. He simply responded that it was big. There were 1000 plus people at the service. That is how much Alex had affected those around her and those who just knew about her. Her dad saw me after the service and said, "Now I know why you wanted to know the size of the church." He couldn't believe the number of people who attended.

I still wear a rubber bracelet with her initials AVB and the word Courage engraved on it so that I have a daily reminder of what courage and what a proper view of life look like. Her loss and legacy, her gift to us, were her words, always live life "from a deeper spot". I can't count the number of times I have used that phrase since her chapel address.

## 9/11

I think those of us of a certain age remember exactly where we were when we heard about the attack on America on 9/11. I was sitting in the office of the Head of School, Jay Crawford, when his secretary entered the office and said, "I think you two need to turn on the television right now." We did so just in time to see the second plane hit the second tower. The school's crisis team was quickly called into a meeting and we worked out a plan for the day. Crisis response and management is one of the things our school does very well.

Our Lower School and Middle School students would remain with the director of their units and their teachers. They were free to come to the chapel from time to time to pray and spend some time with one another in that setting. Parents were free to pick up children from school at any time. Chapel was the center point of help as we asked our school psychologists to remain in chapel along with my chaplain colleagues.

Our Upper School students attended class or came to chapel for solace. Their teachers came as well. It was quite a sight to see, as many students formed groups of friends to offer support to one another, making sure that no one was left out.

A good many people had personal connections to what was going on at the twin towers. Some of our students' family members worked in the financial district. Our basketball coach and his wife, who worked in our athletic office, had two sons who were potentially involved in the tragedy. One son worked in one of the towers and the second one was flying over New York City about the time of the attack. As it turned out the son who worked in one of the towers was held up and was late arriving to work. The other son whose airplane flew over New York City also escaped the tragedy. There were tense, seemingly interminable moments, as the community awaited to hear whether they had survived. Bringing it close to home, my brother, a research physicist, was working at the Pentagon. It was his part of the building that took a direct hit from one of the airplanes controlled by the terrorists.

What I didn't know at the time was that my brother who had a high security clearance was deep in the Pentagon working on a project. He did not even know the attack was occurring. When he discovered that the building had taken a hit, he did as many others did, and crawled to safety over the Pentagon lawn. Since his part of the building was hit, he told me that for weeks all that he did was attend funeral service after funeral service for his colleagues.

When we look back on this event today, we forget that cell phone use was not possible immediately after the crisis. The system was flooded and there were too few towers to handle phone traffic. This made the situation worse for those who were attempting to contact loved ones in New York City or Washington.

I spent the day in the chapel where members of the school community came and went to gain solace. Parents came to pick up their children and made their way to the chapel as well. The chapel was truly a sanctuary or safe place for all in our school community to begin to process one of the most devastating events in the history of our country. It was people helping other people to get through this terrible time.

It is surprising that with all of the members of our school community who work in New York only one school alumnus was killed in the attack. Jeff Coale, '88 was the sommelier for the Windows of the World restaurant at the top of one of the towers. Jeff was rarely there at that time of the day, but on 9/11 he decided to check on his inventory of wines.

In our chapel services each year on 9/11 we continue to remember those who were killed that day and the lessons that we should learn from this event.

### Understanding Islam

Recall that Islam itself came under attack after 9/11. There was so much misinformation in the public domain about the nature of Islam that I decided to have our school sponsor a national conference. The title of the conference was "Understanding Islam". I put together some of the best scholars regarding Islam, including both men and women. These experts had an international reputation for their knowledge of such topics as Islam and the Law, what the Koran really says, and the controversial topic of Women and Islam. I couldn't have done the conference without the assistance of Dr. Roger Allen from the University of Pennsylvania, a good friend and Middle East language expert, and Emily Cronin who managed public relations for EA.

I was warned that a professor at a college in New Jersey had received death threats when he sponsored a similar conference. I did not receive any threats, but I did have angry people in our school community who thought I was being insensitive to the people who had lost loved ones on 9/11.

I saw things differently. I subscribe to the view of psychologist Bruno Bettleheim, "we tolerate (meaning can move forward) that which we understand." Understanding is the key to growth and acceptance of diversity in a tragic time.

I didn't anticipate the number of Black Muslims who attended from the Philadelphia area. There were some tense moments during the conference given the topic. At the very end of the conference I was standing in front of the theater when a tall black man dressed in black attire made his way toward me down the center aisle. I had no idea what was on his mind. He hugged me and said, "Thank you for arranging this and for telling the truth about Islam." That was a mark of success for me regarding the conference and made all the effort and risk worthwhile.

When Vicki and I visited New York during a recent spring break we saw the musical "Come From Away" which is the story of the people in Gander, Nova Scotia, who took in thousands of people whose planes had to land in their small community during the attack. The next day we went to the 9/11 Museum and joined a private tour led by a guide who had a direct connection to the 9/11 Attack. The guide shared personal stories that put our thoughts and feelings in line with those who were present to witness the tragedy. We also found Jeff Coale's information on a display in the museum. The display listed all who died and included details about each victim such as their hometown and their professional life.

## A Gift From Yemen

One of our alumni, Bernie Yaros, '05 lived in Yemen for a time after his graduation from college. He worked for a newspaper, reporting news in the Middle East. His parents and I were in communication with him and literally had to urge him to leave Yemen when it became too dangerous with extremists taking over.

When Bernie returned home we met in my office. He presented me with Muslim prayer beads and a warrior's belt that he had smuggled out. I thanked him profusely but indicated that I was just glad he got out in time. Standing in front of me, safe and sound, was the greatest gift that he could have given me. What was the source of Bernie's courage? We prayed for him daily in chapel. He had two wonderful parents who supported him in what he wanted to do. He was a terrific squash player who was used to the resilience that was necessary to compete at the highest level. He was a cancer survivor. Put all of that together and you have grit. The first time I visited him in the hospital when he was in treatment for his cancer, his parents were present. Bernie looked at us and said, "I am going to beat this!" And he did. He is heroic.

## Joe Greco Lived Out Loud

Joe Greco lived out loud. He was high energy, kind, and a very engaging student. He died in a tragic accident when he was in Chicago for a wedding weekend. Since he was so involved in school life, his viewing occurred in Christ Chapel. The line of mourners was long and wrapped around the building.

At the beginning of one school year after Joey's death, I received a phone call from a friend who indicated to me that Joey's mother was ready to tell her story, an important message for our community.

Following is my introduction for the address by Mary Greco.

On August 7, 1998 I was away on vacation
when I received the worst kind of phone call from
Jay Crawford, our Head of School. Then a minute

or two later another call came from the police in Chicago. Those phone calls caused me to leave immediately to return to Philadelphia to be with today's speaker and her family regarding the tragic story she is about to share with you.

Mrs. Mary Greco is the mother of two Episcopal Academy alumni, Joe, '90, a classmate and good friend of my oldest son, and Jeff Greco, '93, one of my advisees. There is an old saying that God couldn't be everywhere so he created mothers... God is certainly part of Mary who is one of the most courageous people I know. For her to share her story with you today, she must act on that courage. Please stand to greet Mrs. Greco.

## Dying High

### Mary Greco at EA Chapel 1/29/03

When Rev. Squire asked me to speak to you I was honored, excited and scared.

Where do I begin?
How can I reach them?
This is so important.

If I can save one person's life, if I can spare one mother from this pain, then Joey's death wouldn't be in vain.

Standing in this Chapel, just being on this campus brings back so many beautiful memories. It doesn't seem so long ago that Joey and I sat in the theatre for a pre-prom assembly on teenage drinking. I remember the speaker, a representative from a major beer brewing company, saying that this generation was considered the "TV generation".

There was nothing that could be done to change their thinking. All marketing evolved around drinking as the only way to have fun. I remembered leaving that assembly angry. "How dare he say that about my son"? I can change his thinking: my son won't be a statistic!

I followed all the advice professionals gave on parenting. We had discussions about drinking and drugs. Our discussions centered on weighing the consequences of choices. Every choice you make has good and bad consequences.

Well, we made it to graduation, EA class of 1990.

College and fraternity years were a bigger challenge. Joey assured himself and me that he knew what he was doing. *"I know my limit, mom, you don't have to worry. I worked too hard to get here and I'm not going to do anything to blow it."*

Did he really know his limit?

Did his limit increase each time he succeeded in beating the odds?

How could he know his limit if his judgment was impaired?

Did he get to the point where he felt that he was invincible?

Well, Joey did end up a statistic. All his hard work and accomplishments are buried with him.

I wish you could have known my son. Joey was known for his zest for life, his love of a good time, his outgoing nature, and his generosity toward his family and friends. He was a very special young man. I had no idea how many lives he touched until his death. Strangers thanked me for raising such a wonderful person who had a significant impact on their lives.

One of the best tributes to Joey's charisma is the fact that Mr. Durham, Joey's fourth grade teacher, visited his grave regularly and left beautiful notes and remembrances. He once left a note on an American Flag that read,

*"Joey, I think of the children who will never know you as a father and a grandfather."*

I still can't believe that this happened. My precious little boy is gone. He had so much to live for. I can't tell you what it does to me not to have been able to protect my son from this tragedy. I attended every football and lacrosse game and stood on the sidelines following Joey from one end of the field to the other. Joey used to laugh at me because I didn't really understand the games; I just did it because I wanted to make sure that when he fell, he got up. I never dreamed that one day I would stand beside his casket.

The week before he died he made settlement on his first house. The night of Joey's viewing, the president of the company he worked for gave us a sales award that Joey never knew he won. He told us that Joey was up for a promotion to management. On Joey's 1998 Business Plan, under "Professional Growth/Long Term Goals," he listed "To take the necessary steps toward promotion to sales management".

Stories are all I have left. The memories are what get me through each day. The sad reality is that we will never be able to make new memories.

How did Joey die? One might say that he and his friends did everything right. No one drove; they took a taxi. They didn't get into any fights. They were just having fun.

They found the housekeeping closet near their hotel room and decided to goof off by passing the vacuum and doing other silly things. Joey, for some reason, decided to climb into the laundry chute. No one knew whatever possessed him to do that except that his judgment was so impaired by the alcohol that he thought he was being funny. Maybe he thought that the chute was what you see in the movies or on TV, a slide that slides you down into a large pile of laundry. We'll never know what he was thinking.

In reality the chute is more like an elevator shaft. With nothing under his feet he tried to hang on to the wall and screamed for help. One of Joey's friends was so intoxicated that he passed out on the bed and didn't hear Joey's screams. The other one, also drunk, came to help but couldn't get a good grip to pull him out so Joey fell 6 stories to his death.

I never thought that I would have to bury my son. I'm sure that Joey didn't climb into that chute to die. He probably just wanted to be funny. What seemed to be good clean fun turned into a fatal accident. Was this accident preventable?

YES! We need to think about the way we celebrate, the way we party, the way we have a good time.

Remember, if you have trouble making a choice, ask yourself if what you chose is something you would want your family and friends to read about in the paper.

If it is something that you're NOT proud to have them read, then you should think twice.

However, at the time you are making your decision **be absolutely sure** that your judgment is **NOT** impaired.

I pray that I can reach you through Joey's story so that together we can make something positive come from something so tragic.

*Please, please, I beg of you, turn Joey's fatal mistake into a lifetime lesson so he didn't die in vain!!!*

I will end my talk with a poem and then close with a song.

> I asked the Lord to bless you
> As I prayed for you today
> To guide you and protect you
> As you go along your way...
>
> His love is always with you
> His promises are true,
> You know in all your struggles
> He will see you through.
>
> So when the road you're traveling on
> Seems difficult at best
> Take a moment, say a prayer
> And God will do the rest. (Author Unknown)

**GOD BLESS YOU!"**

The song was "Tears in Heaven", by Eric Clapton. (Clapton and Jennings 1992)

### *A Tragedy: Death Of A Father*

I received the call as soon as I entered my office early one day. It was to let us know that Bill Veasey had been shot and killed in South Philadelphia earlier that morning. Bill's son, Billy, '98 was a student at our school. Word travels quickly in any community, particularly a school community. First, there was shock at the news regarding Billy's dad, and then there was the obvious quick question to inquire if Billy was all right.

Billy and his dad had an early morning ritual. Billy's dad would go to Dunkin' Donuts for morning breakfast for both of them and then return home. He was shot and killed while in his car on his way home to pick up Billy. Members of the mafia were the suspected shooters.

This story dominated the news. We always try to cooperate with the press when they arrive at our campus, but our first concern and first priority is to do what is best for our students. In this case, our priority was Billy. We suggested that the press stay in a room in our Administration Building, the first building on our main drive into the school. We wanted only the spokesperson for the school talking with the press. We obviously didn't want them wandering around campus interviewing people in random fashion. The students were our primary concern. The faculty knew that they should direct any questions to our PR person.

The school supported Billy through this entire tragedy. The day and the time for the service for Billy's dad was announced. Students and other members of the school community wanted to attend. The obvious question came up. Would it be safe?

This became a growing concern so I called someone who I knew was aware of mafia protocol and put the question to him. I will never forget his response. "Reverend, that service will be the safest place in the nation." I learned that it is mafia protocol never to go after the family members or anyone else at a service for the deceased.

Being the son of the Chaplain or Head of School is not always easy but this is a time when it helped to have my son, Adam, in school with me. Adam was one of Billy's classmates. I started getting calls as late as the morning of the service questioning my leadership and my sanity for taking students to the service. The attacks were filled with anger as the parents had legitimate fears. All I could say was that my son would be going to the service with me. I would never put him in any danger. A large group from the school community went to support the family. The friend who had direct knowledge of mafia protocol provided good counsel to me. There were no incidents at the service in South Philadelphia.

Billy graduated from EA and went to college out West. I talked with Billy recently about including this story in my book and got his permission to do so. Billy wanted to make sure that I thanked the EA community for their support during that incredible tragedy. That support was an important part of his moving forward.

### *Ricky Whelan: A Model For How We Should Live*

Ricky Whelan,'00 was my advisee when he was at Episcopal which meant that I would guide him to grow in mind, body, and spirit. Ricky was very personable. At times people thought that he was too laid back. That perception immediately changed when he was on the lacrosse field. He was so fast that he was nicknamed "wheels" by his teammates.

Ricky was living at home right after college as he could commute easily to work from there. One night he died suddenly of a malfunction in the electrical pacing of his heart.

When I received the news, I first had to get his younger brother who was a student at our school and take him home. The family was devastated.

The memorial service for Ricky was in Christ Chapel on the Merion Campus. The lacrosse world is a close-knit community. Buses of players came from all over the Northeast and some from the mid-Atlantic. There were over a thousand people present, some viewing the service from a standing room only area in the back of each section of the chapel.

One of Ricky's closest friends was Jamie Biden, '00, nephew of the Vice President. Later in the year I noticed that Jamie had the initials "RW" tattooed on his forearm. I asked him about it, and he said simply that he wanted to wake up each day and see those initials to remind him to be the best person he could be.

Ricky graduated from Brown University where he received the Unsung Hero Award for his role on the Brown University Lacrosse team. After Ricky's death, Brown University changed the name of the award to the Richard Q. Whelan Unsung Hero Award as a tribute to the outstanding character of this very special young man.

Ricky's photograph in his Episcopal lacrosse uniform sat on the windowsill in my office opposite my desk so that I would be reminded of his character as well. Following is the eulogy I gave at the Memorial Service for Ricky on January 15, 2005.

Esse Quam Videri...to be rather than to seem to be...our school motto. In student language it would translate to "be real". We have many awful...full of awe questions of God today. Why do bad things happen to good people? Why Ricky? Where's the justice? How will I go on? We have to hold these questions close to our heart and as the poet, Rilke, reflected "live into the answer in some distant day." (Rilke 1934)

I have a question in addition to these so commonly raised that may help us with our struggle. Why does Ricky seem so real to all of us today even though he can no longer be seen or touched? You will hear much of this "realness" in the Reflections in just a moment. Why can I still experience, as though it is just yesterday, the many conversations with him in my office as his advisor...Ricky leaning slightly forward sometimes sad eyed over a disappointment or that wonderful smile when a goal was accomplished? Why do I remember the very seats and rooms where I taught him? Why do I remember so clearly seeing him in the back of the theatre dressed in black, hands on lighting board...a smile on his face, and why do I remember as though it was yesterday "wheels" running up and down the field...with ball on foot or ball in stick?

Ricky is so real to us now in death because he was so real to us in his life. That word defines him. The expression..."*Esse Quam Videri*"...Latin was a subject with which he struggled while he demonstrated great perseverance and now those Latin words tell us a great deal about who he was.

Where did this realness come from? What did Ricky know in his heart that we should embrace? His mother said something that struck me when I was with the family on Tuesday. Ricky was so grown up yet he had a childlike quality about him. He asked for a back rub before he went to sleep the night he died.

Grown up and being real. I think what his mother meant was that Ricky was mature in the way that Harry Stack Sullivan, founder of modern day psychiatry, defined as simply but profoundly, the "ability to put others before yourself". That made Ricky real. He visited a sick friend in Washington the day before he died.

Childlike...Jesus said, "Unless you become as a little child you shall not enter the Kingdom of God" interpreted by that great theologian Margery Williams in the <u>Velveteen Rabbit</u> with the following words.

"What is REAL?", asked the Rabbit one day, when they were lying side by side..."Does it mean having things that buzz inside you and a stick out handle?"

"Real isn't how you are made," said the Skin Horse. "It's a thing that happens to you. When a child loves you for a long, long time not just to play with, but really loves you, then you become real."

"Does it hurt?" asked the Rabbit.

"Sometimes," said the Skin Horse for he was always truthful. "When you are Real you don't mind being hurt."

"Does it happen all at once, like being wound up," he asked, "or bit by bit?"

"It doesn't happen all at once," said the Skin Horse. "You become. It takes a long time. That's

261

why it doesn't often happen to people who break easily or have sharp edges or who have to be carefully kept. Generally by the time you are real, most of your hair has been loved off, and your eyes drop out and you get loose in the joints and very shabby. But these things don't matter at all, because once you are real you can't be ugly, except to people who don't understand." (Williams 1922)

That story best describes the journey to being Real that I witnessed in Ricky Whelan. His life was shaped by family, faith, friends, and schools. He was as good as it gets. That's where his REALness happened to him…and that's what we are called to do and to be…if we are to struggle to move through those awful questions that rest in our heart today.

Unless you become as a little child…Esse Quam Videri… we are called, as Ricky was, to be real. Let us be inspired by the words which we are about to hear…sacred knowledge that Ricky knew in his heart… for he is so painfully real for us today in death because he was so real for us in life. Amen

## Maura Murphy: She Taught Us How To Laugh And Love

Vicki and I are blessed to be close to the Murphy family whose daughter, Maura, '96 and son, Brien, '00, attended our school. Maura went on to Georgetown and was doing an internship in New York between her junior and senior years when the family received a call that she had died in her sleep. Once again it was an electrical malfunction in her heart. The family and school community were devastated by our loss.

Dr. Murphy, a leading plastic surgeon in the Philadelphia area, was scheduled for heart surgery himself a few days later.

Following is the eulogy I gave as my reflection in celebration of the life of Maura Clare Malone Murphy on June 25, 1999.

We are here today to celebrate the life of Maura Clare Malone Murphy, and we are here to figure out how we make our way through our grief and overwhelming sense of loss...the kind of loss that literally and figuratively has brought us to our knees.

Today I want us to hold fast to a guiding principle in the Christian life...namely that all of life's experiences are to be either enjoyed or learned from.

In the words of the writer of the Gospel of Matthew, "Maura is the light of the world." (Matthew 5:18). She enjoyed life and bringing joy to others.

Maura lived out loud...so loud that you could hear her joy, kindness, and authenticity in the voices of her friends and family.

She had an indomitable spirit. Tell her that she couldn't do something, and you could see her eyes narrow with determination as she would rise to that occasion.

Since she lived out loud, I could hear Maura's voice in the words spoken earlier in the week by her dear friend, Sarah Rosato. Sarah described how Maura checked on her and was so giving to her in a selfless way, helping Sarah in the process of regaining her own health.

Maura's living out loud gives voice to stories that remind us that God loves stories so much that he created us to tell them with our lives. In the days, weeks, months, and even years to come, we will find ourselves beginning a moment in time with the words, "Remember when Maura"...and a story of joy, kindness, and authenticity will be told. She is the light of the world.

All of life's experiences are to be either enjoyed or learned from. What can we learn from this?

What can we do? What do we need to learn to get through this?

Maura was a student at Episcopal and at Georgetown where she learned the importance of the right answers, but she also learned the importance of the right questions.

We here this morning have a lot of questions, and most of them begin with "Why?" "Why Maura?"

As people of faith we recall that questions and answers are the rhythm of life...the ebb and flow of life, but we need to remember the words of the poet Rilke who wrote, "Be patient toward all that is unsolved in your heart and try to love the questions themselves. Do not seek the answers that cannot be given you because you would not be able to live them. And the point is to live everything. Live the questions now. Perhaps you will then gradually, without noticing it, live along some distant day into the answer." (Rilke 1934)

What can we learn from this? That tragedy does not have a ticket into our life. It has a box seat. No one gets out unscathed. It is not a question of "if". It is more a question of "when".

That is the awful truth of life that is transformed when we realize the awesome truth of the Gospel of our Lord.

William Buckley wrote an oral history of our times in his book, <u>Firing Line</u>, which contains the written transcripts of interviews he conducted on his television show by the same name for the past twenty-five years. He interviewed anyone and everyone who was important in shaping the world of politics, religion, and ideas in general. Like Maura he was concerned with global issues.

When asked to point out that person and that interview that had the greatest impact on him among all he interviewed, Buckley indicated that without a doubt it was the interview he conducted with Malcolm Muggeridge, a British author and Rector of Edinburgh University. Muggeridge commented on the spiritual nature of learning from hardships. He said, "I've often thought of the following parable that when Saint Paul starts off on his journey, he consults with an eminent public relations man, 'I've got this campaign and I want to promote this Gospel.' And the man would say, 'Well, you've got to have some sort of symbol. You've got to have an image. You've got to have some sign of your faith.' And then Paul would say, 'Well, I have got one. I've got this cross.' The public relations man would have laughed his head off, 'You can't popularize a thing like that...It's absolutely mad.'"

"But it wasn't mad. It worked for centuries and centuries, bringing out all the creativity in people, all the love and disinterestedness in people; this symbol of suffering, that's the heart of the thing. As an old man, Bill, looking back on one's life, it's one of the things that strikes you most forcibly...that the only thing that's taught one anything is suffering. The only thing that really teaches one concerning what life's about...the joy of understanding, the joy of coming in contact with what life really signifies... is suffering and affliction. When I realize this, I am also free to realize how incredibly beautiful and wonderful this life is." (Buckley 1989)

How do we get through this? We have already been taught much about the key ingredients of joy, kindness, and authenticity by Maura, but we can learn much from her sister, brother, father, and mother who, quite ironically, in suffering the most, teach us the greatest lessons with which to move forth.

F. Scott Fitzgerald commented that there comes a moment when we discover who we are and we realize that this is what we have always been and what we will always be. I saw and heard those life defining moments in the Murphy family early Wednesday morning in the form of questions.

Maggie, whose first words to me were, "What would we do if we didn't have our faith?" That's the very question we need to firmly grasp today as we leave this liturgy. We need to hold it fast for the rest of our lives in celebration of the gift of the resurrection.

"Where is Brien?", I asked Maggie. "He's out cutting roses for Maura." Brien Murphy, a man who creates beauty in the operating room and garden, considers a first gesture to his daughter, to bring her a rose loved and cared for by his hands. What beauty, a rose of truth, kindness, joy nurtured by us, will we bring to others this day and for the rest of our lives?

Maura's brother, Brien, '00, who has learned the value of teamwork from friends and teammates reflected, "We (my family) have to hold each other together." How will we hear those words mandating us to hold on to one another for it is in doing so that Christ promised us and Maura, whose voice is still heard in our hearts, that He will be truly present with us?

Maura's sister, Megan, recalling her last conversation with Maura, asked somewhat wistfully, "Did I remember to tell her I loved her?", implied that she always did. What would our lives...the world...be like if that question burned as fervently for us in the days ahead as it did for Megan in that moment in time. Did I remember to say I love you?

Moments...questions...answers...Maura

Maura...joy, kindness, authenticity...lived loudly the school motto of Episcopal...*Esse Quam Videri*...to be rather than to seem to be. I close with the words of Bishop Bennison's final benediction at the June 17th Commencement Exercises at the Episcopal Academy...words that family and friends feel describe perfectly the gift of the life of Maura Clare Malone Murphy.

> "True worth is in being, not seeming
> and in doing each day that goes by
> some small good, not in dreaming
> of great deeds to do by and by.
> For whatever folks say in their blindness
> and spite the fancies of youth
> there is nothing more royal than kindness
> and nothing more regal than truth. AMEN"
> (Carey 2018)

Maura's legacy was the power of presence particularly her presence and how it can bring light, love, and good times to others.

## Frank McAlpin: He Taught Them How To Run And Much More

When Frank McAlpin, Hon. complained of severe pain, Len Haley, a member of the faculty, and I took him to the emergency room. Frank was a highly regarded language teacher and our cross country coach. Technically Frank never left the hospital. He was diagnosed with lung cancer that had metastasized to his spine, thus causing his intractable pain. He received treatment to palliate his pain but was never able to return home. He died within months of being admitted. During Frank's treatment our cross country runners went to the hospital and hung their running shoes around his bed as a tribute to all he meant to them. The theme expressed by all was that Frank taught them more about life than he did about running. At his service held in Christ Chapel those who spoke applauded his contributions to the life of the school. I recall a year end faculty meeting where Frank was honored for his contributions to the school.

Following that faculty meeting he raced to my office, burst in, and said, "You know, Jim, this is amazing. People really do pay attention to what you do around here."

## The Hands And Heart Of A Surgeon: Thursdays With Ernie

Dr. Ernie Rosato, one of the premier surgeons in the nation and a past parent as well as a friend, contacted me by phone to request a meeting. At that moment he did not elaborate on the reason for the meeting.

As the meeting began we both let silence wash over the room. When I asked him how I could be of help, Ernie disclosed the he had been diagnosed with pancreatic cancer just before Thanksgiving. The Rosato family had been down this tragic road before. Sarah, one of two daughters out of a total of nine Rosato children, lost her battle with Ewings Sarcoma a few years before. Ironically she died at Thanksgiving. Ernie simply said, "Jim, I want you to help me get to the other side."

Ernie was an academic as well as a deep thinker. We set in place a process for our time together. I provided readings for him that served to guide our discussions. He also felt free to take the discussions in any direction he needed. Ernie was the ultimate father and husband and was more concerned about his family than he was about himself. He was blessed with a terrific wife, Gerry, who is also the ultimate loving mother. All eight of the remaining Rosato children have carried on the legacy of family first as they go about their professional lives.

The treatment for pancreatic cancer was a harsh and a difficult path for Ernie and the family to go down. Our time together lasted for two years. It was deeply personal and deeply spiritual. I am sure I gained more from our time together than Ernie did. During those years I often thought of the book, Tuesdays With Morrie. (Albom 1997) For me it was "Thursdays with Ernie". His colleagues planned a dinner to honor Ernie for his work as surgeon and teacher. When we met the week of the event he was worried because he had heard there would be ten people speaking. His concern was that it would be a boring time for the captive audience.

As it turned out about twenty people spoke and the time passed like a snap of the fingers as his colleagues described what it was like to work with Ernie during his long tenure.

When Ernie would watch a resident perform surgery, he would ask, "Now why did you do it that way?" He was a teacher and a student. For a record number of years, Ernie was voted as "The Faculty Person of the Year" by his Penn Medical School students. One year he requested that his name be taken off the ballot to give someone else a chance. The students wrote his name on the ballot and voted for him anyway.

When Ernie died, the service for him was held in the Class of 44 Chapel on the new campus. One of the speakers was Dr. John Morris, Chief of Surgery at Penn, someone who had been mentored by Ernie. A thousand people attended the service.

About a week later I received a framed photograph from John Morris. It was a photo taken of Ernie's last surgery and inscribed below the picture were the words "The Last Surgery That He Performed October 3, 2011". Ernie was standing on the right with scalpel in hand, John was on the left, and in between was a surgical resident, symbolic of Dr. Rosato's love of teaching. It hangs in my home office today.

Following are the words I spoke at Ernie's memorial service in tribute to him.

> Ernie came to my office shortly after he was diagnosed with pancreatic cancer and sat across from me. He let silence fill the land for his question to emerge. You who are present here today, and there are many who learned surgery from him, know that when he asked a question, you better have an answer ready. In your case his question was, "Why did you do it that way?", as you stood next to one another during surgery. In my case the question was, "Can you help me through this and maybe even help me get to the other side?" I said, "Yes!"

Like you, his students and colleagues, I learned much more from him than anything he learned from me. Ernie possessed a deep spirituality and faith. He represented the best of humankind. I was supposed to be the guide, but he became that to me. He was selected as teacher of the year at Penn Medicine for many years, and even when he requested not to be put on the ballot, as I understand it, you wrote in his name anyway and awarded him that distinction.

He was always the guide. He could be no other. The role and context were the only thing that changed...teacher of surgery, surgeon, chief of the division, husband, father, grandfather and friend, to name a few.

Whenever I called Ernie's home, I constantly confused Catherine and Gerry. They sound so much alike. I can't do the imitation as well as I have heard some of you, but when he would call me he would say, "Jim, this is Ernie," with that voice. Like who else could it be! That voice...that voice at the end bypassing our ear to be heard by our heart. Let me keep it simple. We loved him, for that is the response he elicited from the powerful and the powerless and everybody in between. The time was set today as late as possible so that hospital workers as well as many of you who are conducting interviews today for our future physicians could be present. This points to the awareness and sensitivity of the family to all of you.

Ernie died one hour before his beloved Sarah's birthday. He died on January 6th, the Feast of the Epiphany. What a symbolic time for him to leave this world to take up residence in the next, albeit a new native land. He died on Epiphany, a time when we celebrate the wise men coming to see the Christ child and then taking a light of love and new wisdom out into the darkness. Ernie was a wise man who did just that. He brought his light forward to lighten the darkness of disease and disorder.

Many of you here know of that. There are others here that know him in a different way, as a family man who, with Gerry, oversaw a rambunctious group. His girls, Sarah and Catherine, were perfect. His boys and nephews were not. I was faculty advisor to Philip, David and Frank. I cannot tell any of the Rosatos' student days' stories here in chapel. The telling would take too long. Know that as adults I couldn't be more proud of what each sibling and nephew has accomplished in the world as parents and spouses. These alumni are the best!

But I have one story that will highlight Ernie's Solomon-like wisdom. It will come as no surprise to anyone, just look around, that his children had a large, great group of friends. I was standing with Gerry at an athletic event. When one Rosato was competing, all of the Rosatos were there. You could take attendance! During the game Gerry described a problem she had dealt with. She never knew how many people would be at dinner each evening since the kids would always invite their friends, and she liked to have enough food for everyone. She shared her concern with Ernie who solved the problem.

His solution: each child had to make a dinner reservation by three o'clock or they couldn't bring their friends to dinner. It was the only house on the main line where dinner reservations had to be made.

There have been famous couples down through the ages, but none wiser than Ernie and Gerry. Harry Stack Sullivan, the father of the interpersonal theory in psychiatry, was asked the question, "What makes someone mature?" He responded before a blink of an eye with, "It is the ability to put someone else first." One could see in crystal clear fashion the heart of their love for one another made more evident certainly in the days since his diagnosis. Ernie would say, "I want to do what is best for Gerry." She would say, "I want to do what's best for Ernie." That was expressed in word and action.

Ernie and I talked about his heritage as an Italian and as a person of faith.

I want to close with the words of the chorus from the third act of the opera, "Nabucco" by Guiseppe Verdi. The chorus is called *Va Pensiero* that means "Fly thoughts on wings of gold". It was written in 1842 and celebrates Italian patriotism. Many people regard the song as the unofficial Italian National Anthem. When you listen to it, your heart soars, uplifted by the words and music.

The words of the chorus are:

"Fly thoughts on wings of gold
Go settle upon
The slopes and the hills where, soft and mild, the sweet air
Of our native land smell fragrant." (Verdi 1842)

Our beloved Ernie now rests in his other native land to which he has been called by God since his birth, a native land with the fragrant smell of resurrection and redemption. God bless you, Ernie! Amen

Ernie was often seen as the last stop. He would see patients and do surgery on patients that other surgeons would not. Dr. Ernest Rosato has cast a long shadow of legacy as a dad, husband, and surgeon. He was humble and gifted in all things that a husband, father, and surgeon would need to be to make a powerful impact on others.

### Sacred Timing: Kairos God's Time

In the late spring I blessed the marriage of a couple whose wedding was supposed to occur the fall of that year. Some time in March I received a call from the couple requesting that I bless their marriage a few days later that week on a Friday. The couple had planned the wedding for the fall, but the most important consideration for the couple was to have the bride's mother present. Her mother was suffering from an aggressive brain tumor. They had just been informed that the cancer was progressing faster than expected. The bride's mother only had days to live. Her mother's goal had always been to make it to her daughter's wedding.

During the first premarital counseling session the couple plus the bride's father came to the session to bring me fully on board so I knew how tenuous the life of her mother was. They asked if I could be flexible and I said, "Yes." The change in plans was no surprise.

We had the wedding on a Friday in the living room of the bride's home. Only family members were present for both the bride and groom. There were a dozen or so people gathered around the mother's hospital bed. She was alert. The bride was in her wedding gown and others were dressed in appropriate attire for a wedding.

At the conclusion of the wedding service we gathered for a brief reception of food and drink. The suffering of the woman in the bed became transformed into one of the most emotional moments in the lives of those gathered.

I got a call two days later on Sunday letting me know that the mother of the bride had died. Her goal had been to see her daughter marry a truly wonderful man. She achieved that goal.

### An Unbridled Spirit: Death Too Soon

Richard Crockett was an Episcopal alumnus who had an energy and zest for life that was contagious. He felt excitement for everything in life, particularly his family. He was a devoted father, husband, and passionate advocate for his school. Sports of all kinds, especially golf, were a source of great joy for him.

Rich attended the Kentucky Derby with friends, an annual excursion for the close-knit group. The following Monday he was at home, preparing to go to work when he died of a massive heart attack. He left a wife and two young children.

Each year during Kentucky Derby weekend, my thoughts focus on Richard and his family. I always text my prayers and regards to his wife, April. She gives new meaning to the word courageous. She centers her life around her children and is committed to giving them the best of herself, continuing their dad's legacy.

Following is a letter I wrote to the school community to inform them of Rich's death.

May 3, 2010

Dear Members of the class of 1982 and other members of our Alumni Society:

It is with great sadness that I must inform you of the sudden death today of Richard Crockett, class of '82. Rich had a massive coronary in his home at approximately 7:15 this morning. Medics on the scene as well as medical personnel in the emergency room at Bryn Mawr Hospital were unable to resuscitate him.

I was able to have prayers for Richard's departed soul and prayers for the family in the ER. His wife, April, Georgia, his first grader, and Scottie, his third grader, are very much in need of all of our support and prayers.

We spent quite a bit of time together at the hospital where family members and friends reflected on his life. He was someone who "would give anything to be helpful to anyone". It is now time for us to extend this gesture to April and his family and friends. It was also indicated that Rich "never met a stranger". He welcomed everyone into his midst. It is now time for us to gather together as family and school and offer that kind of support to one another.

Rich will be buried sometime this week at his beloved Wellfleet, MA, a place filled with many memories of the importance of family, friends, and his love of our school. The plan at the moment is to have a Memorial Service here at the 1944 Chapel at a yet to be determined day and time. His children were quick to point out the necklace their dad had brought each of them back from his tradition of going to the Derby. It was a heart design with a horse in the center. Maybe that would be our symbol for Rich as someone who loved much with an unbounded energy and spirit.

"May light perpetual shine upon, Rich, and may he rest in peace with his Lord. Amen."

Sincerely,
The Reverend James R. Squire

I flew to Wellfleet with the family and conducted the interment on Rich's beloved Cape Cod.

### Hockey, Rocky, And Livestrong

Marc Mandeville, Hon. was one of EA's ice hockey coaches and an outstanding member of our science faculty. He was held in high regard and respected by students and faculty for his constant support of others and his dedication to giving his best in all endeavors. While his children were very young, Marc was diagnosed with an aggressive colon cancer. He continued to give his best to the school and his family during the years he fought the disease. To honor Marc, his supporters formed a team within the Livestrong Foundation. During his battle with cancer Marc devoted much time and effort to that organization, promoting, support, and fund raising for others facing the same challenges. Just weeks before his own death he spearheaded a large fundraiser for the foundation. Marc was a wine connoisseur and a skilled poker player. He formed a poker group consisting of faculty and staff. They met weekly for an evening of fun and camaraderie. He was a people magnet attracting adults and students alike who just wanted to be around him.

Marc refused to let cancer stop him. He was responsible for once causing me to laugh so hard that it hurt my stomach muscles. Each fall for our annual EA-AI-Haverford Day, Marc volunteered to create a video geared to fire up the troops for the two days of competition between our rival schools.

This particular year Marc had chosen the theme of "Rocky" for the video. He asked me to play the role of Rocky and I agreed to do it, not knowing exactly what he had planned. Since I am a runner, I asked him if I should go for a run the day before the shooting and he said, "Sure, no problem! You will be just running a small amount for the shoot the next day."

Contrary to his prediction, I think we covered a whole lot of miles as I ran through campus, around campus, then through the city. My city route included the streets of South Philadelphia, through the Italian Market, and by the landmark, Pat's Steaks. Of course we had to capture that iconic moment of Rocky ascending the steps of the Philadelphia Museum of Art, culminating with the sound of victory as I jumped up and down with arms high above my head. The filming took six hours to complete.

Marc had two student video experts along with us who sat on either side of his young son in the back seat of the car. The students kept us laughing as they entertained us with imitations of faculty, Marc and me included. Our adventure created a special bond among us. There was nothing that was laugh filled about Marc's rigorous treatment for cancer. Our school community supported him throughout his entire battle with cancer.

When Marc knew his death was near, he asked if he could address chapel. He was very ill, but he managed to express his thanks to the school for all that was done to encourage and support him. He died a week later. An ice hockey jersey with his name on it hangs in the school fitness center. The service for Marc was in the Class of 1944 Chapel. One of the keynote speakers was Middle School Chaplain, The Reverend Albert E. R. Zug, '78 who provided great spiritual support for Marc and his family. Bert was a member of the faculty poker group and thus had a special opportunity to experience Marc's fun loving and giving nature.

## *Leadership, Family, The Larva Dei*

Fred Haab, '55 had a significant positive impact on the school and the greater community. For as long as I can remember the Haab family has been important to me and to the life of the school. Fred was a pillar of leadership. He was Chairman of the Board and CEO of the F. C. Haab Fuel and Lubricants Company. His two sons who are EA grads assisted him at the company. He was a trustee and Chairman of the Board of Trustees of the Episcopal Academy. He also served as trustee or chairman of other boards in the community too numerous to mention. He was an inspiration to all the organizations that were fortunate enough to have him as part of their leadership. Fred and I were friends, and I do not use that word lightly. Fred died after a long battle with lung disease. His wife, Gabby, predeceased Fred by a few years. She was vibrant, gregarious and a great spouse, friend, and mother. She was a people person enjoying a wonderful life with family and friends.

Following is the address I gave at Fred's memorial service.

A few weeks ago I went to pick Fred up to come to my home for dinner. It was the proverbial awkward moment since he was being taken out the front door of his home in a wheelchair to go to a birthday party for Chris as I was coming in the door to get him. There was miscommunication and I assured Fred that I would call again and arrange another time for us to get together for dinner.

As I turned toward my car, Fred called my name, I looked back and he said, "Jim it's a family matter"... and repeated for emphasis, "It's a family matter!"

We have all been taught the aphorism, "It is not what you say but how you say it that counts." That is what I thought about...the how...on my drive

277

home. "It's a family matter"…the fact that family mattered and was essential to his soul. That was Fred's spiritual center. I found myself smiling. One word defined Fred…family. Family first and foremost, but there were more groups that were important to Fred, including the people at his work, at Cornell, Cornell's 150 pound football team to be specific, the congregation here at St. Christopher's Church, the Episcopal Academy, and many more.

Family matters…Fred and I shared some important times together, and he spoke lovingly about Judy, Gabby, and his children and grandchildren. He spoke of the care they provided him particularly during these last challenging years. Fred was Fred and he had definite ideas about what he did and did not want to do. What an understatement. I could almost hear the voice of Frank Sinatra singing "My Way" as a backdrop of our conversations.

But let's be clear, Fred was decisive and empathetic, but empathetic in the way that the Dalai Lama describes empathy. The Dalai Lama teaches that, if we see a person who is being crushed by a rock, the goal is not to get under the rock and feel what they are feeling; it is to help to remove the rock. Empathy is not passive. It is active. We see this clearly in the life of Fred Haab who spent a lifetime removing rocks from others…whatever burden was pressing down on them.

He spoke about his love for his father and mother. I quickly learned the origin of the family work ethic that demanded forward movement in the face of hardship. Don't let anything stop you! Fred was such a presence…sophisticated but sometimes a bit rough around the edges, but always a person of integrity.

Family matters…Fred was old school which included an unfamiliar distant relationship with his cell phone...losing it, speaking into it when it was turned off or upside down. Where most companies employ consultants to provide direction that includes much wringing of hands and focus groups to provide feedback, Fred got great pleasure in sharing that the five year plan for F. C. Haab Company was normally handled over a lunch with his children.

Family matters...There was a special place to which Fred was drawn to fill his cup of peace and to feel oneness with God. That was the farm. He and Gabby loved animals as witnessed by the menagerie of animals they cared for including Paco the parrot and the family dog who traveled back and forth to the farm with them. Picture that scene in the car as I understand that Paco was quite loquacious. Through the assistance of Meredith and Steve, Fred had one last trip down to the farm a few weeks ago. When I asked him how it went, he simply said, "Fair, I couldn't do anything," but Meredith shared that a baby goat named Wyoming was presented to him at the farm and his joy could not be exchanged for all the riches in the world. The farm was where Fred and Gabby would go to get their hands dirty which brings me to the religious significance of that part of their lives, blended with family matters.

There is a word, larva, those repulsive things that crawl along the ground, tree, or plant, a part of their life on the farm. *Larva* is a Latin word that is translated as "mask" or "disguise". It describes a phase in the development of an organism that masks the mature form. The caterpillar masks the butterfly.

Martin Luther used the term as well but expanded it to be the *larva dei,* the mask of God, as a description of family life where God is accomplishing his purposes often in quiet and hidden sorts of ways....nothing fancy...words and actions, like the many times the Haab family exchanged words and deeds with each other and with their family of friends and colleagues.

Family matters…the *Larva Dei*…the mask of God…once God perhaps seen through a glass darkly but for Fred now seen face to face…here with us still in our hearts but thanks to the resurrection of our Lord…transformed into eternity. Amen

### Ted Stone: What Price Are You Paying?

Ted Stone,'78 was diagnosed with head and neck cancer. His treatment required multiple surgeries that left his face quite disfigured. In addition, he underwent the most rigorous chemotherapy and immunotherapy to treat the residual and relapsing cancer as he and his doctors sought a cure. I noticed something after my conversations with Ted over a long period of time. I forgot about his disfigurement. Ted died after a courageous battle against the disease. Following Ted's memorial service I was with friends of Ted at a reception.

I mentioned to one of his friends that I completely forgot about his facial disfigurement after we spent time together in conversation and the friend reflected that he had the same experience. This demonstrates that when we connect with someone at a deep level, all labels fall away and we see the person for who and what they truly are. This allows us to focus on their character, moral fiber, and grit. Ted was a source of inspiration to many. His wife, Liz, his children, and extended family members embodied great courage as well.

Following is the sermon I gave at Ted's memorial service.

Homily at the Memorial Service for Edward Chase Stone, '78

The Reverend James R. Squire

Ted's life's work was as an actuary. He spent his professional life analyzing the financial consequences of risk. Sometimes this is referred to as cost/risk/benefit analysis.

Each day of our lives we enter into this equation that Ted used in his professional life with simple but profound questions, "What is the price you and I are paying?" More important, "Is it worth it? What is the cost?"

These became the questions that would dominate his life since his cancer diagnosis as decisions regarding the path of his treatment had to be made. They are the most difficult decisions that one could imagine. He drew a line in the sand when he indicated that he would not have his second eye surgically removed since it would result in blindness.

Bert, Tim, and I marveled at how he would move through the terrain of these questions with such courage and grit. These questions are Ted's legacy and a gift to us gathered here today. We need to take time to reflect on them as we live our lives. What is the price that you and I are paying? Is it worth the cost?

Ted approached his life and his pending death as an actuary of faith, to use a turn of phrase, in what tomorrow would bring.

Recall the book, <u>Profiles in Courage</u>, written by John F. Kennedy when he was hospitalized for a long period of time. We know from the profiles described in Kennedy's book and from our own lives lived that courageous people have their faults and their failings. Ted was not perfect. None of us are. I really don't think he wanted to be perfect. He just wanted to give what he was confronting in life his best effort, whatever the challenge happened to be.

One of the things I have learned in my life is that we live life the way that we view death.

"There is a story regarding the Headmaster of Eton, the fine British Prep School, who was confronted by a very angry parent who did not feel her son was progressing fast enough. She laid that responsibility at the feet of the school. Her emotions emerged in an angry question, 'Just what are you preparing him for?' The Headmaster took the wind from her sails by responding to her with, 'We are preparing him for death!' The boy was wasting time and was unfocused." (Squire 2017)

The Headmaster wanted him to appreciate more the time that he had on this earth and to use it better. We live life the way we view death.

Ted tried to redeem each moment he was given by filling each minute with 60 seconds of meaning. Some days because of the chemotherapy he couldn't do this. He was often bored and yearned to have more richness in his time. This was a daily challenge for him.

What is the price you and I are paying? Is it worth it? Is it the price of love?

Weeks ago he heard from his medical team perhaps the worst eight words in the English language, "There is nothing more that can be done."

Ted was religious in an unconventional way. The root of the word religion is the Latin *ligio*, the same root for the word ligament, a structure that connects parts of our body. Religion means that which connects us to God, self, and others…and those others for Ted were, first and foremost, Liz and his children, Elizabeth, Andrew, and Will, along with the extended Stone family.

Someone who has spoken eloquently about these holy connections and questions raised by the risk/cost/benefit ratio of life is Dietrich Bonhoeffer. He was a German pastor, theologian, and anti-Nazi dissident who stood up against Hitler. He was imprisoned in 1943 and hung on April 9, 1945 as the Nazi regime was collapsing. Bonhoeffer sets the stage for his ultimate sacrifice in his book, <u>The Cost of Discipleship</u>. He paid a price for his convictions. I believe his decision to stand up against Hitler was the cost of his love for the Gospel and for the people of Germany.

Think of Ted as you listen to these words of Bonhoeffer in his book, <u>Letters and Papers from Prison</u>. These two sentences are essential to hear today. "It is only because Christ became like us that we can become like him. We must learn to regard people less in the light of what they do and more in the light of what they suffer."

And suffer Ted did, but let us not forget the quiet suffering of Liz and his children as each day went by. If you are looking for a modern day hero look no further than Liz.

Moving forward from his committal service... earth to earth and ashes to ashes...held earlier today at the Church of the Redeemer, everyone of us now must choose our own way down the corridor of grief to encounter the light of life mixed with regrets but always lessons learned.

I will conclude with the following words. I think they say it all.

> Grief never ends, but it changes
> It is a passage. Not a place to stay.
> Grief is not a sign of weakness.
> Nor a lack of faith
> It is the price of love. (Parkes 2010)

Words made more real as we remember and celebrate the life of Ted Stone, a time to remember a legacy of those questions which will yield us new life now and, I dare say, eternal life in our last hour.

I believe Ted is experiencing that gift of eternal life now…on his own terms…in his own religious way.

What is the price you and I are paying? Is it worth it? Is it the price of love?

## A Driven Spirit And Problem Solver

Harry French, '44 was a pillar of our school community. He served in various leadership capacities. He lived life to the fullest, drinking from the well of various experiences with his family, friends, his company, and our school. Within his last year of life, Harry broke his leg after missing a step. We stayed in contact during his recovery and rehab.

During his recovery I had a conversation with Harry that sums up his drive and spirit. I asked him how his rehab was going and his response said much about his attitude toward life. He told me that rehab started at 8 in the morning so he would wake up at 6 so that he could run through two hours of his exercises before he went to a regular two hour period of rehab with his physical therapist. I wasn't surprised when I asked him why he was doing his rehab that way, when he responded saying, "I think I will get better twice as fast if I do twice the work."

I think it was this attitude that enabled him to take a struggling flashlight company and transform it into the largest of its kind in the nation. Harry and I had a close relationship so it came as no surprise that he wanted to make sure I would do his burial service when that time came. Harry's death came quicker than his family and I expected. Given his indomitable spirit, we expected him to bounce back and return to rehab after his most recent illness.

Following is the homily I preached at the memorial service celebrating his life and legacy.

Today we do something unique and rare in this celebration of the life of Harry French. Our service today is here in this place because of the vision and commitment of Harry and the Class of 1944, including the architects Robert Venturi, '44 and his wife and partner, Denise Scott Brown. How often does the person who was, in part, responsible for building a chapel have his memorial service in that same place?

I called Denise on Saturday past to inform her of Harry's death. She was grateful for the call. She is as productive as ever but stays close to home these days. She talked about architecture in general and specifically about the joy of designing our chapel. As part of the conversation she shared with me the key ingredients that every building should have. They are Firmness, Commodity, and Light.

I said to her, "You have just described Harry French." She simply replied, I am sure with a twinkle in her eyes, "Yes!"

I learned a great deal by just listening to her describe her passion for the art of architecture.

Firmness: The building must be structurally sound and have a firm foundation. Harry was described in his EA yearbook page by the following words, "Harry may be best remembered as bustling around the <u>Scholium</u> room or bawling out a dilatory classmate for not paying his dues. Direct in his efforts, he was occasionally overbearing. In spite of his boundless energy and exuberance, he has shown himself capable and reliable in everything he has done. In his many executive capacities Harry has demonstrated his deliberation and forcefulness." That is a concise description as well of his life following his time here at the Episcopal Academy, a self-fulfilling prophecy if you will.

I found Harry to be a rock and, obviously, so did many others. He did not have an ambivalent bone in his body. He told us exactly what was on his mind, but he did it in such a way that he wasn't asking us to do something that he himself was not willing to do.

Harry would call and we would meet to talk. There was no agenda hidden or otherwise but there were occasional requests. His friends and colleagues didn't say "no" to him out of fear. They said, "yes" because they cared for and respected him. He didn't ask much unless it was something that was very important to him such as the dilatory classmate in arrears for his dues.

The love for him was palpable in his hospital room last Friday morning when he died. Stories were told and I led the service for the departed with family members around his bed. His foundation was based in an abundance of love that he shared with the people who worked for him, his family, his classmates, this school, and his friends.

Commodity: A building must have usefulness. It must be able to meet the demands and the many expectations of those who will use it. Can we think of a better way to describe Harry's endeavors and motivation as an electrical engineer, a stockbroker, an entrepreneur, a CEO, and a chairman of various boards? All of his life was about creating something that would be useful to others. I am sure that many of you have been the recipient of various kinds of flashlights he would pull from his pockets and gift to us.

My family and I built a home on the Chesapeake. We should have had Harry with us to get it right for there is one hallway that is darker than it should be. The hallway is where our thermostat was placed. Due to the lack of lighting it is difficult to read. For the longest time there has been a red flashlight about an inch and a half long that sits on top of the thermostat. You twist it to turn it on. It is easy to use. Problem solved by a very useful gift from Harry.

In architecture light equals love in the schema of this sacred space. "You are the light of the world."

That is what we are commanded to be. When we enter this sacred space we should remember that mandate and carry it out into the world when we leave.

This chapel was designed with light as a theme. It pours through the high story. Jesus' words move throughout and touch all that enter here with the importance of responding to the needs of others and the awesome responsibility of doing so. "You are the light of the world." A call to action! Harry did not have a passive bone in his body. You are the light of action. Not just any action, but the action to love. Denise also indicated that the light of a building must contain the light of delight. We must enjoy being in it. Can you think of a better word... delight...to describe Harry...he saw opportunity where others saw potential failure. He had that unforgettable smile and laughter that could not be contained. His glass was always half full.

Was it an accident or intention that his company of 350 or so is called "Streamlight"? The family wanted to make sure there would be an opportunity to meet and greet the personnel from his company to share condolences. He loved them, and they loved him. He had one of the core ingredients of a happy life...to love others and to love his work combined with his faith. How many people do you know who can't wait to get to the office, even with a walker, at the age of 92?

His family, his friends, and our school, the Episcopal Academy, shaped him in his formative years with the same ingredients that are contained in this chapel, firmness of foundation, commodity of usefulness, and the light of spirituality wrapped in the cloth of love and the moral life. Those characteristics are what he has given back to us and they are what Harry would want us to emulate through our lives.

"A city built upon a hill cannot be hid. It gives light to all in the house. In the same way let your light shine before others, so that they may see your good works and give glory to your father in heaven." (Matthew 5:14-16)

A signature command...a signature chapel...a signature life...Harry French. Amen.

## Reflections

Do you conduct your life in such a way that your good deeds are unknown to others?

Do you observe that once you get to fully know another, labels are discarded? Or are they reinforced?

Have you ever been surprised about what you thought a person you know could achieve?

Think of examples where you have not been quick to judge but have rather sought to understand?

How did the examples in this section of Loss and Legacy and Life and Legacy move you to a better place in life? Did they inspire you?

What would it take to move you toward living life from "a deeper spot"?

Do you have a physical object that was given to you that reminds you how to live life from "a deeper spot"?

If you met a famous person would you be likely to see that they are just like you?

Do you remember where you were on 9/11?

Was there an occasion in your life where you were unable to move forward until you understood (not agreed with) a person or situation?

If you drink alcohol, do you drink responsibly and encourage others to do the same?

Has someone in your life who has died continues to inform how you live today?

Is there a song that makes you immediately think of someone special in your life?

Alex Bilotti Receiving the Class of 1890 Prize for the Best Essay in Religion at Her Graduation from EA

Shells Given to Honor Life and Legacy. Both Shells Have Won in National Competitions.

Rev Throwing Out the First Pitch on Senior Day with Kyle Verbitsky

Dr. Delvin Dinkins and Rev Sporting Letter Jacket and Letter Sweater During Spirit Week

Soccer Shirt for EA-Haverford Day 2015. Pictured with Rev are Matt DePillis and Zach Viscusi

Spirit Week T Shirt for EA-Haverford Day 2015.

Spirit Week 2015

Marriage of Greg and Cos in the Princeton Chapel

Christopher Row, Rev, Bishop Rodney Michel, Reverend Zug, and
Reverend Gavin

Bert Zug Provided the Wood and Steve Muir Built This Table, a Special Gift
Upon my Retirement

Christ Chapel on the Merion Campus Designed by Vincent Kling

Altar Guild Luncheon 2015

Altar Guild Presentation of Stole and Altar Hangings

Jay Crawford, Head of School 1973-2002

Ham Clark, Head of School 2002-2013

Lou Fryman, Board Service 1979-1992, Chair 1989-1992

Fred Haab, Board Service 1975-1999, Chair 1992-1999 Pictured with his Wife, Gabby.

Rev, T J Locke, Rush Haines. Rush Haines Board Service 1985-2005, Chair 1999-1995. T J Locke Head of School 2013-

Gretchen Burke Board Service 2001-2013,
Chair 2005-2011

Gary Madeira Board Service 1994-2016, Chair 2010-2014

Ed Vick Board Service 2002-2012, Chair 2014-2017

Bishop Bartlett Preparing for the Service for Graduation

Architects of Class of 1944 Chapel, Design Meeting. Matthew Conti, John Hunter, Denise Scott Brown, Robert Venturi

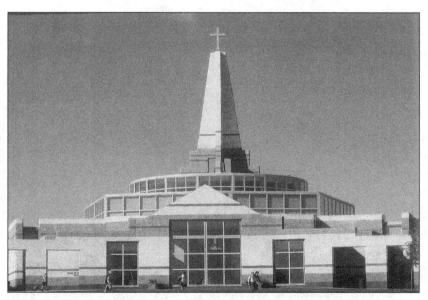

Front View of the Class of 1944 Chapel

Side View of the Class of 1944 Chapel as Seen Upon Entering the Campus

Interior View of the Class of 1944 Chapel

Rev Addressing Chapel

Interior View of the Class of 1944 Chapel

Rev Speaking in Chapel

"Physical Therapist", Sadie, Overseeing My Physical Therapy at Home

My Favorite Photo, Capturing the Spirit of Vicki, the Light of My Life.

# FREEDOM IN

# CHAPTER 8: LOVE, RELATIONSHIPS, MY FAITH, THE SHEMA

## Seven Aphorisms On The Nature Of Relationships

To introduce this section on relationships, I wish to share how I have experienced God and my Lord in my life. I turn to the very core concept of religion itself and one of its important tenets: relationships are an integral part of religious experience. A central tenet of Judaism and Christianity is the *Shema*: Jesus is asked, "Which commandment is the first of all?" Jesus answered, "The first is Hear O Israel: the Lord our God, the Lord is one; you shall love the Lord your God with all your heart, with all your soul, with all your mind, and with all your strength. The second is this, You shall love your neighbor as yourself. There is no other commandment greater than these." (Mark 12: 28-31)

The word "religion" comes from the Latin word, *ligare*, which means "to connect". Religion describes our relationship or connection to God, to others, and to self. This is why there is an emphasis on relationships in this book. This emphasis is noted also because ethical decisions never occur in a vacuum. All decisions affect others in some way, shape, or form.

In the Gospel of John, this central point of the *Shema* is underscored with Jesus' words, "This is my commandment. That you love one another as I have loved you." (John 15:12)

I believe our faith in God comes about in at least two ways, the way we treat self and the way we treat others. Many years ago I was taught that if you want to know the deepest truth about a person, ask them what they would like you to pray for. For me prayer can occur in the most unusual settings such as staring out into a sunset over the Chesapeake Bay or having a run where I see the nature of God in ways that I had not experienced before. Prayer is central to corporate worship. This is the first part of the *Shema,* "Love God!", meaning to love God with a sense of gratitude for all aspects of life.

The second part of the *Shema* is very important as well, "Love your neighbor." We experience significant physical pain in the world, such as illness, hunger, and war along with all the many forms of injustice and pain that often seem to be wrought by others on us. Jean Paul Sartre, the founder of modern existentialism, in his play, <u>No Exit</u>, writes, "Hell is the others!" (Sartre 1955) A lot of our pain is emotional in nature and caused by our relationships with others. But just as relationships can create pain, they can also create a sense of heaven coming into our lives.

I believe healthy relationships are critical to happiness, joy, and the spiritual life. Relationships are contracts we make with others. Since the dynamics of these contracts assist our spirituality--Love God! Love your neighbor--they are also a covenant so they can be stated as "we will" or "we'll". Covenants have two parts. You need to be living *both* parts of the *Shema* not just one or the other. Loving God and loving others are the central ingredients to Christianity and Judaism.

Consider the following Seven Aphorisms on the Nature of Relationships as an important part of your living the *Shema*.

## 1. Be present.

**We will be present.** When I was a boy assigned the unwanted task of cutting the grass, I would ask my father to sit outside and watch me cut the grass. I cannot imagine a more boring thing to do, but he would watch me. What I wanted was for him just to be present. He did not have to do a thing. I just needed him to be there. But as I look back on the situation today, it was also a way for me to get his undivided attention. One of the ingredients needed to build solid relationships is giving another our undivided attention.

Paying attention to another is not as easy as it seems. Being able to be genuinely interested in another requires some work on our part. Work must be done to empty ourselves so that we can fill it with the meaning created in a relationship. When we are truly present, we are able to enter another's world. People like to feel that someone else is there just for them. We must listen and not be thinking of the next thing we will say when it is our time to talk. People can sense when we feel that our words are more important than their words. We empty ourselves so that we can be filled. We empty ourselves so that we can fill another with the gift of being there.

There are times when a person will arrive in my office and they will be so overcome with emotion that they will cry during most of the time we are together. When the time is up they will stand and say, "Thank you very much," even if I have not done much of anything at all. In that moment of crying, what they want and need is just someone to be present.

**We will be available to one another.** It is important to communicate availability to those with whom you wish to build significant relationships. Availability is a state of mind. It is an attitude on our part and an important perception on another's part. To be available to another does not mean that we are always on call. The other's wish is not our command. Availability means that one should see interruptions in one's day as an opportunity to be an agent of change. Life is not packaged neatly; the real opportunities to be helpful come most frequently when we least expect them. When we communicate a willingness to make adjustments to be with another, we communicate a strong message about how we value that person. We make ourselves available to another when we communicate an investment in finding time to meet the other's need. Notice that those who are busiest, in the most creative use of that word, are usually those whose door is always open for you.

**We will recognize the power that is present when two people are in a relationship.** We will recognize the political nature of relationships, acknowledging that relationships are concerned with distribution of power. When people think of politics, they immediately think of groups or nations establishing their power or trying to determine the nature of the relationship that they will have with their people and each other. The same is true when two people meet. There are three positions one can take: one up, one down, or equal.

When one begins a relationship with another, there is often an investment in one or the other being in the one up position, putting the other person in a one down position. When someone is in need, that someone is usually in a one down position. This is the position we might experience when we go to a doctor or a teacher for help. They have knowledge or expertise we need. Contrary to what one would think, people strive to appear one up when they really feel one down or inferior. People also may put themselves in a one down position when they are not confident about their abilities, when they feel that the other has the ability to rescue them from a problem, or when the other holds power or authority over them. It is very lonely to be in either position, one up or one down. Real intimacy occurs when we meet one another on equal ground and are able to reveal our vulnerabilities to each other. When power and vulnerability are shared, we feel in control of our lives. We feel we have the ability to be masters of our destiny together.

**We will realize that our feelings and thoughts are not always known to another person.** Because we feel or think strongly about certain matters, we assume the other person must be aware. Our thoughts and feelings are like a radio within us. If the intensity or volume of the sound increases, we make the mistake of believing that those around us surely must be hearing what is going on within us. This fault in relationships is usually accompanied by the words, "But you should have known". Few of us have been given the gift of reading minds. Strong convictions, intense feelings, and important thoughts need to be shared with clarity and directness in order to avoid misunderstanding.

**We will understand how perceptions can influence our relationship with self and others.** Several studies of teacher/student relationships have proven that the way in which a teacher views a student can determine the relative success or failure of that student.

In one study, a teacher was told that a group of students who had a high ability rating was inferior in intellectual capability. The result was that those students performed significantly below their academic ability. Another teacher was told that a group of students who had an average ability rating was superior in intellectual capability. The result was that those students performed significantly above their stated academic ability. There is a tendency to become who we and others think we are.

## 2. Be empathetic.

**We will know our hot buttons and try our best not to push hot buttons in others.** All of us have hot buttons. They concern how we want to be seen by others. For example, let's say that you are a gifted musician and someone criticizes your ability to play your instrument. You may not react to this situation at all as you know that it is not true. You know how good you are. But let's say that you secretly are unsure about how attractive you appear to others. If this is the case, and someone indicates to you that you are not attractive, you may respond in anger to protect your ego.

**We will be empathetic toward others.** Empathy is so much more than sympathy. I love the Dalai Lama's description of the paradox of empathy, "If we see a person crushed by a rock, the goal is not to get under the rock and feel what they are feeling; it is to help to remove the rock." Empathy is not passive. It is active. It tries to make a situation better.

When I began my training in counseling, the approach that was very much in vogue was Carl Roger's Client Centered Therapy. In this approach the counselor is to mirror back to the person in need of help the thoughts and feelings they are expressing. The catch phrase is, "What I hear you saying is…" The challenge with this approach, in my opinion, is that it is never as active as it needs to be. It is great to have empathy, the ability to walk in their shoes, but it is equally important to accomplish understanding so that the person feels there is a solution.

**We will have each other's back.** When I am in a relationship with another, I need to feel that the other person is on my side and ready to support me unconditionally. People respond to us when they trust that our actions will be in their best interest. In other words, we want what is best for one another, even to the point of putting our own needs second. Maturity is the ability to put the needs of another before our own. We must learn to value ourselves but also be able to put ourselves second to the sanctity of the relationship. I have found that the more we put others first, the more they do so for us. It becomes a wonderfully energizing, positive cycle. But it is all a matter of the intent. Another can sense when you are giving in order to get something back. It will always feel as though there are strings attached.

**We will seek to understand more and to evaluate less.** It is always helpful to attempt to understand a situation first and to assess its ethical ramifications second. When we remove judgment from a situation or exchange, we are free to do the right thing. The human impulse is to do good; it is our basic human nature. We tolerate what we understand, even if we don't agree with it. When we understand a situation, we can move forward. Richard Chessick who wrote How Psychotherapy Heals indicated that empathy plus unconditional positive regard are the two things that are essential for someone to grow in a relationship. (Chessick 1965)

**We will affirm a person's fundamental need to be recognized and to feel needed.** Everyone needs to feel recognized, and in a more meaningful sense than Andy Warhol's statement that we all get 15 minutes of fame. Fame and recognition are very different, yet they are often confused. In fact, those who seek fame and find it often feel empty. Fame reflects more on one's reputation and less on one's character. Those who seek fame are on the wrong track. What we actually desire is recognition. Recognition is more profound; it indicates a life of purpose. We need to know that what we do matters. This recognition should come from those around us, but it must also come from within. Self-validation is necessary. We must know that our actions have meaning apart from external feedback, or we will constantly be looking for affirmation from others, making our personal happiness too dependent on the whimsical nature of the world. One of the ways to receive self-validation is to serve others anonymously. Real fulfillment comes from this kind of action, which in turn nourishes the self and leads to higher self-esteem.

**We will realize that those who shout with loud words or actions do not feel heard.** Since our thoughts and feelings are like a radio within us, we need to realize that people turn up the volume when they do not feel their sound is being heard. Those people speak louder and louder to the point of screaming. Some may also speak loudly by acting out their dissatisfaction in not being heard with behavior that causes others to notice them since this prompts a response. Their own internal radio needs to be heard before they reduce the volume of their words or deeds. We must remember that there are two ways to turn a radio down. You can pull the plug, which is similar to rejecting the person, or you can gradually lower the volume, which is similar to attempting to hear what that inner radio of the other is really saying.

**We will acknowledge that our parents play an enormous role in determining who we are.** Parents, or people who occupy that role in our lives, are the transmitters of values, behavior, and attitude. They become the reference points in all relationships. Even when we say we will not do a thing that our parents want us to do, they still remain the reference point for the opposing behavior. Sometimes this is because the parent's behavior is such that we don't want to emulate it. We are in a constant state of evolving our relationship with self and others. Expectations can assist us in setting personal goals. "I am…" "I want to be…" "I need a friend to be like…" "My image of my lover is…". But often these expectations are formed at a time in our life when we were not able to be realistic about them. If the expectation for self or others is not realistic, we may feel, "I just don't measure up," "I'm not good enough," or "He/she isn't quite what I need or want." The ideal self states, "I must be perfect" and "You must be perfect." The real self says, "No one is perfect" and "Our flaws are what unite us and makes us human." By nurturing us along, guiding us with realistic expectations, parents teach us how to form more loving relationships. What more important role could one have?

## 3. Maintain hope.

**We will help each other see the big picture and sustain hope**. I have spent a great deal of time pondering this statement or its cousin, the question, "Why do bad things happen to good people?" I face this question daily both professionally and personally.

My response now in life is, "Get over it!" The key word here is over. That said, we do not have to go it alone. This is where relationships come in; we need to rely on our relationships to help push and pull us out of adversity and the depths of challenge. Like comrades in basic training helping each other through the obstacle course, there is no shame in reaching to relationships to lend a hand to get over any wall that is in our obstacle course of life. We often become too absorbed in our troubles and see them as unfair or we see other's lives as better than ours, the grass is always greener on the other side of the meadow. Consequently, we need friends, colleagues, spouses, and even strangers to help us gain perspective. We need to help each other carry our burdens, to help us see that our burdens are not as large and overwhelming as we may think. To every struggle, there is an end. We can only grow in a relationship when we come to accept our own sorrows. There is a story about the Tree of Sorrows. Once people die and reach heaven, they are free to walk around the Tree of Sorrows and place their sorrows on the tree. After they place their sorrows on the branches, they must circle the tree again and remove someone else's sorrows from it. Once they circle the tree and see the sorrows of others, they wind up choosing their own from the tree.

Some of the great experiences in life are captured in those moments when someone believes in us when we temporarily fail to believe in ourselves. We do not forget those people. We all need a person or persons who support us unconditionally.

**We will realize that relationships are often a mutual admiration society.** Two people who are very much alike enter into a relationship because they have the same interests and the same style of personality. They seek validation from each other. We may hear two young people say with great pride, "You and I are the ultimate party animals." Two other people may look at each other and say, "Isn't it great that we don't feel the need to be competitive with others?" They feed off one another by supporting either the parts of their personality that they want to encourage as ideal or those parts of their personality that they are insecure about and question in their own minds. This can be a mutually supporting and reinforcing dynamic. It can also have a dark side, if negative or mutually harmful traits are reinforced and left unchecked in a relationship.

**We will turn shortcomings into strengths.** We all have personality traits that may seem annoying, detrimental, or just plain wrong to others. But some negative traits can become a strength or an asset in the right context. I had a very bright student who always seemed to get things done at the very last minute, but he would get the assignment in just in time. People knew this was his standard mode of operation. He drove his parents and teachers crazy. So what is he doing today? He is an editor of a newspaper in New England. He loves deadlines. We must always strive first to turn the negative we see in self and others into assets. If that fails, we must help each other see how we might change behaviors and attitudes in ways that lead to greater benefit. However, not all negatives can be transformed into something positive.

**We will not major in minor things**. We need to be aware of the fact that what is important to one may not be important to another. One of the ways of empowering a relationship is to take seriously what another person takes seriously, to honor those things that may not seem as important to us. It is equally important to identify issues that are regarded with mutual importance to be the focus of our communication in a relationship. Overlooking something that both parties feel is important, while caught in the swamp of the trivial, is unhelpful. I found myself often dealing with a particular life or death issue within our school community. At the same time, I might be speaking with a student, whose greatest concern would be which college would accept them, whether they would win their tournament that afternoon, or how well they performed on a test. All circumstances are relative, and we should never judge someone's concerns as more or less important than ours.

## 4. Live fully.

**We will control our own feelings and reactions.** Often in our relationships we try to change the other's behavior in a particular way. We think that if we could only get them to act differently or feel differently toward us, everything would be all right. The old adage that "you can't make someone love you" is true. We can't change how another person feels about us, but we can change how we respond to that person or situation. We can have influence but not ultimate control.

**We will live life with a sense of urgency and passion.** We have only been given today. For that matter, we have only been given this moment. When people are confronted with personal tragedy, they cope by living moment to moment. We see this most graphically in a critical care waiting room. This is where you witness what a passionate commitment to the now means. A shared experience of intensity can be the glue that holds a relationship together.

**We will initiate in the relationship.** We will care enough to begin. Beginning is the gesture that leads to healing. In situations of wanting something from another, there is power in the hands of the person who will not give us what we want. Withholding is an act of power. Power produces a sense of security, however false it may be. When we feel threatened in relationships, we fight or flee, and often that fleeing takes the form of withholding what we know the other wants. Initiating takes courage, for we must risk rejection, but it is the only gesture that brings healing. In my experience, this is one of the greatest contributors to stability in a relationship.

Not only do we become what we intend to be, but relationships become what we intend them to be as well. When I was reading to my young son, I often did not remember the content of the story. My intention was to give him the joy of hearing the story. My intention was not necessarily to remember the content. Relationships are similar to reading to a young child. If we go about the relationship with an intention of just having routine exchanges, largely based in function, the relationship will become routine, without much grounding in feelings or affection. If, however, we wish to create a relationship with shared mutuality, like when reading to a child, we need to have meaningful follow up and discussions about the book. This creates true dialogue and genuine shared interest.

**We will understand that we learn the most from our challenges or even failures.** We learn the most significant things about life when we don't get what we want. The hard times we encounter with another, when seen as opportunities to learn and grow, will become important pieces of nourishment for relationships. A muscle grows and develops by being stressed, and then by being given the opportunity to rest and heal. After the healing process, the muscle is stronger than ever. The same is true in relationships between people.

In relationships, we fear rejection, guilt, and vulnerability. Anger or personal pain can produce all three. In these instances, we must look for opportunities to rest and recover. Rest in this analogy means to seek renewal. The kind of rest we need is to listen to one another. After the rest of understanding comes the gain of a relationship based in new and perhaps more reality based strength to care for one another.

**We will acknowledge the power of the familiar in our lives.** We tend to enter into relationships that are comfortable, that enable us to feel at home. At home is a good expression here, for most of our "feeling environment" was developed in the context of the home, where parents were the key formative factors of our emotional life. If we were raised in an environment where criticism was a common ingredient, we may look for a relationship later in life that contains that element, even though that critical environment may not be best for us. We choose that emotional environment because it is familiar.

**We will claim the importance of friends in our lives, since we all need to belong.** Friends are the best relationship investment we have. Whatever you invest in the relationship with a friend, and it can be relatively small, you get so much more in return.

The power of friendship lies at many levels. Our sense of self, identity, and belonging are vital to our emotional health. Inclusion counters fears of rejection. A group of friends can make good intentioned people better and bad intentioned people worse. Friends have great power to help and to hurt. Sometimes a group of friends can have shared communal values that can set them against society. True friendship is unconditional.

Regardless of whether the dynamics are positive or negative, friends provide us with the important experience of being part of something greater than the self, and when we experience this, we feel personal satisfaction and meaning.

**5. Be interdependent.**

**We will understand independence as essential to interdependence.** Often we want the person with whom we are relating to be an extension of our self, but people resist becoming something that others want them to be. We should seek a relationship with someone who will help us discover who we are. This is essential to independence. When a person achieves independence, they are better able to achieve a positive state of interdependence in a relationship.

The relationship that begins with any form of dependency must move to a relationship of two independent persons becoming interdependent. The job of one person is to empower another to become truly who they are so that they reach their moment of authenticity. This is true for friendship and also for parenting.

**We will remember that we need emotional sustenance.** Sometimes those who are most hungry for the food of emotional response from others push people away through neglect, abuse, or other means. The more they need, the more they push away the potential givers of sustenance, to the point that they almost starve. If we find ourselves in a relationship with such a person, we may need to push through their resistance so that they truly feel our response.

Many who grew up during the Depression of the 1930s went without adequate food. Later in life many of these same people, after achieving financial stability, would still keep stockpiles of food in their homes. Past deprivation was still influencing their lives. This is also true of our emotional life. Many of us did not get the emotional food we needed as young people. We still hunger for it today. We need to identify moments of starvation in each other and feed that emotional hunger. At times we strive to give to others what we have not received in our lives. We have all heard someone say, "I'm not going to be like my parents when I have children. I am going to treat my children differently."

We must empower each other to discover our own way of seeking and providing this much needed emotional food. "Give a man a fish and you feed him for a day; teach him how to fish and you feed him for a lifetime."

**We will acknowledge that we look for emotions or characteristics in another person that we ourselves do not possess.** The old adage holds true that opposites attract. The outgoing person may seek as a friend or partner someone who is quiet and reserved. The risk taker may seek out another who is more cautious. What we are attempting to achieve within ourselves is a vital balance or homeostasis. For example, since risk takers may not have developed a cautious side, they seek someone else in a relationship who will stop them when they have gone too far out on a limb. Likewise, people who are very organized and have every minute of their life planned may choose for a friend or lover someone who is very spontaneous so that they, in turn, can feel a sense of spontaneity and freedom through the attitude and actions of another.

We tend to live vicariously at times through the emotions of another. I am not much fun at parties although I love to be around people, engaging them in conversation. So what did I do? I married someone who is the life of the party and is always upbeat and loves to play. Many say that she is the party. She balances this with the ability to work very hard as well.

**We will realize that another person can be a mirror of our own internal self.** Because we want to see ourselves in an ideal way that conforms to our own self-image, we are at times prevented from seeing all of the many aspects that make up our inner world. In a very real way, we do not want to know all that we are, for we sense that there are desires and wishes within that we simply do not wish to claim. They may be too repulsive for us to think of or feel; however, an emotion or desire left unacknowledged has a power over us. Awareness becomes the key to new understanding.

One may think, "I can't stand Jane. She is so selfish. She only looks out for herself." Jane may, in fact, be all of those things, but we tend to feel particularly strong about those parts of others that are also parts of ourselves.

This process is also seen in our identification with another. We think some elements of our inner life are good and desirable, but for reasons that are beyond our awareness, we are not able to claim these parts of ourselves. It is said "imitation (the process of identification) is the highest form of praise."

**We will realize that people in relationships are like questions and answers for one another.** When we enter into relationships with others, we raise certain questions for ourselves and for others, and we provide certain answers for each other about the truth of our own inner life. Questions are raised in our relationships with others. "How much do I trust her?" "Would he continue to be my friend if he knew that…?" Answers are provided by relationships as well. "I have earned your trust." "I can accept that part of you that you are struggling so hard to accept yourself." When question and answer become one unconditional love is present. My ability to love you is deepened when I experience your ability to love me.

When you think of it, an important part of the marriage service are the questions and answers. Will you have this man/woman to be your wife/husband? Will you love her, honor her, and keep her in sickness and in health? Who gives this woman to be married to this man? Her mother and I do. Will all of you witnessing these vows do all in your power to uphold these two persons in marriage? We will.

**We will acknowledge a fundamental drive in people: the more we have, the more we want, whether it is matter or emotion.** Part of us has a consumer mentality toward possessions and people. We want more things, and we have increasingly higher expectations for emotional return in relationships. Our culture has sold us a soap opera definition of love based in sentimentality and not in sacrifice. The mature person is someone who can put the needs of others first. This results in the kind of joy that cannot be experienced when we are the primary focus.

**We will acknowledge that intimacy requires distance.** We see this lesson graphically displayed in the animal world. Porcupines need to huddle during the winter months to keep warm. They need that kind of intimacy for survival. But soon they begin to stick each other inadvertently with their quills, and they must distance themselves from one another in order to survive. Our relationships are similar in that we engage in the ebb and flow of intimacy and distance. Both the warmth of intimacy and the autonomy of realizing our own uniqueness in the world are needed. One without the other would put our emotional survival into question. We can only experience intimacy when we encourage the other to experience his or her individuality. We will be most able to truly experience our individuality, to move to interdependence, when we have a base formed in an intimate relationship.

**We will acknowledge that in the relationship between two people, a third person is present.** For example, relationships between lovers are always love triangles. Two people cannot enter into a relationship as lovers without an invisible "third person" overseeing the relationship. That third person, referred to by some as our conscience, comprises all those people who have influenced our values. Our conscience speaks to us constantly as we consider what is right and what is wrong, what we should and should not do. Hollywood depicts the issue by showing someone contemplating doing something wrong with hand on chin. Next, we see the devil appear over one shoulder saying, "Go ahead, do it." An angel quickly appears over the person's other shoulder saying, "No, that's not right. Don't do it." Simplistic as it may seem, that visual image points to a reality in our relationships.

There is a saying, "all of our relationships with others become part of who we are." These internalized images and voices become incorporated into our identity and personality.

## 6. Confront challenges.

**We will not avoid feelings of guilt, rejection, and vulnerability.** We spend enormous amounts of energy avoiding these emotions. We do anything to belong. We try to avoid feelings of vulnerability by building structures of permanence and success. Since these emotions can dominate our decision making and actions, we need to be mindful of when they are determining too much of our lives.

All of us who are engaging life find ourselves under constant evaluation. For example, we are evaluated regarding our appearance and our ability to be successful at some task. Guilt and rejection come with the territory of being evaluated.

All of us feel guilt. It was referred to in the Middle Ages as "O Happy Guilt" for it kept human beings morally in check. But we need to be careful not to let guilt become shame. Guilt is "I did something wrong". Shame is "I am something wrong". Shame can take us to a very dark place for there are times when we mistake shame for guilt, so we must be aware of this danger.

**We will realize emotional pain in relationships stems from challenges to our self-esteem and our sense of belonging.** Examine your self-esteem or your desire to belong when you are experiencing emotional pain. We all need to feel good about ourselves. Belonging and self-esteem are closely linked. We all yearn to belong, particularly when our self-esteem is low. The group to which we belong becomes our primary identity as we seek to carry out a shared purpose. We want to belong because it is one of the best emotional investments available. A group that we long to be part of can bring out the best or the worst in us. As a counselor, I always sought to analyze both belonging and self-esteem; if neither were present, I knew that much help would be needed, and fast.

**We will examine the price we are paying in our relationships.** We are all paying a price in life. What is it? Is it preparing us to love? If not, should we change our course of action? What are the values that are determining the nature of this price? Everyone is getting something from a relationship. We know that there are givers and takers in the world. Givers do things without thought of getting something back. Takers, on the other hand, do things so that they will get a return on their giving. Friendships and relationships of all kinds rise to the level of greatness when two givers are giving mutually.

**We will strive to assist one another in achieving greater self-acceptance.** We are at our best when we operate from the premise that we do not have to justify our feelings or any other of our personal attributes. Your hair color is your hair color. Your feelings are your feelings. Period. Those feelings (like hair color) should not be up for debate. When we deny a negative feeling or emotion, we give it more power. When we acknowledge a negative feeling, we can bring it into the light and transform it to a higher good. All evil is good waiting to be transformed.

By recognizing all feelings, we are free to change them or to continue to involve them in our repertoire of life, but acknowledgment or "emotional ownership" of these feelings or parts of ourselves must come first. We all possess an inner ideal of who we think we are. Sometimes this inner ideal does not conform to the feedback others give to us. If this is the case, we become defensive, not allowing the outer picture that others have to touch our image of who we are. The more we get in touch with our true inner self, the better we will be able to realistically assess our role in the world. Does this outer feedback conform to our truth or not? Blaming, denying, rationalizing, and placating are several common ways we attempt to change the outer impression to match the inner perception.

**We will acknowledge the importance of the role of criticism in our lives.** The criticism of us by others can teach us some important lessons about how we truly feel about our own selves. We tend to react defensively with great anger when we secretly believe that criticism by another is describing who we really are. I turn again to Randy Pausch's words of wisdom in the <u>Last lecture</u>, "When people criticize us they communicate that they are still invested in us. We should start to worry when people are not criticizing us for that may communicate that they have given up on us." We should try to remember that there is always an ounce of truth in any criticism that comes our way. We just need to find it and address it.

Imagine someone coming up to an Olympic runner and stating, "You're really out of shape and not very motivated, and you have to be one of the slowest people who I have ever seen." The runner—and anyone who overheard this accusation—would probably shake his or her head and wonder what planet this individual making these outrageous comments had been living on. The words of criticism would not stick. It would not register, for an Olympic runner is sure of his or her physical prowess and motivation to be the best.

Now let us take a look at another situation where the criticism sticks. A particular student does extremely well in all of her courses. By everyone's assessment she is a gifted thinker. But this student secretly feels that she has fooled others into believing she is intelligent. She may be saying to herself, "If they only knew how stupid I really am, they would laugh at me." Her internal perception does not conform to her external reality. She receives the highest marks on tests in all of her courses. Then one day she gets a B on a math test. A classmate makes the offhand criticism, "You're really not so smart after all!" The criticism sticks. It registers, for no amount of external reinforcement of how well she is doing can combat that inner voice of doubt about herself. Ninety-nine people could say to her, "You are the finest student in the school." One could say, "You are not so intelligent." She will believe the one. This criticism hurts and stops her. A change of perspective is needed. She needs help from herself and from others to see that she needs to work just as hard correcting her "inner grading system" as she works in achieving high grades in her courses.

**We will acknowledge the fact that life is a two edged sword.** One of the basic principles of life, and in particular of relationships, is that every dimension of a relationship can work for us or against us. However, it is more helpful to see these opposites as one positive charge and one negative charge. It is not helpful to think in terms of categories such as good or bad. Like the battery, when both polar aspects are acknowledged, they can bring power to the relationship. If we deny or repress feelings regarded as negative, these negative feelings will increase in power.

For example, let us look at independence/dependence, compliance/defiance, and responsibility/irresponsibility. People who communicate extreme independence are often guarding against feelings of dependence. People who are so compliant, doing everything we wish them to do, will manifest a defiant part of themselves in some way. Likewise, extremely defiant people have a compliant side they keep secretly hidden from public perception. Those who are highly responsible enjoy the relief of being able to be childlike or irresponsible in their behavior. Hence, some of the most driven people will seek a means to allow their irresponsible side to take over.

The key is balance. We see this in the basic elements of fire and water. Fire can burn you or provide heat for survival. Water is essential for life, but too much can cause a destructive flood. The key balancing agent is experiencing love in the unconditional sense from God or another or from within our own self. As a theologian once said, "When we discover how to love, we will have discovered fire for the second time." (Teilhard deChardin 2008)

### 7. Develop trust.

**We will recognize that trust is the steel with which the bridge of a relationship is built.** When adolescents are asked to comment on what they feel is the most important aspect of friendship, they are quick to indicate that trust is essential. The same is true for adults. We only share those inner feelings we cherish with another when we know they will be treated with ultimate respect and care. We need to be the bearers of each other's secrets. A survey conducted in our school revealed that over 90% of the students in Middle and Upper School thought trust was the most important ingredient in their relationships.

Honoring expectations is essential to build trust. When you think about it, a great deal of anger is based in unfulfilled expectations. If someone says that they will pick you up at 6 in the evening and they don't arrive until 7, you become angry. The negative power of unfulfilled expectations creates that anger. Think of the last time that you were really angry with someone. Was an unfulfilled expectation the cause of that anger?

**We will acknowledge that we have an underlying need to possess material things and people.** We want to say, "You are mine." There are various reasons for wanting others to be ours. Parents, friends, and lovers want others to be exclusively theirs because they always "know what is best for the other". From our own perspective, we know what has brought meaning and joy to us, and we assume this experience, idea, attitude, or value must be good for others. Often it is, but often it is not. Indeed, the way to hell is paved with good intentions.

For parents, friends, or lovers, the other could be what provides them with meaning, so they wish to have control over that important feeling. "Without her, I am nothing." "Without him, I would be alone." The goal of relationships should be to move from an attitude of strings attached to an attitude of unconditional acceptance. This creates a movement from conditional to unconditional love. In conditional love, people act out of fear; in unconditional love, people act out of respect. Their goodness is all-encompassing, existing in both the private and public domain.

**We will acknowledge the fundamental importance of responsibility and balance in our relationships.** Responsibility is a direct outgrowth of respect. When we feel respect for self and others, we also feel accountable to act in the best interest of all concerned. Best interest is defined by our values, principles, and personal code of behavior. Relationships are in many ways like contracts. As relationships evolve, rules develop. Certain subjects can be talked about, others cannot. Relationships change, and so must the rules. If change does not occur, the relationship becomes stagnant and oppressive. If rules do not change, conflict occurs because of mixed expectations. Clear contracts assist in the development of clear expectations. Clear expectations assist in turning conflicts in relationships into a creative experience.

Relationships are a balancing act. The image of a juggler comes to mind. We are like the juggler. The more we become intent on balancing the many items in our life—desire to possess/desire to empower, desire to love/desire to be loved, desire to give/desire to get, strings attached/strings cut, fear/respect, and so on—the more exciting and meaningful our lives will be. The more successful we are in balancing the polarities in our lives, the more we will be able to succeed in our relationships.

## Love

Love is a difficult word to wrap our minds around, but we over use it. We love pizza. We love baseball, etc. It is a word that needs to be understood. In my Ethics course I taught the nature and characteristics of love, that love is one of the two pillars that support ethical action. The other pillar is Justice. I based my observations on the Greek understanding of the four loves that were explored by C. S. Lewis' in his book, The Four Loves. (Lewis, 1960) I added to his thinking by exploring the Greek words in greater depth with the application of the tenants of psychology, theology, and philosophy. I also incorporated what I learned from students and adults along life's way.

*Storge* is the Greek word for the love of parents. Parents have shaped us more than anyone else in our lives. When I ask students the question, "Who has determined the most of who you are today?" They answer 99% of the time that it is a parent or parenting figure.

I witnessed situations in my 38 years as a school chaplain in which an older brother took on the role of the parent. Sometimes we desire to become exactly the opposite of our experience with our parents. Still, parents are the reference point.

Parents tend to love their children unconditionally. They can see the good in their children when others cannot. They love the ostensibly unloveable. They produce a warm and familiar environment for their children. They also have the need to say "mine" and be possessive in their approach to their children.

For example the parent who has always been a great athlete will, at times, want his child to become an extension of his dream. This cannot occur when the child has a more intense interest in playing the violin. Parents can want their child to be an extension of their own self. They assume that what they find enjoyable is what will also be enjoyable to the child. It may be or may not be. This is natural. Think about when you saw a great movie and one of your friends was not able to attend. The tendency is to encourage them to attend because you enjoyed it. They may see the same movie and think that it is terrible and wonder why you recommended it.

*Storge* assumes much! This is an important characteristic. You don't really have to wonder whether parents are going to let you into the house to have dinner. Parents on the other hand don't worry that you won't come home. But something that is assumed can be taken advantage of. Parents can take advantage of children and children can take advantage of parents. *Storge* is a dynamic in friendship as well. We can assume that a friend will do one thing and they surprise us and do another.

*Philia* is a Greek word that means friendship. There are many different levels of friendship. Some friends are people that you hang out with while others may be part of your inner circle where you can discuss issues that are very important to you.

Friendship always begins with a shared purpose. In some way, shape or form, the friendship is forged by doing something, usually important, together. The troops in Vietnam were very diverse in nature in terms of backgrounds and interests but once they left the military they became friendly with one another based on their common experience of war. They choose people who were right there with them because they did not have to explain what the experience was like. Research suggests that their war experience became a glue that bonds them together.

Friends tend to have a moral code or an immoral code. It is not written down but you know exactly what you can and cannot do. It is a set of covert rules.

Whenever there is a group of friends there is always an in group and an out group. Anytime we say "us", we are implying that there is a "them". Anytime we say "we", we are implying that there is a "they".

Friendship is a powerful emotion. The two emotions that are most essential in our lives are self-esteem and a sense of belonging. These are primary emotional needs. Notice that I say a "sense" of belonging. There are times when we can have a large number of friends but don't sense that we belong for we harbor thoughts of, "if they only knew what I really believe they would reject me."

Think about it. With friends you get two things at once. It is like that favorite item in a grocery store when we can see that we can buy the item and get a second one free. We give a boost to our self-esteem with friends. We tend to gather with people who make us feel better not worse. It is one of the main reasons we have friends. They know what it is like to be us. There is also the sense of belonging that we get by being part of the group. We feel surrounded by support and that can take us out of ourselves. Loyalty to friends is what creates peer pressure. Alone I may not be so great, but together we are magnificent. The power of the group can be seen as a driving force making well intentioned people better and bad intentioned people worse. Think of the power of a cancer support group with power to do good, and think of the KKK as a group with power to do bad.

Friendship can be the basis of all "isms" and prejudices. When we find an innocent victim who did nothing to deserve our contempt, friendship is a powerful glue to hold the group dynamic together. The best way at times to feel included is to push someone out of the group. The most up to date analysis of bullies is that they engage in this behavior for they have such low self esteem that they feel as though they don't belong.

*Eros* is the Greek word for sexuality. Here I am referring to something that is beyond the sex act itself. I am referring to the chemistry of human sexuality. When passion enters a relationship, reason usually leaves the equation of this kind of love. Adolescence is a time when hormones are raging for both the male and the female. Sometimes their actions have us wondering about their sanity. Again passion causes reason to step aside. Our behavior makes perfect sense to us while our friends may see our behavior as self-destructive. Why would a happily married man leave his wife and children for her? Why does a public servant lose the respect of his constituency by having an affair with someone else?

*Agape* is God's love for us seen by C. S. Lewis as holding the natural or biological loves mentioned above together. Each love is like a magnet wherein both the positive and the negative charge are needed. Sometimes this is expressed as, "Life is a two-edged sword." Everything can work for us or against us. The Love of God is the source of all love, and our loves are a reflection of God's love as the primary source.

### Reflections

What do you consider to be the heart of your faith?

Are their particular ways that you connect with God, others, and yourself?

Think of examples.

Choose three "We will(s)" that you feel describe what you believe is important to you in your relationships with others. Recall examples of when each of these "We will(s)" occurred.

Consider examples of when the dynamics of *Storge, Philia, Eros,* and *Agape* were helpful to you in understanding your life.

# CHAPTER 9: PERSPECTIVES FOR A FULFILLING LIFE

## Temporary and Permanent Mindsets

Have there been certain ways you thought you should act in order to be accepted by yourself or by others? How did you handle those behaviors? Do you feel you were successful in incorporating them into who you are today? Did you turn away from those behaviors when you thought they were no longer helpful to you? One negative behavior that comes to mind is the quest to achieve perfection. People who chase perfection never feel that they measure up to this unrealistic standard. The quest for perfectionism tends to go along with the whole human package whether we like it or not. Perfectionism can be deceitful. It can creep up on you when you least expect it. One of my mantras for learning has been "learn to fail or fail to learn".

In the 2018 French Open, Sloane Stephens was defeated by the number one tennis player in the world, Simona Halep. Sloane had a high regard for Halep and following the match paid her opponent a great tribute. After taking time to reflect on her own performance, Sloane posted an inspiring message, "You win or you learn, but you never lose." (Stephens 2018)

In my years of teaching I have observed that the students who struggle the most are those who have not had a "positive failing experience" from which they have learned and grown. Carol Dweck has a model that is very helpful in framing one's life in a way to address failure and create a positive experience from it. If you have failed a test (or submit where you think that you have failed) and

333

feel that it is a permanent issue for your life, you will be find yourself depressed, possessing a negative attitude toward yourself, and the inability to cope with moving forward. (Dweck 2006)

If after failing a test you say to yourself or others, "I am stupid. I will never be able to do well in this course," you lock yourself into that mindset. If, on the other hand, you feel that your poor performance is a temporary condition and that you have identified the issues of why you didn't do well, then you will be able to say to yourself, "I didn't do well on this test, but I know what I need to do to correct things in order to do well on the next evaluation." This attitude will enable you to see life as a challenge but one that you feel confident in addressing as you move forward.

People who frame life in a temporary way as they address issues take baby steps. That is one of the key tenets of Alcoholic Anonymous, still the preferred treatment platform for alcoholism today. They stress the mantra, "Take one day at a time." That approach can also be applied to most problem solving.

The person who has a permanent mindset feels that change is not possible. All of us feel this way from time to time. This mindset destroys hope. Individuals with permanent mindsets take a long range view that stifles progress. I once met with a parent who was paralyzed by the thought that her child would not be admitted to Princeton. The child was in first grade. Taking the long haul perspective is not the way to problem solve.

The work of Edison and Einstein that led to their scientific discoveries illustrates that even for the greatest problem solvers, baby steps and many failures along the way were the reason they achieved so much. There are few overnight successes in life. The people that seem like overnight successes usually combined years of practice or work that met with good luck or providence!

## *Positive Psychology, Mindfulness, Flow, And Christian Mysticism*

There have been times when I have attended a function where minutes felt like hours, as though I were crawling through a desert. I also have had the opposite experience where hours seemed like just minutes and time seemed to stand still. We call this latter experience "flow", a psychological phenomenon studied extensively and presented by Dr. Mihaly Csikszentmihali in his seminal book, <u>Flow: The Key to Unlocking, Meaning, Creativity, Peak Performance and True Happiness</u>. I was invited to attend a seminar of a small group of people at Princeton where I had the opportunity to engage Mihaly Csikszentmihali, Marty Seligman, Tal Ben Shahar, and Barry Schwartz. The purpose of the seminar for me was to learn more about some cutting edge perspectives in psychology and how they intersect with religion. Most world religions, along with the experience of mindfulness, contain elements of mysticism that are found in the ideas of Csikszentmihiali's flow. (Csikszentmihalyi 2008).

Certainly such experiences filled that part of me as psychologist, but something was missing. That something was mindful Christianity, also referred to as Christian mysticism, a practice that dates back to Jesus himself. Christian mysticism is the direct experience of God.

Jim Burklo refers to my missing ingredient as Christian spirituality or "mindfulness plus". Burklo explores such mystics as the unknown author of the <u>Cloud of Unknowing</u>, and the work of Meister Eckhart. Instead of learning about God, Christian mysticism, is knowing God directly. ((Burklo 2014) It does require living in the present, as we are informed by our past, and having trust in a hopeful outcome in the future. An important passage of scripture, "God comes as a still small voice" (1 Kings 19:12), calls us to begin a mystical journey. I would also suggest a careful reading of Psalm 46 that includes, "Be still and know that I am God." Galations 2:20 describes the state of Christian mysticism as "It is no longer I who live, but it is the Christ who lives in me."

A large group of teachers at EA were trained in Mindfulness Studies. This initiative was based on one of the important books on mindfulness by Jon Kabat-Zinn, <u>Full Catastrophe Living</u>. (Kabat-Zinn 1990). The goal was to reduce stress in both students and faculty and to guide students to practice living in the moment. Our hope was that this would result in students focusing better in class.

One of the past members of the Religion department, The Reverend Timothy Morehouse, a brilliant scholar, practiced ways for the meeting of the religious with the secular. He is now Chaplain and Chair of the Religion Department at the Trinity School in New York City. Tim would begin each class with what students and he referred to as the "Morehouse Minute". The lights would be turned off in the classroom. The students were encouraged to think about nothing. Although they found it hard to do initially, they increasingly found this to be an important part of their day. You would think this minute of silence would be an easy task but it wasn't. In the beginning students were more comfortable with the noise that usually surrounded them.

During the last several years before my retirement we would have silence in chapel as part of the prayers. The students valued their time in chapel, referring to it as the "pause that refreshes". They took prayer seriously as could be illustrated by the length of our prayer list. A lot of the names on the list were by student requests. We were blessed to have had faculty and students speak in chapel about the benefits of this practice of silence and mindfulness, giving guidance on how to incorporate it into everyday living.

I have always been interested in the relationship between science and religion. I like the image of one man, the scientist, climbing a mountain and another man, the religious leader, climbing up the other side. They meet at the top and shake hands with one another.

I remembered this image from words I read by Robert Jastrow in his book, God and the Astronomers. In a statement that concludes the book he describes this relationship between science and religion best. "For the scientist the story ends like a bad dream. He has scaled the mountains of ignorance; He is about to conquer the highest peak; as he pulls himself over the final rock, he is greeted by a band of theologians who have been sitting there for centuries." (Jastrow 1992)

One of our students gave a chapel address about the importance of mindfulness. She referred to FOMO, Fear Of Missing Out. FOMO has become a problem in our culture. The goal in reaching success in this context is to have many Facebook connections so we can constantly check on people or receive updates from them.

FOMO is also problematic because you only see smiling faces as you check on the people you have friended. The message transmitted is that everyone is happy and has a better life than you. If you are struggling in your life, you could come to the conclusion that you just don't measure up. This can lead to sadness, envy, and depression. We have a culture of "noise" that is in need of more silence.

There has been much written about the perils of being constantly connected via our iPhones. This constant connection is the modern day version of the temptations that confronted Jesus in his forty days in the wilderness where he had the possibility of many distractions related to power. I feel it is time to offer an option of silence in our schools. A suggestion would be to guide the students to focus on their religious connection if they have one. This could be facilitated if their school has a religious heritage. In my case it would be Christianity. Psychology and Christianity could come together to reach the peak of a mountain of challenges. What better place than a school to begin this cultural change in young people. EA faculty members are evaluated by students. One of the most important pieces of feedback I have received from a student is, "You teach this course as though my life depended on it." I believe their souls and psyches do depend on interactions with faculty, staff, and fellow students.

### Family

In my address at the Burial Office for Fred Haab, Board Chair and friend, I indicated that Fred's focus in life was on his family even though he made significant contributions to the business world and to endeavors in the community. Family life is at its best when it becomes the *larva dei,* the mask of God, meaning God is at work in the relationships that make up family life. I share that focus with Fred and others. The following is a snapshot of my family who "light up my life".

## *Thaddeus and Meredith*

Thaddeus was your usual first child and a parent's dream. He was engaging, caring, and full of energy with many varied interests. He was easy at all levels. He loved music and was drawn to the classical realm, even at a young age. He inherited his great grandfather's baritone horn, beginning lessons at only 7 years old. His teacher could not believe a child that young could get such beautiful music out of such a large instrument. A few years later Thad added piano lessons and soon became highly proficient as a pianist as well. He was not so interested in sports. When he was 6 years old we signed him up for T-ball. He spent his T-ball time in the outfield, either looking up at the sky or in the grass searching for bugs. One day he raised a most important question, "Exactly why am I doing this?" We removed him from that torture at once.

Thad had many interests mostly focusing on his love of nature. He collected and catalogued rocks and shells and he took great delight in sharing this passion with anyone who would listen. A theme throughout his early years was that he took full advantage of every opportunity to learn.

He was a student leader at EA, '90, where he was elected by his peers to serve as the Senior Warden of the Student Vestry. Thad went on to Princeton University where he really came into his own. He double majored in Music and History of Science, each semester taking the maximum number of courses allowed.

Thad was the student conductor of the Princeton University Orchestra his senior year. He planned and led a tour of England and Europe for the orchestra. This was no small undertaking. The experience required great detail and a business sense. Jay and Rosemary Crawford went with us to see Thad conduct the Princeton Orchestra. We lived across the main drive of the school from the Crawford Family so for years they listened to Thad practice the baritone horn. In the beginning it sounded like the mating call of a moose. We wanted them with us to see the reward for their patience and to be present for a very special moment.

On the weekend of Thad's graduation from Princeton, we were ushered into a room before the graduation service. In that room he was inducted into Phi Beta Kappa. Before that moment we didn't know he had achieved this distinction as he just never brought it up.

After Princeton Thad was awarded a Fulbright Scholarship. He had applied to study orchestral conducting at the University of Leipzig, Germany. After his time there he returned stateside to apply for admission to Yale in the PhD program to continue his study of conducting. Yale accepts just two or three students from around the world into this graduate program each year. Thad made it to the final round, but was ultimately passed over twice after his years of preparation. When he returned home after his first attempt to gain admission, I asked him what he was going to do. There was not a pause. He replied, "I guess I will have to work harder."

When he was denied admission to Yale to study conducting, Thad then decided to take his passion for music and the arts and use it to advance those elements in Philadelphia. Over the past 15 years he has founded and built Culture Works Greater Philadelphia, a management services organization for the arts. It is based in Philadelphia but has morphed into Culture Works Commons Management, a national initiative. He works tirelessly, always with a passion in his quest to bring enrichment to others through the arts. Thaddeus founded Culture Trust Greater Philadelphia, an affiliate of Culture Works, which is a shared non-profit administrative platform for projects and organizations. It is the first of its kind serving arts and heritage in the country. He was hailed as a visionary voice in contemporary arts by the <u>Philadelphia Inquirer</u>.

Thad also finds time to serve his community is other ways. He has served on the board of the Russell Byers Charter School and he heads the community association, Overbrook Farms Club, in his neighborhood. Thaddeus is married to Meredith Rainey. It was a joy for me to bless their marriage in a location that is near our home on the Chesapeake. What a wonderful memory I have from that occasion!

Meredith has been a member of various ballet companies. He began in the Pennsylvania-Milwaukee Ballet just after graduation from an arts-centered high school. Once that company split he became a permanent resident of Philadelphia and a popular member of the Pennsylvania Ballet. His skill resulted in his promotion to become the first African American soloist in the company. We delighted in watching his performances and observed that he always got the loudest applause from the audience. He is a crowd pleaser as his warm, kind personality shows through his art. Meredith's accomplishments and popularity have been memorialized. He is the central figure in a mural installed on a building at 13th and Locust Streets in Philadelphia.

Since Meredith retired from the Pennsylvania Ballet, he has focused his talents on choreography and teaching. He has been commissioned to create works for the Pennsylvania Ballet, Ballet *Classico National de Columbia*, the Brandywine Ballet, Ballet X, Hubbard Street 2, and Phrenic New Ballet. His work is performed throughout North and South America and Europe including the Miami International, and the International Ballet Festival of Ecuador. His work has also appeared at the first and second International Ballet Festival of Cali (Colombia) and Madrid, Spain.

Meredith has taught ballet at Bryn Mawr College, Swarthmore College, and Muhlenberg College. He is an adjunct professor at Drexel University and Master Lecturer at the University of the Arts. He traveled to France for two summers to fulfill some of the requirements to receive a Masters of Fine Arts in Dance. He brings his charisma to all he does. His expectations are high for the students in his classes. His loving nature and kindness have added much to our family life.

## Adam and Courtney

Adam, born 13 months after Joanna's death, was a loving, sensitive child. His love, energy, and high-spirited personality helped move our family along in our process of healing. Two words that come to mind to describe Adam are warmth and grit. In his initial years at EA he exhibited a learning difference that defied identification at the time. The psychologist who tested him told us that, in her opinion, Adam would never be able to get through EA. She further stated that she felt he would never be able to attend college.

We set about getting him help to compensate for his learning difference, as it was called, but we were advised to withdraw him from EA for a few years. We enrolled him in the local elementary school because we felt it offered proper support for Adam's learning needs. Our home was on the main drive of the EA campus so each day as Adam waited for the school bus, he had to watch his friends arriving at the school where he yearned to be. This situation planted the seed of grit in him. He did well at the public school, integrating skills to compensate for his learning difference, but his goal during the four years he spent there was to return to EA for sixth grade.

Adam did return to EA in the 6th grade. He graduated from EA in '98 in good standing and went on to graduate from Temple University with high honors, having studied in their honors level program. Adam's sense of adventure and his high spirits presented us with challenges as he grew and matured. Later in life I received a letter that all parents would want to receive. In it he stated, "Thanks for not giving up on me. I don't recognize the person I was then." Adam was a Religious Studies major at Temple, but after graduation he decided to defer graduate school for an entry level job at Whole Foods. He started with the company in the seafood department and soon became the Mid-Atlantic manager for that division. Adam completed his work for Whole Foods, managing a local store, but his grit and courage led him to embrace his true passion.

He and his wife, Courtney, bought an organic farm in Connecticut. Watching him work the long hard hours that he does is interesting and inspirational because he goes about all the hard labor like a little child filled with joy and wonder. He is a mainstay in his church and enjoys the special life of being part of a farm community in which the members take care of one another. He is surrounded by beauty as their farm is located on a designated scenic road.

Adam's extensive knowledge of organic (regenerative) farming is almost totally self-taught, and he shares his knowledge by giving lectures on organic farming and sustainable food culture. He has been recognized for his intellect and ability to make complicated theory simple. He has also traveled to Guatemala with his church group to assist those who struggle with abject poverty.

Our daughter in law, Courtney, also worked for Whole Foods. Like Adam, she began at an entry level position and finished her work with the company functioning as the manager of the Whole Foods store in Providence, Rhode Island. She did this for the first four years of their farm production, as they were establishing the business. She is now Executive Director of Marketing, Communications, and Customer Relations for their business, Unbound Glory Farm. She does those tasks when she is not working side by side with Adam in the field. Courtney is strong and loving. She is a talented University of Pennsylvania graduate, a school that many of her family have attended. She was just inducted into the Hall of Fame at her high school for being part of her championship field hockey teams.

She is quick to laugh and sees the positive in all her endeavors that now include teaching yoga, nutrition counseling and writing about sustainability of food production in different magazines. Back to my cousin's words of wisdom, she has more energy than anyone and can also outwork anyone.

Adam and Courtney make a perfect pair as they share the same interests, purpose, and dedication to their farming business. Their wedding occurred at Lighthouse Point Park in New Haven. I was honored to officiate. The wedding service itself was on the beach, and the reception was held in an historic, glassed-in structure that houses a carousel. Vicki and I hosted a beach barbecue the following day at Hotchkiss Grove where many of Courtney's family members live. The wedding experience was perfect in every way, one of the best weeks of my life.

## Spencer

My youngest son, Spencer, was born into our family when Adam was 9 years old and Thad was 16. Vicki has achieved distinction among her sorority sisters as being the sister who gave birth at both the youngest age and at the oldest age. This spacing resulted in the feeling of having three separate families. Thad went off to Princeton when Spencer was just two years old. Still Spencer is so much like his brother with regard to his musical talents and creativity that it demonstrates nature over nurture. He studied piano from an early age, progressing into proficiency that enabled him to enter competitions. Spencer was driven from his earliest years. He also declared early on his passion for movies and theater. He thrives on being always engaged.

Spencer, '07 took the most demanding course of study at EA selecting AP courses whenever possible. He had the lead role in his first grade play, The Frog Prince, and continued as a major cast member in nearly every production throughout his years at EA. He excelled in all academic pursuits and won the prize for excellence in History at graduation. He knew his next educational experience would have to include both theater and academics.

Spencer was admitted to the Tisch School of the Arts at New York University, but he ultimately decided to study at Northwestern University where he could experience the balance he desired. He graduated from Northwestern with high honors, majoring in theater and business. He also earned certificates in musical theater and marketing. We delighted in our trips to Northwestern to see him perform in the student productions. He had leading roles in Bye Bye Birdie and Ragtime. Spencer's passion for movies and theater continues. He has spent the time since college pursuing this passion first in New York but mostly in LA. He is constantly going to auditions for acting roles, but the part of the industry that is coming together for him is writing. He is discovering his gifts in that realm.

LA is a tough town and his choice of profession is a high-risk, potentially high reward, journey. He is resilient and focused. He has scripts in the works that are progressing through the very slow process of production. He is being mentored and encouraged by wonderful friends. At the time of the writing of this book Spencer has completed his first short film. He wrote the script, directed the filming, had the leading role, and wrote some of the music for the sound track. He declared the project was the hardest work he had ever engaged in, but it allowed him to experience all the aspects that must come together to produce a movie. Feedback from the cast and crew was glowing. Participants indicated to him that they felt empowered by the experience. During the shooting of the movie, we had a phone call from him during the filming where he said, "This is the best day of my life. This is what I was meant to do." This hard work was duly rewarded. He was awarded the distinction of Best Actor and Best Short Film at the Brentwood and Pacific Palisades Film Festival.

As I write these brief statements, I am reminded that all three of my children and their spouses have lived lives with the common thread of "taking the road less traveled". They have the ability to outwork me and to take risks that I would not have had the courage to take. What more could I ask for? They are passionate about life and enjoy helping others. All of them are deeply moral and ethical in their deliberations and actions. In a recent discussion my oldest son, Thaddeus, said something that staggered me. He said, "Do you know how we were able to do everything we did as your children? We had major back up in you and mom."

As I mentioned before there is a standard family joke that I am always trying to give them vocational advice or link them up with various connections I have. The biblical maxim holds true that "a prophet is not welcome in his own land". They all want to do it themselves. No surprise to me!

There are certain things about me that annoy my children, but when I think of the big three, they would be as follows: I can't help but give vocational advice to them or their spouses. It is just what I do. I know a famous dermatologist who has the same experience. If she spotted something on the skin of one of her children and pointed it out, they would brush it aside. Meanwhile her patients have to wait a long period of time to see her as she is so highly regarded.

When we planned to travel to a foreign country, I would study the language enough to cover the basics, but when I tried to speak to a native somehow my conversational style lacked much to be desired. My children got very good at acting as though they didn't know me. Imagine their embarrassment when I acted out my words as if I was playing the game of charades.

Whenever I would be with one of my children's friends who I didn't know well, I would ask what they majored in at college. When the friend would leave, they would be quick to point out,

"Dad, nobody asks people what they majored in at college. You are the only one!"

I was brought up short on this issue when I was with one of our alumni, John Salvucci '98, who had served as the Senior Warden of the Student Vestry. He was a great leader and a fun person to be around. Everyone loved him. When he was a student at Penn I knew he was on their soccer team but I didn't know his major. In typical form I inquired about his major. He replied, "International Relations!" When I asked him what that major was all about, he got a smile on his face and said, "I have no idea, but doesn't it sound good when you hear it."

## The Road Less Traveled

There is an underlying dynamic in people that creates this ability to take the road less traveled, to work hard, and to take risks. I learned about this underlying dynamic from Chaim Potok, the author of The Chosen and other novels. Chaim Potok authored popular books and was a rabbi in the conservative tradition. All of our students on the Merion Campus were required to read The Chosen.

Potok was influenced by Evelyn Waugh's book, Brideshead Revisited. It is a story about different cultures that co-exist on an English estate. All of Potok's novels deal with the confrontation of different cultures and difficult choices that need to be made as a result of encountering different perspectives.

I asked Rabbi Potok to come to our campus and to speak about his novels and the values in life that are necessary to confront different cultural values. As a result of this invitation, we became friends. We certainly represented two different cultures, but somehow we found a lot of common ground. He told me a story that I have passed on to my children and others so that they would know that I understood their effort and passion on the road less traveled.

Chaim shared with me that in the conservative Jewish culture it is frowned upon to become a writer of popular fiction as opposed to scholarly works for academia. In this manner, he experienced his own core cultural confrontation. He wanted to write novels.

His mother discouraged it. Then his popularity took off and he was recognized as a brilliant novelist. His book, <u>The Chosen</u>, sold 3,400,000 copies. He still felt his mother's disapproval. Once on a visit with his mother at Miami Beach, Chaim walked down the beach and saw many people with his book in hand. He asked one person if he could see the book. It had an inscription inside which read, "To _____ signed, the mother of Chaim." She had come around to supporting his passion.

This gave me the perfect opportunity to ask the question that was burning inside me. "Chaim, what empowered you to go up against your culture, and more importantly, your mother, to become a popular novelist?" He looked at me. There was silence. A smile came over his face and he proclaimed, "I wish I had a choice."

In a recent exchange with one of my sons I told him that I would always support him one hundred percent. I also expressed my worry. His response was, "Don't worry. I am fine!" I told him that it is natural for parents to worry when they watch their children struggle, but it is my job to let them know I am with them. Still a part of me wishes they chose a more conventional path in life.

### Forming A Network To Help Others: Three Degrees Of Separation

One of the joys of working in a school community is that it has produced various connections that enable me to help others. Our students and alumni come to me to assist them with job searches. They reason is that I am able to connect them with a good resource since I know over 38 years of alums and parents. When I connect them to the right person, they are very grateful. When I have been asked to be a reference for an alumnus who is seeking higher security clearance in our government, the FBI has come to my office to interview me. They never interview references by phone.

When I receive an expression of gratitude, I always follow their thank you with a statement that I may need them sometime in the future to be helpful to another member of our community. They get it. At the risk of sounding like Marlon Brando in "The

Godfather", it really is not only expertise but it is also who you know that counts.

My oldest son, Thaddeus, in a tribute to me at my retirement, said, "Most people have six degrees of separation from people who they know. My father has three degrees of separation. People either know him or know of him." I have been blessed to know the most powerful, the most powerless, and those in between. My joy is to be able to make the connections to help them all.

## *Reflections*

Have you successfully transformed any perfectionistic desires so that you are now able to give everything you do your best effort and claim, for that moment in time, it is good enough?

Can you think of a positive failing experience you have had that promoted learning and insight?

In what way does the framework of *storge, eros, philia*, and *agape* assist you in understanding relationships?

Consider situations where you have had a temporary mindset, and a permanent mindset.

Do you see yourself on a conventional or unconventional path in life?

Have there been certain paths in life you felt compelled to pursue?

# CHAPTER 10: FUTURE CONSIDERATIONS

## Challenges And Opportunities For Change

When I retired, I had person after person say, "Congratulations." I can't imagine myself saying to someone, "Congratulations on your retirement." I've never said it myself. I was leaving a community that had become my family, and I enjoyed every aspect of the job. For this reason, the notion of retirement seemed odd, if not irrelevant.

So why congratulate me for leaving something I loved doing? The well wishers were expressing appreciation for my years of service and wishing me well as I moved on to spend more time with my family, and to discover a new ways to share the gifts that I had developed during my 45 years as parish priest and school chaplain. What I have discovered is that you never really leave work that has been so significant in your life. Your role simply changes.

I have had some tough critics over the years. People in our community are well informed and have strong opinions about certain issues. I once had a parent call me to express her criticism of a fellow parent with a strong personality. I responded by saying, "All of our parents have strong personalities." It introduced some humor into a tense moment. Looking back I realize just how challenging my job was. When you are the spiritual leader of a diverse community, you must be ready to celebrate that gift and all that comes with it. For some I was not Christian enough. For others I was too Christian. For those who were on the liberal side of things, I was too conservative. For those who were conservative, I was too liberal. People actually counted the number of times I had female versus male speakers in chapel, democrats versus republicans. They would let me know if things were out of balance. But for the most part people knew I was committed to supporting them even if I did not agree with their stance.

I recommended the first woman clergy person to be a chaplain at our school, the Reverend Daphne Killhour-Polys. Women's ordination was a controversial topic at the time. The response to Daphne joining our chaplaincy staff was, for the most part, positive but there were challenges. Donors withheld money and members of the community protested her appointment. It was great to have the support of an outstanding Head of School, Jay Crawford, who fully endorsed this important step forward. Daphne had a pioneer spirit and could not be intimidated. I told her she would have the support of the school community by Thanksgiving. I was wrong. She had the community in the palm of her hand by Halloween.

When John Yoo, EA '85 came to speak, he addressed the community in the theater. We knew his message would have a political bent and we thought it best delivered in a neutral space. John was a controversial member of George Walker Bush's administration, providing legal counsel. He is now a professor of law at Berkeley in California. In contrast, a parent in our school arranged for Chris Matthews to speak. Chris is the very liberal talking head for the show, "Hard Ball". We had him speak in the theater as well. I would rather have had them speak in chapel, as both touched on subjects at the heart of social justice. Both John Yoo and Chris Matthews were terrific. They treated the students with the utmost respect and seriousness in addressing their questions. We had a parent who accused me of having only liberal speakers in chapel. I suggested that she submit her own suggestions for chapel speakers. If the student chapel leaders and I agreed that her desired speakers had something to say regarding religion, ethics, character, faith, or social justice, we would invite them to speak. We did invite one of her recommended speakers but he cancelled on four separate occasions. I drew the line at four cancellations and the speaker was not invited to reschedule.

I received a call one day in August from a parent who stated he was representing a group of parents who did not like the direction in which the school was heading regarding sexual equality and support of LGBTQ people.

Whenever the issue of sexual equality arose, I did not disclose that I have a gay son. That disclosure would have made the issue personal and would have taken the focus off of the moral mandate for inclusivity for our school. I listened to the caller and told him to get back to his large group to determine a time and place for me to meet with them. I never heard from him again.

There are a few things to keep in mind when you are in a diverse community with the above tensions. First and foremost, know where you stand. Never let a label define who you or others are. Second, work hard at getting into the shoes and world view of the person or people with whom you disagree. There is always some good there to be discovered. I think this approach would help any community or nation find their way forward.

Let me give you a personal and timely example from my own life about not judging a book by its cover (literally) or a person by their label.

I was not a fan of George W. Bush. I watched TV news and read extensively about his leadership or, as some would say, his lack of leadership post 9/11. The TV cameras at the time of the event focused on him reading to little children in a Florida school. The images communicated that he was out of touch and clueless.

Portraits of Courage: A Commander's Tribute to America's Warriors (Crown 2017) chronicles how President Bush became a painter after he left office. He threw himself into his efforts, had several teachers, and developed a passion for creating portraits on canvas. The portraits in his book are of veterans and with each portrait is a statement describing the veteran's courage and commitment to our country. President Bush brings home the plight of returning vets in a very graphic way. It cannot be ignored.

I also read President Bush's book, Decision Points. (Bush 2010) In the book he describes his thought process behind how he handled 9/11. I was prepared to put the book down after a few chapters, but I found it enlightening and compelling. He takes you inside the storm that was the decade following 9/11 and also gives credit to

President Obama. It is a fascinating journey of history and of one man's leadership during it.

I now see him in a very different light and feel he is a man of great courage and conviction. Yes, he was born with a silver spoon in his mouth while living in Midland, Texas, but quickly I hear that voice, "Yes George, and you didn't miss anything."

My liberal friends may be thinking, "Yes but..." As human beings we are conditioned to hear the negative and not the positive. Think of the last time you did something that you felt was great. But then you heard one voice of criticism, and it is that voice that you remembered for the rest of the day. We all have a "gotcha" inclination within us that is quick to find fault in others while forgetting to focus on the good.

### Gordon Gee: The University As A Spiritual Place, The University As Similar To Faith

The Murphy Family established a Lecture Series to honor their daughter, Maura, EA'96 who died tragically the summer after her junior year in college. The family desired to have the lectures address moral issues in the lives of students. The Murphys and I planned the lecture together and on a particular year we decided to invite Gordon Gee, President of Vanderbilt, to speak. Their daughter, Megan, attended Vanderbilt so Gordon was delighted to accept the invitation and to honor the legacy of Maura Murphy by speaking to our students.

There was a press release to announce Gordon's upcoming lecture. Shortly thereafter, I was at a fundraiser and was asked repeatedly, "Jim, have you read the Wall Street Journal today?" The answer was, "No," but I went online when I got home. The article reported that Gordon Gee had spent $6 million dollars rehabbing his home on campus, and that his wife, who was a member of the faculty, was caught using marijuana. It was said that she was using it for medical reasons. That explanation didn't go down well with the rest of the faculty. Of course, my phone started to ring and the common theme was, "How could you have him here?"

Regarding the money spent on his home, the remodeling was planned and executed with the goal of having it be the location for fundraising events. This follows the custom in many southern institutions of higher learning. My standard response to those who questioned the decision to invite Dr. Gee was that I think students should experience civil discourse so, if you disagree with him, come to the lecture and ask him some questions. I wanted our students to hear from people on the many sides of an issue. Here is Dr. Gee's address to the community. I share it because of its importance to students and its emphasis on the university as a spiritual place.

I wish to thank Headmaster Hamilton Clark, and Chaplain Jim Squire, for inviting me to come to Episcopal Academy.

And please allow me to express my deep appreciation to the Murphy family and to their friends for making this lecture series possible, in honor of their daughter Maura. The gift that they make in her memory, a gift of allowing you access to moral thinking in action and in practice, and the gift of allowing you to ask questions about it, is a great one.

And I doubt you will be shy when the time arrives to ask questions, because I have seen in my experience that your generation is a deeply moral and spiritual one.

Why would you be shy about asking important questions? I know what my conversations with Vanderbilt's students have taught me, and I doubt that Episcopal's students are very different: I know that you love your families, and I know that you love each other. I know that you think of yourselves as members of communities: whether those communities be your classmates, or your teammates, or your Friends List. I know that you want to make this a better world. I know that you have a sense of something that is higher and bigger and vaster than one person's narrow desires.

And I know that you are bold – an invitation to an adult professional to reveal to you the most basic foundations of his daily practice is indeed bold! Is it an invitation, or a challenge? Can I be as good as you deserve to have me be?

From my pre-speech reconnaissance, I know what your stripes mean. So you can know what mine mean. This is only fair. You want to know how I make my decisions as a university Chancellor, and as a person. I spend so much time at my work, that those categories are actually inextricable!

I noticed as I considered my remarks that my thoughts began to take on a spiritual tinge. I realized that <u>everything</u> I might have to tell you about, that all of my stripes, the way I have spent my life and how I learned to make appropriate decisions, and what gives me any authority at all to speak to you in a Chapel capacity, comes from my upbringing as a Latter-Day Saint. (That is the official term for 'Mormon,' by the way!) That was an intense realization.

And I also realized that my wanderings in this world, and my time spent <u>outside</u> of the safe and rich haven of Utah, which is, for Latter-Day Saints, a homeland, are what have made me more aware of the merits of my own faith. Those wanderings have made the practice of my faith personal. They have made it something I chose for myself, and choose every day, instead of something that I do just because everyone I know does it, everyone I know believes in it.

To say that my faith 'had not been tested' before I left Utah would not be entirely accurate; Latter-Day Saints have much field-testing in our principles and duties of mission (you may have seen us in your neighborhood, being field-tested!). But I should say instead that in my case, my faith, that is a legacy of my family and their gift to me, had not fully been <u>proven</u> to me, until I had seen it exercised in my dealings with others as a university president.

What we learn in our life eventually connects back up to where we stand spiritually – to what we know about ourselves in relation to the religion in which we were raised or in which we have come to believe. So I may say that everything I know about being a Latter-Day Saint, and beyond that – everything I know about living a good life, I have learned from running universities.

Now, unless you are a paleontologist, you might not have heard of Vernal, Utah, which is my hometown, and also home to Dinosaur National Monument. Basically, the hippest characters in town have been extinct seventy million years – it took me until I was eighteen years old to meet anyone who was not Mormon, or Republican, or a dinosaur!

So you can see how being on a mission would be a particular grace to someone like me, to bring me out so that I could look around! I went on my first mission after my first year at the University of Utah. But it turned out that my life's work would be the most deepening mission of all.

Anyone who is acquainted with the responsibilities of a university presidency can attest that it is a role that hyper-accelerates your existence: you can make hundreds of new acquaintances in one day, and each one of those friendships has its own demands; you have a heightened accountability, because you are the <u>one</u> person who cannot outsource blame or praise for anything that happens at your university; and so often is attention on <u>you</u> that you have to attend very closely to the details of your private persona.

So, as you can imagine, I received, probably before I was ready for it, a crash-course on what kind of person – and even what kind of Saint – I wanted to be.

The first lesson I learned, that deepened my understanding of my spirituality, is that, as a University President, I have to be comfortable with what I am and what I represent. I am a unique and highly symbolic figure on campus, and several years of being <u>that</u> has inoculated me to any suspicion others may have about me as idiosyncratic, or exotic, or as a member of a religious minority.

On any campus, the chief executive officer is something of a unicorn – in your uniqueness, there is no anonymity; everyone knows who you are, and everyone has something to say about how you should lead, or how you should spend your time, or even how you should dress (as you can see, I have chosen to ignore that last category!). After more than twenty-five years in this position, I know that if any human can handle that level of scrutiny, he can bear up as a representative of what he believes in his innermost heart of hearts.

To that end, I have learned to have thick skin, nerves like sewer pipes, and a good sense of humor. Fielding criticism is part of the nature of a university presidency, but remaining <u>calm</u> in the face of criticism can be excruciatingly difficult, as is not feeling stampeded by the emails, telephone calls, and letters flooding in to your office!

I wonder if it was the experience gained on my mission that has made me appreciate the strength of character that is required in such situations, or if it was being in such situations as a university president that helped me to understand exactly what was taking place inside my heart on my mission.

I learned that my experiences in mission had been intended also to impart strength to me, that going door-to-door, that not knowing how I would be received by the people I met – whether I had that strength at the time, or even whether I acquired it later, I now realize part of the benefit of those trips, what they were intended to do for me.

From presiding over five universities, I learned <u>humility</u>. I learned not to believe the hype about <u>myself</u>! I learned that it is possible for a university president still to possess all the frailties of humankind. I learned that although I needed to be serious about my position, serious about my vocation, I could not let that seriousness turn into seriousness about myself – because then not only would I have been unbearable to be around, I would be vulnerable to puncture at any moment!

But I also had to acknowledge that I do have an experience that is different from that of other people at Vanderbilt, and that difference demands that I make an effort to understand the experience of others. It is easy to fall into the habit of enclosure, of assuming that no one could possibly have obstacles or problems that you don't already know about – or conversely, gifts that you do not already know about! So, over the years, I have learned the value of appreciation for all of the talents it takes to run a huge and complex research university. I have learned to recognize humans in their worth and dignity, not just as a theory, but by actually watching – and by being in <u>awe</u> of! – the skills and the dedication of all the people around me.

From that recognition, I learned to treat everyone within the institution as a teacher, no matter what that person may do. I have gained the ability to see that students are partners in the University's efforts, that all individuals on campus are members of a community that depends upon them. I have learned that respecting the worth and contribution of each individual is the only way to live not only the intellectual values of the university, but also the values at my core.

Another realization I had is that the expectation of excellence I have of myself as a Latter-Day Saint is similar to the expectation of excellence that must be upheld at a University. But I also realized that to expect high things of people is not just punitive; it has a real, practical application to the way people work together and the quality of their working relationships with one another. Lowering your standards to support people who are not passionate, enthusiastic, or engaged with their work hurts everybody, because first resentment brews, and after that stage comes one even worse: when no-one is inspired to try their hardest.

I learned that the spirit of a community matters, for the sustenance and health of a community's long-term life. And in that, I learned that I myself must also believe unequivocally in the institution I am fortunate enough to lead. I made the mistake very early of trying to restrain my involvement with the university, trying to keep my heart separate from my work. I discovered very quickly how dry and unfulfilling that is. Every day I realize that passion for vocation, passion for mission, is what invigorates an institution and enables it to thrive. Your passion is proof that you believe in what you have committed yourself to do.

And from working with different 'casts' of academic and administrative personnel over the course of my career, I learned that the people with whom we surround ourselves, with whom we collaborate, are visible evidence of the invisible qualities that we value. A work community often also becomes a community of faith – if not faith in a religious sense, of faith in shared purpose and mission that is constantly renewed and renewing.

I learned not to honor traditions for their own sake, but to practice them because they are relevant. I learned that a university, just like a faith, is not a museum, but that tradition should be alive, should be authentic, should be living and dynamic, and should enhance the lives of those who observe its traditions.

And from the times I have gone about trying to demolish university traditions, I have also learned the opposite: to keep clear of change for change's sake, and to acknowledge that whatever might be the needs of my ego, or my desires for immortality and fame, they cannot compete with the importance a university has in the minds and hearts of those loyal to it. Respect for others, above all else, is how to live in the world.

I am frequently asked by people of belief how I can sustain my core faith amid so many different kinds of people who do not practice the same beliefs as I do, or believe the way I do, whether they are of different religions or no religion at all. How can I believe in anything in an environment where so much that is fundamental about the universe is questioned, proven, even disproven? How can belief exist surely where everything is subject to debate and discussion?

Ladies and gentlemen, if you take anything with you when you graduate and go to university, take this: know that open discussion is what brings the human spirit to transcend its selfish impulses and its limitation and its narrow view – know that honoring others by listening to them is one of the surest ways to 'get over yourself' – something we all need to be able to do!, and, perhaps, the greatest, deepest, and most spiritual gift of universities.

The most important lesson that I have learned, I learned from being around universities – which is how much the enterprise of a university is like faith.

The mission work I did when I was young granted me the opportunity to experience the complexities of the world. Not only did it train me to trust in who I am, it also trained me in complexity. It taught me that I belong to an international community, to a planetary community, and that there are many ways within that community not only to view a problem, but also to solve a problem.

In my own life, I traveled from the land of the dinosaurs through presidencies at five major Universities. At every one of those Universities, I knew how blessed I was to assist in an enterprise which throws people from many different cultures together in one Utopian environment and then allows them to talk, think, and work together with the common aim – however they might approach it – of making our world safer and more humane.

My mission of understanding the world did not end when I returned from my first mission in Germany. It continues, for at universities, I learn every day that it is possible for me to co-exist in good faith with people who are not like me. Everything I know about why my beliefs work, about respect for others, and about appreciation for the variousness of the world, comes from life and is sensed through my doing what I do.

Like faith, universities are chosen. They are at their richest and their best when you engage in them on purpose, and with full knowledge of what you are getting into – instead of just because they are customary to do! And the secret is that, at a university, knowing what you are getting into means accepting that you have no idea of what you are getting into! You simply have to take it, as they say, on faith.

This occasion is denoted a lecture, but I know as you know, ladies and gentlemen, that what chiefly recommends it is the dialogue it has been designed to turn into. And now is our occasion for that dialogue. What questions would you like to ask me? What would you like to know?

There was great give and take and respect for others during the question and answer session until a woman student raised her hand and asked, "Since you are a Mormon how many wives do you have?" I choose to believe that the question was real for her. My colleagues on the faculty, however, did not share my positive take on the situation. They thought she was being disrespectful. You could hear a pin drop. He simply replied that he had one wife, never missed a beat, and moved on.

I must admit that I called an EA graduate who was studying at Vanderbilt and asked what she thought of President Gee before I invited him to speak. She reported that the students loved him. She stated that on Friday nights he would bring cookies to various corners of the campus to treat the students. Once I heard our graduate share her thoughts, I felt much safer with our choice. How an educator treats students is an important barometer for me.

### Are We Pushed Or Pulled Through Life

From a religious perspective St. Augustine had powerful words to guide our future considerations, "Thou hast made us for yourself, O Lord, and our heart is restless until it finds its rest in thee." (Augustine 2011) This describes a God-directed life, a focus that guides me. But there are other perspectives that need to be considered in looking to our future.

The question is, "Are we pulled through life or are we pushed?" I have written extensively in a previous book about how the past informs our present decision making. The present shapes each moment we are here. Jean Paul Sartre and Simone de Beauvoir, the father and mother of modern day existentialism, professed that people are the meaning makers and we must make that meaning in the now.

I realized I was missing something important by failing to put proper consideration on how the future shapes my life and decision making in the now. Ernest Becker in his book, <u>The Denial of Death</u>, states, "the way we view death is the way we view life." (Becker 1973) Jesus says, "This is eternal life, that they may know you, the only true God, and Jesus Christ Who you have sent." (John 17:3) Eternal life is inextricably linked to how you are viewing it as a future consideration as well as in the present.

## *Logotherapy*

Years ago when I was studying in New Haven I came across a slim volume of a book concerning the Holocaust, <u>Man's Search For Meaning</u>, by Victor Frankl. The book has two basic parts. The first shares what it was like for him to be in a Nazi concentration camp. The second part of the book describes a type of therapy pioneered by Frankl, "Logotherapy". The book seeks to answer the question, "How can people find meaning in their lives under the worst possible conditions?" Frankl quotes Nietzsche, "He who has a why to live can bear almost any how." (Frankl 2006) The book is a vivid account of life in a concentration camp. In this extreme setting he learned how to survive and thrive in any situation.

There are two ideas at the heart of what Frankl discovered and that form the basis of Logotherapy. The first tenet is the value of love and loving as a key ingredient in one's life. Frankl thought that love was the be all and end all of life. In other words, we all desire to love and be loved. Beck Weathers, who was part of an ill fated climb up Mount Everest, was able to survive when so many others didn't because he constantly thought of his wife and children. He could not imagine life without them. He was driven to this reality as a result of traveling the world over looking for meaning. Then in his quest for survival on Mt. Everest he was led to discover that meaning had always in his own backyard. (Weathers 2015)

The second idea at the basis of Logotherapy is that one must have a future goal to look forward to. Mankind is the only species whose life is future directed. Hope is future oriented and beckons us into our future.

## The Importance Of A Sense Of Future In Slavery

The history of slavery in the United States holds many similar survival stories that reflect Frankl's findings. Enslaved people were often criticized for having an unrealistic view of their situation. Their religious fervor and music focused on the Promised Land, not on the justice they needed more immediately. But I believe it was that future consideration of heaven or a better life in the future that enabled them to survive.

The goal of the Underground Railroad was described as getting to the Promised Land. Any enslaved person dreams of being with loved family members and friends. That was part of their identity and a daily dream. Spirituals that were sung by enslaved people had covert meanings. The codes often related to how to escape to a free part of the country. There are many metaphors of "home", for a home is a safe place where everyone can live free.

The "Gospel Train" includes a direct call to get away.

> I hear it just at hand
> I hear the car wheels rumblin'
> And rollin' thro the land
> Get on board little children
>
> There is room for many more
> I hear the train a comin'
> She's loosed all her steam and brakes
> And strainin' ev'ry nerve
>
> The fare is cheap and all can go
> The rich and poor are there.
> No second class aboard this train.
> No difference in the fare.

"Swing Low Sweet Chariot" describes the identity and destiny of an enslaved people. It is filled with hope to connect them to a new future.

Swing low sweet chariot
Coming for to carry me home.
Swing low, sweet chariot
Coming for to carry me home.

I looked over Jordan, what do I see,
Coming for to carry me home.
A band of angels coming after me,
Coming for to carry me home.

Swing low, sweet chariot
Coming for to carry me home.
Swing low, sweet chariot,

Coming for to carry me home. (www.negrospirituals.com)

## *Future Considerations In Judaism And Christianity*

The enslaved people in the United States were influenced by the biblical traditions of both Judaism and Christianity. These traditions played very important roles in their spiritual lives. One of the central elements of Jewish scripture is the story of the Hebrews escaping the bondage of Egypt to enter the promised land "of milk and honey". This event is celebrated every year as Passover. Foods served for Passover symbolize the event. For example, unleavened bread is used to symbolize the haste with which they had to leave Egypt. They had their sense of a future goal to reach the Promised Land. This story is repeated each year across the world. The service of Passover deals with the central question, "How is this night different from all other nights?"

The Reverend Dr. Martin Luther King, Jr. proclaimed these famous words.

Well I don't know what will happen now; we've got some difficult days ahead. But it doesn't matter to me now, because I have been to the mountaintop. And I don't mind. Like anybody, I would like to live a long life --longevity has its place. But I am not concerned about that now. I just want to do God's will. And He allowed me to go up to the mountain. And I have looked over, and I have seen the Promised Land. I may not get there with you. But I want you to know tonight, that we, as a people, will get to the Promised Land. So I am happy tonight; I am not worried about anything; I am not fearing any man. Mine eyes have seen the glory of the coming of the Lord. (Delivered on April 3, 1968 in Memphis, Tennessee at Bishop Charles Temple)

The heart of the Christian tradition is the Resurrection. It is the core of the Christian identity. Just as Jesus was resurrected so will those who believe in him now be resurrected. They will have eternal life, the ability to be alive in the fullest moral sense, and to look to a future at a heavenly banquet. The Christian identity is clear and the future destiny of the Kingdom of Heaven is just as clear.

In the Gospel of Matthew we hear, "Do not store up for yourselves treasures on earth where moth and rust consume and where thieves break in and steal; but store up for yourselves treasures in heaven where neither moth nor rust consumes and where thieves do not break in and steal. For where your treasure is, there will your heart be also." (Matthew 6:19-21)

Apocalyptic literature in the Bible says that God will have ultimate control over all future events. In the book of the Revelation of St. John, we see the description of this kingdom which we are drawn to as a future home, "After this I looked and there was a great multitude that no one could count, from every nation, from all tribes, peoples, and languages, standing before the throne, robed in white with palm branches in their hands. They cried out with a loud voice saying, 'Salvation belongs to our God, who is seated in the throne, and to the lamb.'" (Revelation 7:9-10)

One can see how a future perspective could be envisioned for those who are undergoing hardship, "They will hunger no more and thirst no more; the sun will not strike them, not any scorching heat; for the lamb at the center of the throne will be their shepherd, and he will guide them to springs of the water of life, and God will wipe away every tear from their eyes." (Revelation 7:16-17) Identity and destiny are essential to surviving and thriving in this life and the life to come.

## Marty Seligman: Positive Psychology

One of the great thinkers in the world of psychology and one of the most intelligent people I know is Dr. Martin Seligman who founded the Penn Center for Positive Psychology at the University of Pennsylvania. Marty is a lifelong learner. He went from treating people with depression to founding a new movement in psychology. He never settles in a comfortable place. He is always challenging himself and others. He received the Lifetime Achievement Award from the American Psychological Association in 2017.

The most popular course in the history of Harvard University was a course on Positive Psychology taught by one of Marty's disciples, Tal Ben Shahar. Students flocked to the course by the hundreds so the class had to be moved to a large amphitheater. Marty is always looking for ways to interpret the human dilemma. Recently Marty co-authored a book, Homo Prospectus, that made a case for how our sense of future impacts our everyday decision-making.

*Homo Sapiens* is translated as "wise man". *Homo Prospectus* is translated as the person who looks to the future like a prospector would look for gold. Marty describes the two principles of Homo Prospectus, "(1) Because action always stretches forward in time, so must the mind that reliably succeeds in action. (2) In the game of life, life must win every moment of every day, while death has to win only once." (Homo Prospectus, Seligman, 2017)

I was teaching Marty's children in a course in Ethics and I met his wife, Mandy, when she came to parents' night. I described the ethics course curriculum. Mandy approached me after the period ended and said, "I have to get you, your wife, and Marty and me together! Would you come to dinner?" I said, "Of course!" Two days later she called, and we arranged a time. She apologized that leaders in education in Britain and Australia would be present as well, but she thought that would make for a great evening, and it did.

A conversation with Marty causes you to soar into an innovative and creative world. He has a way of challenging current thought and turning ideas and experiences upside down so that you can see them in a new and different way. On a subsequent occasion, my son and I were having lunch with Marty at his house. Marty's youngest children had set up a restaurant in our midst to play chef and waiter. Marty stopped the conversation, looked at my son and me, and, with all seriousness, asked, "Do you think we are interfering in their playing working in a restaurant?" Most people I know would have tried diplomatically to get the children to leave the room. One of Marty's beliefs is that we should have something in our lives that is bigger than us. One of those things is the care of children and love for others, including the possibility of our relationship with God.

I recently wrote a book, <u>Watch Your Time</u>, in which I describe how the past and present shape our decision making. Certainly the past and present influence our identity and how we make decisions, but Marty and his co-authors make a case for current decisions being guided more by future considerations. It is how we view the future that also is significant in shaping our decisions and identity now and in the future.

I repeat the following section from my previous book. It highlights this thought.

> The importance of time is directly linked to no time left, or death. There is a story about a difficult parent who met with the Head of Eton, the fine English prep school. She was disappointed in her son's performance at every level. She raised question after question with the theme, "What exactly have you been preparing him for?" The headmaster's

response, after giving her ample time to express her anger, was "death." What the Headmaster was underlining was that the student really needed to use his time well. His time was limited.

It was his most important commodity. He had to be better about watching his time. His view of death would make his decisions better and his identity as a student clearer. (Watch Your Time, Squire, 2017)When I consider the research Marty Seligman and his colleagues have examined, I think immediately of the messages of Judaism and Christianity. I think as well of the horrors of slavery and the Holocaust and how people coped with that. I also consider the writing of Victor Frankl in Man's Search For Meaning.

So how have all of these future considerations affected me? How have my future plans shaped my identity and decision making? The answer is, in ways that I was not aware of at the time. When I was simply reacting to what life served up I certainly was not future focused. Consider life as a car. I have tried to determine how much time I was looking out the front window and how much time I was looking into the rear view mirror. I am afraid that too much time was spent looking into the rear view mirror to make sure I was getting away from all I found troubling. I was not goal oriented for the most part, but recall that the one place I wanted to be was the Episcopal Academy, based on my experience with one student. Like my cousin, Noble, that student was a model of the very best of humankind. Consider how one person, you, can impact the life of others without you being aware of it at the time. Recall that "you may be one person in the world, but you may be the whole world to one person". (Geisel Website) What an awesome opportunity and responsibility you and I have for our actions each day of our lives.

When I consider the future and its effect on my life I look out the front window of the car to the resurrection of Christ and the afterlife. Because of my life and ministry I have seen enough death to last several lifetimes. It has compelled me to live a certain way today. I am aware of the precious nature of my existence, and the moral mandate that I have to help others and to live each day as if it were my last. Those thoughts certainly pull me forward. When have you and I made a significant difference in the life of someone else without even knowing it?

When I looked into that rear view mirror I was also looking for that back up that never arrived in the way I thought it should. Philosopher and theologian, Soren Kierkegaard, wrote, "life can only be understood backward but must be lived forward." (Kierkegaard 2009) There is a blend of the past, present, and future in our decision making and understanding of life. Each of the times of my life play a critical role.

Let me return to the emergency room metaphor that described a lot of my ministry. I had to be focused on what was in front of me. What I had within my soul was a drive to never give up or give in. I did live with hope although that was dashed at times. I was given that gift of grit by others, both young and old, who inspired me.

## *Gattica: A Metaphor For My Life*

There is a movie that is a metaphor for my life. Gattica is regarded as one of the best bioethics movies of all time by the Penn Center for Bioethics. It is science fiction and deals with a time in the future. There are two types of births. You can be a God child or natural birth known as an "invalid" as opposed to a "valid" whose genes are engineered, creating a being who is the very best of what one could be.

As the story goes, the child who had a normal birth, Vincent Freeman, is compared to his brother who had a birth guided by the geneticists. The "invalid" never measures up and because genetic testing is required for every job, he is relegated to cleaning toilets across the country. But what he longs to be is an astronaut traveling through space. He reads everything available to him, works out until his body glistens with sweat, and then changes his identity to a "valid" named Jerome Morrow, by using hair samples and urine samples from Jerome. Jerome chased perfection, failed, attempted suicide, and now is relegated to a wheelchair. Against all odds, Vincent finally makes it into Gattica, the space training facility.

Vincent's "valid" brother, Anton, is a detective. There has been a murder in Gattica, and Vincent, who is now posing as a "valid" by the name of Jerome, is the prime suspect. Keep in mind that your identity is not based on a photograph. Your identity is based on your genetic makeup. Vincent's brother, Anton, who is in charge of the investigation, recognizes his brother and confronts him. They had swum together when they were teenagers. Anton's question is, "How did you ever get in here?" The detective brother can't believe that an "invalid", Vincent, has become one of the elite in Gattica.

They meet where they met as boys and start swimming out to sea to see who is strongest. The detective brother, Anton, asks his "invalid" brother, Vincent, to stop for fear of getting them both killed. Vincent doesn't stop. He keeps swimming, forging ahead of his detective brother who cries out, "How have you done this? How have you done any of this, Vincent?" Vincent responds with the most important line in the film. Vincent, the "invalid" says, "You want to know how I have done any of this, Anton? It's because I never left anything for the swim back." In other words, the "invalid" did not seek the perfection that the detective brother supposedly had with his genetically manipulated material. He simply gave everything that he had to achieve his goal to live out his dream and fly into space.

That line, "I gave it everything I had", expresses my heart seeing into my future and my view of creating my identity and destiny.

The future forces us to focus on the path to our goals. But it is true that the journey is as important as the destination. This has been true for my Christian ministry. When people ask how I did what I did for 38 years at EA plus 7 years in the parish before that, I can simply say, "I never saved anything for the swim back to shore." How did I go from the home that I psychologically fled to the rarified world of some of the best schools in the nation and living a challenging life in attempting to help others? It was my looking to the future, my faith, and my regard for time as a precious commodity.

A future orientation helps us to discover what is needed in attitude, decision making, identity, and hope right now. It is a process that makes one's journey through life meaningful. Vincent, the "invalid" in the movie <u>Gattica</u> had no backup! He just left home and tried to make it in the world without backup. In fact, no one tried to stop him from leaving his home. He had to leave. His posture was freedom from, freedom to, and freedom within.

The "invalid" created his own back up, himself. I also created my own back up supported by God incarnate in Jesus, family, and others who have become a part of me.

At the point in the movie when the detective "valid" brother, Anton, is about to go under, Vincent swims back to him and brings him to safety. As Vincent looks up to the heavens, he sees the stars. He sees his dream. His future goal is clearly in sight, but it is just as important to get his brother safely to the shore. What a moment of cognitive dissonance! The stars above are symbolic of the dream. His brother in his arms is a powerful image as he chooses to risk all for his brother who he loves. (Gattica 1997)

In my own life I have certainly felt like the "invalid" or non-elite and have done the same thing that Vincent did but with a different vocation and different life.

Maybe we need to reverse the humor mentioned earlier. While John F. Kennedy was campaigning, the young man yells out, "John, you were born with a silver spoon in your mouth." Another shouts from the crowd, "John, you didn't miss anything."

What if we changed things to, "John you were born without back up in a working class world, not an elite world. Yes, John you did not miss anything except having the hope, faith, and back up on your own to shape your future."

We look to the sky to see our dream in the stars. Does helping others help us to keep our eyes on the prize? Or is it the dream in the stars that enables us to help others? These are questions for the ages. I believe the ultimate future consideration is that we all want to love and be loved, as Vincent did. Vincent falls in love in the movie with someone who loves him unconditionally. Some say that the pursuit of happiness should be our future consideration. Perhaps, but what may take us even further in looking for our future is to love and be loved. For me that may be who we are and whose we are, as said so well by St. Augustine and St. Paul.

Not that I have already attained this or reached
the goal; but I press on to make it my own, because

Christ Jesus has made me his own. Beloved, I do
not consider that I have made it my own, but this
thing I do. Forgetting what lies behind and straining
forward to what lies ahead, I press on toward the
goal for the prize of the heavenly call of God in
Christ Jesus. (Philippians 3:12-14)

You have made us for yourself, O Lord, and our
heart is restless until it finds its rest in thee." (St.
Augustine in <u>Confessions)</u>

## *A Question That Gets To The Heart Of The Matter*

As I mentioned earlier, we built a home for our family on the
upper Chesapeake Bay in the early 1980s. One day we were on my
deck overlooking the bay with a group of friends. It was a stunning
view of the water and sunset. Apropos of nothing, one of our guests
turned to me, looked me directly in the eyes, and asked me point
blank, "How did you go from "Conshy" to here?"

She knew that "Conshy" (a nickname for the Philadelphia
suburb of Conshohocken) was a blue collar, depressed area when
I lived there in my youth. No one had ever asked me that question
so directly and in such a setting of absolute beauty. I stumbled over
some words to respond to her. I realized how difficult it is for me
to discuss that question. There were times, as I indicated, when I
had to just stop writing this book because I would become overwhelmed by emotion.

Maybe if she picks up this book, she will have a partial answer
to her question.

As I draw this memoir to a close, remember that it is for your
reflection and personal growth and to help you to connect to your
story. It is also for my children, their spouses, and our close friends
who didn't know very much about what I have written in this book.
I hope that they may benefit from my reflection in their own search
for their future and answer to the most basic but profound question,
"How did I get here from there?" It is our pursuit of the answer to
that question that is the essence of a life fully lived.

## *Reflection*

How closely do you listen to people who disagree with you? What does it take for you to understand what is really going on in the life of another?

Do you actively seek to encourage civil discourse?

What does your heart yearn for?

Are you pulled or pushed through life and do you take time to live in the moment?

How do you view death? Is it the end or a new beginning?

How much do you look into the rear view mirror of the car of your life? How often do you look through the windshield at what is directly in front of you? How often do you look further down the road as far as your eyes can see?

Do you know who you are and what you stand for? Do you have a sense of your destiny?

Can you explain how you got to where you are today? Where do you dream you could be?

Do you have a sense of destiny and a clear sense of your identity?

# CHAPTER 11: EPILOGUE

## A Medical Journey

I went on an unwanted medical pilgrimage from June 2016 until the present day. After my retirement from EA in June of 2016, I began to feel intense pain in the upper area of my right hamstring muscle. I have been running as long as I can remember so the initial presumed medical diagnosis was a severe hamstring pull. This made sense to me, but what confused me was that the pain only came when I was lying down in bed to sleep.

I consulted a physical medicine specialist and a sports medicine practitioner attempting to find the cause and to treat the problem. One of the doctors noticed a weakness in my right leg and ordered an MRI of the spine. I was having difficulty walking. The MRI revealed a large, hard, benign synovial cyst on my lower spine that was affecting the sciatic nerve.

I had spine surgery and pain relief in the leg was immediate. A few weeks later I was at a family gathering when I began to feel very ill. When I got home I was shaking uncontrollably and running a high temperature.I went to bed for I thought I had the flu. Vicki called my surgeon to report my symptoms and he indicated he should see me the next day. That same night I collapsed on the bathroom floor injuring both knees and my right ankle.

The next day my surgeon determined that the surgical incision was infected and admitted me immediately to the hospital. I needed surgery to cleanse the surgical site but it had to be delayed for two days to allow my blood thinner to clear my system. During the delay the goal was to keep me from going into septic shock. It was a race against time. I felt as if the grim reaper was standing by my bed. My skilled surgeon along with the infectious disease specialists at Lankenau Hospital pulled me through.

The injuries to my knees and ankle still needed to be addressed so I began physical therapy just to be able to walk again without pain. One morning shortly after my release from the hospital, as I started down our stairs at home one of my injured knees gave out. I tumbled down the entire 13 stairs head first onto a slate floor.

Vicki and Spencer, who was home for the holidays, came running to see what happened. My mind instantly focused on the hope that I had not injured my spine. Thoughts of two former students who became paraplegic flashed into my head. I could remember each step and the last crack as my head collided with the flagstone at the bottom of the stairs, but I remained conscious. I asked Vicki and Spencer to help me to stand so that I could see if I had function in my legs. It was a long few seconds until I realized that I could stand. That was all that I cared about.

But I noticed a look of fear on Vicki's face. When I touched my head, there was a lump the size of an egg. I was on a blood thinner again so she rushed me to the ER. The grim reaper was kept at bay once again as the CT scan revealed no bleeding in the brain. I never know when memory of the fall will wash over me in slow motion. Sometimes in my nightmares the fall does not have a positive ending.

Once I recovered from the fall and the second surgery, I turned my focus to rehab, going from physical therapy in the home to physical therapy at Excel working with Michael Quintans. So in the midst of fighting to get back to being able to ambulate without pain from the injured knees and ankle, I did what I usually do. I went to work as hard as I could and I prayed.

All of that determination and hard work did not resolve the pain that was now focused in both legs. My legs felt very heavy like I was carrying 50 pound weights on each ankle. My podiatrist was actually the one who urged me to get an MRI of the lower spine and to return to my spine surgeon for a consultation. Without any hesitation my surgeon diagnosed spinal stenosis. It was the cause of all my dysfunction. One week later I had a laminectomy L2-5 with bone fusion L4-5.

I always advise people to take someone with them when they go to an important medical appointment. I was a living example of the validity of that recommendation. I downplayed the seriousness of the surgery in my mind, but Vicki heard and ingested it all. After surgery I couldn't deny the nine inch surgical incision in the lumbar area of my spine nor the accompanying pain.

My surgeon is a terrific guy and tried to brighten my spirits by indicating that he had to use four saw blades to get through the removal of the facets to open up the spinal canal. This is the upside for those who have been running for a long time. Exercise increases bone density.

After the surgery to correct my spinal stenosis, I continued to have knee pain that severely impacted my quality of life. I discovered the problem was caused by more than the impact of the fall I had while septic. I was paying the price for my years of running and my genetics. Knee specialists tried numerous injections and procedures including a scope of the MCL in an attempt to address the problem with my knees. When nothing reduced the knee pain, it was recommended that I plan for knee replacements. Those surgeries occurred on March 15, 2018, and June 14, 2018. My goals were rather simple. I wanted my active life back. I wanted to go for walks with Vicki and our dog, Sadie. I wanted to return to running, the elliptical machine, and the bike. I wanted to begin to enjoy the pleasures of retirement including world travel. We actually had a trip to New Zealand planned for my first year of retirement but had to cancel it after my post surgery sepsis.

Rehab has helped me reach a state of recovery. It is a lot of work but I had my goal of returning to an active lifestyle. As one friend told me regarding her knee replacement surgery, "Jim, it is not for sissies." Another friend indicated that I should have both knees done at the same time or I would never go back for the second one. I can see the truth in that counsel, but I was highly motivated and, as I indicated above, went back for the second surgery.

I never saw a downside coming as I pushed through each of these surgeries. I counted on moving forward with no problem. Then it hit. It was a form of "Post Traumatic Stress Syndrome" that set in after being in great pain for two years and having six surgeries during that time. To top it off, I recently spent a week in the hospital with pneumonia and had surgery for a kidney stone. At some point I hit an emotional wall and struggled a great deal to keep moving forward. It was devastating! I wouldn't have been able to work through it without Vicki's support and prayer. As I understand it, it is not unusual for heart surgery patients as well as others with serious diseases or injuries to go through the same phenomenon. You reach your limit.

My next book may focus on what I learned from all the medical challenges of the past two years for I believe that "life is to be enjoyed or learned from". Norman Cousins, a longtime editor of the <u>Saturday Review</u>, wrote <u>An Anatomy of An Illness As Perceived By the Patient</u>. It was the first book to explore the human spirit as an integral part of the healing process and explain the importance of the patient being his own advocate. His book, written in 1979, is still as relevant now as it was then. It was written after he was diagnosed with a crippling and irreversible disease. He conquered the disease by working closely with his doctors. The book focuses on the importance of a patient taking responsibility for his medical care and becoming a partner with his caregivers. Cousins communicated that attitude, grit, humor, and faith are essential to the healing process. (Cousins 1979)

I am pleased to say that was the way my doctors and I approached my medical dilemmas. They worked closely with me. I wouldn't want anyone to go through what I have gone through, but it has an upside to it as I have realized that illness or injury can be a great teacher. Suffice it to say that I have learned a lot. Thank you to my medical team who got me through it all. They are simply the best. "It takes a village" has become a bit worn as a metaphor, but in my case it did take a number of people who cared for me as more than a patient but as a friend.

The overseer in all my treatment was my medical general contractor, Vicki Squire, who gave me months of private duty nursing care. Thank you to Dr. Scott Rushton, surgeon extraordinaire, Donna Garrison, BSN, RN, MSN, Dr. B J Smith, Dr. Jay Siegfried, Dr. Robert Benz, Dr. Gary Gilman, the Infectious Disease Department at Lankenau Hospital, Dr. David Vegari, Dr.

Jeffrey Gerland, Dr. Behzad Pavri, Tansy Briggs, and the team at the Rothman Institute including Dr. Michael Ciccotti, Dr. David Pedowitz, Dr. Ari Greis, Dr. Jess Lonner, and Dr. Lonner's physician's assistant, Sophia Matthews. The person who was there with me from beginning to end is Michael Quintans at Excel Physical Therapy. He is in a league of his own and is a great teacher who combines toughness and care. There is none better. The grim reaper did not have a chance against this talented bunch. I am now back to my active self, better than ever.

## A Paradox: A Seeming Self Contradiction

Never forget where you came from. Live in the now. Always remember where you are going. Keep these three balls in the air at the same time like a juggler of life.

An analogy I mentioned in the book that can help you to visualize this paradox is a ride in a car. There are times when you are right in the moment, but at the same time, you have to look through the front windshield to see where you are going, and also check the rear view mirror to see where you have been, particularly in the heavy traffic of life.

or

Consider the interlocking gears on the front cover.

## Don't Forget Where You Came From

In the midst of all of this I wanted to touch the roots from where I came. Vicki and I went back to Conshohocken to locate the Alan Wood Steel Coke Plant where I was employed in the summers to earn money for college. It was a place that provided a formative experience for me. We drove up the Schuylkill River that runs along Conshohocken, the blue collar town where I was born and raised, and couldn't find the coke plant so we went to the borough hall. No one remembered it. They were all pretty young. They suggested that I walk down the street to a frame shop where the local unofficial historian of the town worked. I asked to talk with him. He was enthusiastic about the history of the town and its surroundings so I told him that I couldn't find the coke plant. I asked where it was. He pulled out some books that contained pictures of the plant and then said, "It's gone!"

I couldn't believe what I was hearing. I asked, "How could it be gone? It was an iron edifice complete with tunnels, ovens, and conveyor belts that reached to the sky?" It took up miles of space. He said just one word, "Dynamite." The area is now filled with new industry such as the <u>Inquirer</u> newspaper printing plant. He let me know that a professional demolition company destroyed the plant and carried the remains away, earning a great deal of salvage money.

It was gone! How funny! It can't be gone because I can remember every inch of the place and the cast of characters who inhabited it. My only regret was that I had wanted Vicki to see it!

We then drove past my family home that was built by my grandfather. He raised a family of twelve children in that tiny home. There is a narrow alley in between my home and our neighbor who introduced me to the world of boxing. The home is where I was born and raised. We lingered in front of the home remembering times we visited my parents there with Thad and Joanna. We then passed the bar where my father was a too frequent customer when I was young. We continued on to A.A. Garthwaite Field, one of the first lighted stadiums in the area. It was Conshohocken's version of "<u>Friday Night Lights</u>". Everyone came to the games. The air was always electric with excitement!

I remembered everything being much larger than it really is. Perhaps the past looms larger in affecting our lives than I was willing to admit. I should have taken the advice that I have given to so many others, "Don't forget where you came from." I will now repeat that statement with more enthusiasm, intensity, and importance.

I believe that we as human beings are more alike than different no matter what your life circumstances, race, or creed. I hope this book has helped you to connect to important parts of who you are, both large and small, by the questions that are raised. The answers rest in you.

# END NOTES AND REFERENCES

Albom, Mitch. <u>Tuesdays With Morrie</u>. Doubleday, 1997.

Becker, Ernest. <u>The Denial of Death</u>. New York: Simon and Schuster. 1973.

Bettleheim, Bruno. <u>The Uses of Enchantment</u>. Vintage Books, 2010.

Bonhoeffer, Dietrich. <u>The Cost of Discipleship.</u> Touchstone, 1995.

Bonhoeffer, Dietrich. <u>Letters and Papers From Prison</u>. Touchstone, 1997.

Bogle, John. <u>Enough: True Measures of Money, Business, and Life.</u> Wiley, 2008

Brooks, Joseph. "You Light Up My Life". UMG Publishing, 1977.

Browning, Robert. *Andrea del Sarto*. Watham Saint Lawrence, Emg;and: Golden Cockeral Press, 1925.

Buckley, William F. <u>On the Firing Line: The Public Life of our Public Figures</u>. Random House, 1989.

Burke, Gretchen. "A Message From Gretchen Burke, New Chairman of the Board of Trustees', Inside.Episcopalacademy. org/drum/admin Website 2005

Burklo, Jim. "Mindful Christianity". "Huffpost", 2014.

Bush, George W. <u>Decision Points.</u> Crown Publishers, 2010.

Bush George W. <u>Portraits of Courage</u>. Crown Publishers, 2017.

Carey, Alice. Poems of Alice and Phoebe Carey. (Classic Reprint) Forgotten Book, 2018.

Chessick, Richard. How Psychotherapy Heals. Science House, 1965.

Csikszentmihalyi, Mihaly. Flow: The Key to Unlocking, Creativity, Peak Performance and True Happiness. Canada: Harper Collins, 2008.

Clapton, Eric and Jennings, Will. Tears in Heaven. Warner Brothers, 1992.

Coleman, John. Blue Collar Journal: A College President's Sabbatical. Philadelphia, Lippincott, 1974.

Collins, Larry and Lapierre, Dominique. Or I Will Dress You in Mourning: The Story of El Cordobes and the Spain He Stands For. New York: Simon and Schuster.

Cousins, Norman. The Anatomy Of An Illness As perceived By The Patient. W.W. Norton and Company, 1979.

Dweck, Carol. Mindset: The New Psychology of Success, Random House Publishing Group, 2006.

DeBeavior, Simone. The Ethics of Ambiguity. Open Road Media, 2011

Frankl, Victor. Man's Search For Meaning. Beacon Press, 2006.

Fink, Sheri. Five Days at Memorial Hospital. First Edition, New York: Crown Publishers, 2013.

Gattica, Movie Released October 24, 1997, Director: Andrew Niccol.

Geisel, Theodore. *10 Quotes to Live By on His 113th Birthday.* Website

Goodwin, Doris Kearns. Leadership In Turbulent Times. New York: Simon and Schuster, 2018.

Grant, Adam. Give and Take: Why Helping Others Drives Our Success. Penguin Books, 2013.

Gawande, Atul. <u>Better: A Surgeon's Notes on Performance</u>, Henry Holt and Company, 2007.

Hong, Harry V. <u>The Essential Kierkegaard</u>. Princeton University Press, 1995.

Jastrow, Robert. <u>God and the Astronomers.</u> W.W. Norton and Company, 1992.

Johnson, James and J. Rosamond Johnson. <u>The Book Of American Spirituals</u>. Viking Press, Inc., 1925

Kabat-Zinn, Jon. <u>Full Catastrophe Living</u>. Random House, 1990.

Kidder, Tracy. <u>House.</u> First Mariner Books Edition, 1999.

www://kinginstitute.edu/king-papers/documents

Kierkegaard, Soren. <u>Fear and Trembling.</u> Feather Trail Press, 2009.

Kushner, Harold. <u>When Bad Things Happen To Good People.</u> Random House, Inc.,1981.

Latourette, Kenneth Scott. <u>A History of Christianity</u>. Harper and Brothers, 1953.

Lewis, C. S. <u>The Four Loves</u>. Harcourt, Brace, and Company: First American Edition, 1960.

Locke, T. J. "New Computer Science Department Announced". Episcopal Academy Weekly, May 25, 2018.

Mahler, Gustav. <u>Symphony #2 Der Grosse Apelle, the Great Calling, the Resurrection</u>, 1895.

Markle, Sandra. <u>Wounded Brains: True Survival Stories.</u> Minneapolis, Minnesota: Lerner Publishing Group, 2011.

McNamee, John P. <u>Diary of a City Priest.</u> Sheed and Ward, 1995.

Mower, O Hobart. Sheldon B. Kopp. <u>If You Meet the Buddha On the Road, Kill Him!</u>. Palo Alto, California: Science and Behavior Books, Inc., 1972.

Pecock, George. https://www.youtube.com/watch?v=oYaveihFlXk
Website www.negrospirituals.com

New Revised Standard Version of the Bible. National Council of
Churches, 1989.

Nietzsche, Friedrich. *Maxims and Arrows,* Twilight of the Idols:
How to Philosophize With a Human, Oxford University
Press, 2016.

Parks, Dr. Colin Murray. Bereavement: Studies of Grief in Adult
Life. Routledge, 270 Madison Avenue, New York, NY, 2010.

Pausch, Randy. The Last Lecture. Hyperion Books, 2008.

Video https://www.youtube.com/watch?v=ji5_MqicxSo.

Pink, Daniel. When: The Scientific Secrets of Perfect Timing. New
York: Riverhead Books, 2018.

Potok, Chaim. The Chosen. New York: Simon and Schuster, 1967

Riemer, Jack. "Perlman Makes Music the Hard Way". "The
Houston Chronicle", February 10, 2001.

Rilke, Ranier Maria. Letters To A Young Poet. New York: W. W.
Norton and Company, 1934.

Rogers, Carl. Client Centered Therapy. Houghton Mifflin, 1951.

Roosevelt, Theodore. "Citizen in a Republic". Createspace, 2014

Sartre, Jean Paul. Existentialism Is Humanism. Yale University
Press, 2007.

Sartre, Jean Paul. No Exit. Mass Market Paperback, 1955.

Schwartz, Barry. The Paradox of Choice: Why Less Is More.
Harper Perennial, 2005

Seligman, Martin. The Circuit of Hope. Public Affairs, 2018.

Seligman, Martin; Raiton, Peter; Baumeister, Roy F.;Sripada,
Chandra. Homo Prospectus. Oxford University Press, 2017.

Shahar, Tal Ben. <u>Happier: Learn the Secrets to Daily Joy and Lasting Fulfillment</u>. McGraw-Hill, 2007.

Shahar, Tal Ben. <u>The Pursuit of Perfect: How To Stop Chasing Perfection and Start Living a Richer, Happier Life</u>. McGraw-Hill, 2009.

St. Augustine of Hippa. <u>Confessions</u>. Brewster, Massachusetts: Paraclete Press, 2011.

Squire, James R. <u>Watch Your Time</u>. Create Space, 2017.

Stephens, Sloan
<u>https://ftw.usatoday.com/2018/06/sloane-stephens-tennis-french-open-inspiring-message-loss-simona-halep</u>

Sunstein, Cass R., Thaler Richard H. <u>Nudge</u>. Yale University Press, April 8, 2008.

Teilhard de Chardin, Pierre, <u>The Phenomenon of Man</u>. Harper Perennial Modern Thought, 2008.

Verde, Guiseppe. <u>Nabucco, Va Pensiero</u> Inspired by Psalm 137, 1842.

Viorst, Judith. <u>Necessary Losses: The Loves, Illusions, Dependencies, and Impossible Expectations That All of Us Have to Give Up in Order to Grow</u>. Fireside: New York, New York, 1986.

Walker, Alice. "Sunday School Circa 1950", <u>Revolutionary Petunias and Other Poems</u>. New York: Harcourt, Brace, and Jovanovich, Inc, 1973.

Weathers, Beck. <u>My Journey Home From Everest</u>. Bantam Books Trade Paperback Edition, 2015.

West, Cornel. <u>Race Matters</u>. Vintage/Random House, 1993.

Wiesel, Ellie. <u>Night</u>. New York: Hill and Wang, A Division of Farrar, Straus and Giroux, 2006.

Williams, Margery. The Velveteen Rabbit. George H. Doran Company, 1922.

Wonder, Stevie." Isn't She Beautiful" in Songs in the Key of Life. EMI Music Productions, Lyrics by LyricField, 1976.

Wonder, Stevie. "You Are the Sunshine of My Life" in Songs in the Key of Life. EMI Music Productions, Lyrics by LyricField, 1976.

# THANK YOU TO THE EDITORS AND OTHERS

Winston S. Churchill wrote, "Writing a book is an adventure. To begin with it is a toy and an amusement. Then it becomes a mistress, then it becomes a master, then it becomes a tyrant. The last phase is that just as you are about to be reconciled to your servitude, you kill the monster and fling it to the public."

Churchill is right! But my experience was tempered by assistance from the people who read it and assisted with the editing. I asked Spencer to read a draft and to tell me what was missing and what he wanted as the reader to know more about. Thaddeus did the yeoman's share of editing the first draft focusing on flow and format of the narrative. Vicki read every word with an editor's eye more times than I can count. I am grateful for the editing skills of Emily Cronin, Former Director of Publications and Public Relations at Episcopal. She was also the former Associate Director of the John B. Hurford Center for the Arts and Humanities at Haverford College. The book is better because of their efforts and feedback.

There was a side benefit to the above process. I got to have meaningful conversations with the above-mentioned three family members that I wouldn't normally have had without the content of the book in front of us.

I am grateful to Lauren Maloney,'10, Director of Alumni Engagement at the Episcopal Academy, who provided photos. Lauren also created the book, Celebrating the Life of the Reverend James R. Squire, I can't imagine how much time and expertise she put into producing that book containing pictures and text from members of our school community. I am also grateful to Michele

Godin, Director of Communications at Episcopal, for her support and in obtaining permission from people who appear in the photos in the book.

I am thankful for Will Forbes, a member of the Episcopal Academy Technology Staff, who has helped me overcome challenges of technology in working with this document. Will is a leader, educator, and one of the most patient people I know. He also taught my Ethics students a key decision making tool called OODA LOOP which was formulated first in the military, but now is used in business, litigation, and one's personal life. It focuses on observation, decision making, and action.

Thank you to Brandy Brixius, Marc Bermudez, Sean Sheehan, and Alexandria Zaldivar, my Project Coordinators with Mill City Press, for keeping me on track and for making sure that everything was moving in the right direction. I also want to thank Cindy Engala, my Publishing Consultant, who was very helpful in the beginning and throughout the entire publishing process.

Author's note: If I have failed to give proper credit where credit is due, I would be grateful for any attributions readers may direct to me. There are people who are not named in this book, but they will recognize themselves in the narrative by virtue of the context. I have contacted people who are named if there was an issue that was not in the public domain or if there was a sensitive nature to the anecdote itself. There were several who could not be reached so they remained unnamed. Any sermons or addresses by me were, by their nature, in the public domain.

# ABOUT THE AUTHOR

The Reverend James R. Squire has spent 38 years teaching Ethics as the Head Chaplain at the Episcopal Academy in Philadelphia, Pennsylvania. He specializes as well in bioethics, faith development, positive psychology, diversity work, and the development of student leaders. He was Chair of the Religion Department. After the 9/11 attacks, he created a national conference on "Understanding Islam."

Squire has served as chief pastor to thousands of people who make up the school community. He was a founding board member and counselor at the Marianist Counseling Center in Chester, Pennsylvania. He has served on the board of the Middleton Counseling Center in Bryn Mawr, Pennsylvania.

He holds degrees from West Chester University, Berkeley Divinity School at Yale University, and Duke University where he was the Jarvis Traveling Fellow to Duke from Berkeley. He was among the first in his family to attend college and believes his work as a laborer in a steel mill to pay for his college education was one of the most valuable learning experiences of his life.

His first book, published in the spring of 2017, is <u>Watch Your Time: An Interfaith Spiritual and Psychological Journey</u>. He has developed an innovative approach to counseling called Lever Therapy for everyone who wants to help another in distress. That model will be presented in a forthcoming book.

He works to assist Episcopal Schools at the national level in any way that he is needed. He is a consultant at Culture Works, Philadelphia, Pennsylvania.

CPSIA information can be obtained
at www.ICGtesting.com
Printed in the USA
BVHW041155201019
561574BV00016B/216/P